MW01253085

Clinton and Blair

The former president of the United States, Bill Clinton, and the current prime minister of the United Kingdom, Tony Blair, have described their style of government as a "Third Way." In this important and timely book, Flavio Romano identifies and clarifies the economic implications of this particular approach to public governance.

Clinton and Blair: The Political Economy of the Third Way tests the validity of President Clinton's and Prime Minister Blair's claims of practicing a Third Way by submitting their economic policies to extensive theoretical and historical analysis. Through careful and detailed examination of their fiscal, monetary, education, employment, and public and private investment policies, overwhelming evidence is presented to challenge these leaders' claim of practicing what they preach. Flavio Romano's detailed study shows that the economic policy practice of both leaders is actually rooted in standard neoclassical theory. Dr Romano provides suggestions for an alternative course which could constitute a genuine third way.

This engaging book will be of great interest to students and practitioners of economics and politics and to those interested in world politics in general.

Flavio Romano is a Lecturer at the University of New South Wales, Australia.

Routledge Frontiers of Political Economy

Clinton and Blair

The political economy of the Third Way

Flavio Romano

Routledge
Taylor & Francis Group

LONDON AND NEW YORK

First published 2006
by Routledge
2 Park Square, Milton Park, Abingdon, Oxon OX14 4RN

Simultaneously published in the USA and Canada
by Routledge
270 Madison Ave, New York, NY 10016

Tranferred to Digital Printing 2006

Routledge is an imprint of the Taylor & Francis Group, an informa business

© 2006 Flavio Romano

Typeset in Times New Roman by
Newgen Imaging Systems (P) Ltd, Chennai, India
Printed and bound in Great Britain by
Biddles Ltd, King's Lynn

British Library Cataloguing in Publication Data
A catalogue record for this book is available
from the British Library

Library of Congress Cataloging in Publication Data
A catalog record for this book has been requested

ISBN 10: 0–415–37858–3
ISBN 13: 978–0–415–37858–1

This book is dedicated to the memory of Adriana and Adriano Romano

[T]he ideas of economists and political philosophers, both when they are right and when they are wrong, are more powerful than is commonly understood. Indeed, the world is ruled by little else. Practical men, who believe themselves to be quite exempt from any intellectual influences, are usually the slaves of some defunct economist.

(John Maynard Keynes, *The General Theory of Employment, Interest and Money* 1936)

Contents

Illustrations

Charts

Figure

Tables

Preface

This study arose out of a lifetime of interest in the role of government in improving the economic condition of its citizens. The Nobel Prize-winning economist Robert Lucas famously observed that once one begins to think about questions of economic growth it is difficult to think about anything else. I have found myself subject to that dilemma, and this study is one of its results.

Acknowledgments

I am grateful for the assistance of Peter Gilbert of the United States Information Service in Sydney as well as for the support of George Argyrous of the University of New South Wales and Mabel Lee of the University of Sydney.

Acknowledgements

Abbreviations

BBA97	Balanced Budget Act 1997
BERD	Business Expenditure in Research and Development
CBO	Congressional Budget Office
CEA	Council of Economic Advisers
DLC	Democratic Leadership Council
EGT	Endogenous Growth Theory
EITC	Earned Income Tax Credit
GDP	Gross Domestic Product
NAIRU	Non-Accelerating Inflation Rate of Unemployment
NEC	National Economic Council
NHS	National Health Service
NSI	National Systems of Innovation
OBRA93	Omnibus Budget Reconciliation Act 1993
OMB	Office of Management and Budget
ONS	Office for National Statistics
PFI	Private Finance Initiative
PPP	Public–Private Partnerships
USDHUD	United States Department of Housing and Urban Development
USDL	United States Department of Labor
WFTC	Working Families Tax Credit

Introduction

President Bill Clinton of the United States and Prime Minister Tony Blair of the United Kingdom have both described their approach to public governance as a "Third Way" that is of neither the Right nor Left but new and different. The concept of a Third Way has also gained currency in Australian political circles, especially amongst the Australian Labor Party, and is particularly associated with politicians such as Mark Latham (*New Thinking for Australian Labour: Civilising Global Capital* 1998) and Lindsay Tanner (*Open Australia* 1999). The Third Way has also been invoked by Liberal politicians such as Tony Abbott as well as popular economic and social commentators such as Clive Hamilton (*Growth Fetish* 2003) and the Reverend Tim Costello.

Current interpretations of Clinton and Blair's Third Way are brief and limited to the philosophical and political. Economic evaluations of the Third Way program are lacking, and it is precisely the purpose of this study to analyze the Third Way as an economic policy program.

The analysis begins by examining the Third Way as an economic program. Chapters 2 and 3 examine theories of economic growth and public finance respectively. They find that the Third Way's economic program is drawn from two very different and potentially conflicting traditions: its program for economic growth is best described as drawing from evolutionary growth theory and endogenous growth theory (EGT), whilst its program for public finance is based on standard neoclassical theory. The potential for conflict resides in the fact that its program for economic growth advocates increased public investment, whilst its program for public finance requires fiscal discipline.

Chapters 4 and 5 analyze the Third Way's economic policy practice in the United States and the United Kingdom respectively. They find that the potential conflict between public investment and 'sound' public finance did emerge in practice and was resolved in favor of the latter, locating Clinton and Blair's Third Way within standard neoclassical theory. Thus, the "Third" Way is found not to be a third way at all.

Chapter 6 concludes by discussing the political dimensions of the Third Way as well as the Australian Third Way debate, in particular its possible origins in the Hawke and Keating Labor Governments as well as its currency among more contemporary politicians. The concluding chapter also offers an alternative economic program which, it is argued, could come closer to constituting a genuine third way.

1 An introduction to the Third Way

President Bill Clinton and Prime Minister Tony Blair have described their practice of governing the United States and the United Kingdom respectively as a "Third Way" that is of neither the Right nor Left but new and different.

Use of the term "Third Way" to describe some style or philosophy of government is not new; it has in fact been used to describe quite an eclectic range of different governments since at least the end of the nineteenth century, when Pope Pius XII called for a third way between socialism and capitalism. It has also been used in more recent times to variously describe Sweden's "social democratic middle ground between capitalism and communism" (Reich 1999: 1); some unspecified form of social democracy between free-market capitalism and centrally planned socialism; as well as by the dictators Franco and Tito to describe their own approaches to governing (Arestis and Sawyer 2001: 2). Since then it has also reappeared in other contexts; in fact the similarity to Harold Macmillan's (1938) "Middle Way," for instance, is notable.

Marxist political philosophers have also used the term. Ota Sik in his *The Third Way: Marxist–Leninist Theory and Modern Industrial Society* (1976), for example, used the term to describe a system where market forces are allowed to operate within the economy but where the government intervenes to redistribute wealth to ensure equality of outcomes. The term has also been applied to examples of attempts to combine a free-market economic policy with a socialist political environment such as China, Vietnam, and Laos (McDonnell 1999: 21).

In the 1980s, the term was adopted by the charitable sector in the United States to describe the development of "social capital," that is, a system whereby communities work together to accrue wealth for philanthropic purposes and to also improve social bonds in the process (McDonnell 1999: 22).

In the 1990s, the United States Democratic Party adopted the term to once again point to an alternative philosophical route between neoclassical liberalism and social democracy:

> We reject both the do-nothing [laissez-faire Republican] government of the last 12 years and the big government theory that says we can hamstring business and tax and spend our way to prosperity. Instead we offer *a third way*.
> (Democratic Party 1992: 690, italics added)

Similarly, US President Bill Clinton announced to the Congress in his 1998 *Report on the State of the Union* that:

> We have moved past the sterile debate between those who say Government is the enemy and those who say Government is the answer. My fellow Americans, we have found *a Third Way*. We have the smallest Government in 35 years, but a more progressive one. We have a smaller Government but a stronger nation.
>
> (1998c, italics added)

Even more recently the term has been zealously adopted by the prime minister of the United Kingdom, Tony Blair, and his self-christened "New Labour" Government. Blair wrote in 1998:

> The "Third Way" is to my mind the best label for the new politics which the progressive centre-left is forging.... The Third Way stands for a modernised social democracy, passionate in its commitment to social justice and the goals of the centre-left, but innovative and forward-looking in the means to achieve them. It is founded on the values that have guided progressive politics for more than a century – democracy, liberty, justice, mutual obligation and internationalism. But it is a *third* way because it moves decisively beyond an Old Left preoccupied by state control, high taxation and producer interests; and a New Right treating public investment, and often the very notions of 'society' and collective endeavour, as evils to be undone.
>
> (1998d: 1)

It is with this last form of the Third Way – that of Clinton and Blair – that this work is concerned. In particular, it is concerned with exploring Clinton and Blair's Third Way as an economic program, with the aim of determining whether it is in fact 'new' or whether it actually adheres to some existing economic theoretical tradition(s). Existing evaluations of the Clinton–Blair Third Way have focused on its philosophical and political nature. Economic assessments are lacking and it is therefore precisely the purpose of this study to analyze the Third Way's coherence as an *economic* program. The importance of the study is that, by exploring the Third Way and its heritage, it seeks to improve our knowledge and understanding of the Third Way and thereby contribute to the quality of public discourse concerned with contemporary macroeconomic policy.

The Third Way as a public philosophy

As Pierson and Castles (2002: 687) point out, it is unclear from the literature exactly what the Third Way is and its proponents are clearest about what it is not – neither the "old" social democracy nor neoliberalism. One interpretation of the Third Way, associated with Anthony Giddens – the Third Way's "chief" philosopher and the person Scanlon (1999: 25) describes as "Tony Blair's favourite intellectual" – seeks to explain it as an emerging public philosophy. Giddens has written very extensively (1994, 1998, 2000a,b,c, 2001) about the philosophy of the Third Way as an alternative public philosophy by reference to the two other "ways" of "classical social democracy" and neoliberalism:

> Classical social democracy thought of wealth creation as almost incidental to its basic concerns with economic security and redistribution. The neoliberals placed competitiveness and the generating of wealth much more to the fore-front. Third way politics also gives very strong emphasis to these qualities, which have an urgent importance given the nature of the global marketplace. They will not be developed, however, if individuals are abandoned to sink or swim in an economic whirlpool. Government has an essential role to play in investing in the human resources and infrastructure needed to develop an entrepreneurial culture.
>
> (1998: 99)

Furthermore:

> Traditional socialist ideas, radical and reformist, were based on the ideas of economic management and planning – a market economy is essentially irrational and refractory to social justice. Even most advocates of a "mixed economy" accepted markets only grudgingly. But as a theory of the managed economy, socialism barely exists any longer. The "Keynesian welfare compromise" has been largely dissolved in the West, while countries that retain a nominal attachment to communism... have abandoned the economic doctrines for which they once stood. The "second way" – neoliberalism, or market fundamentalism – has been discarded even by most of its rightist supporters... neoliberal policies... suggest it is up to individuals to fend for themselves in a world marked by high levels of technological change and insecurity.
>
> (2001: 2)

According to Giddens (2001: 2), the Third Way project must begin with "modernising social democracy" in order to "adapt social democracy to a world which has fundamentally changed over the past two or three decades" due to globalization and the emergence of the "knowledge economy" (1998: 26). The Third Way project consists of a "series of endeavours, common to the majority of left parties and thinkers in Europe and elsewhere, to restructure leftist doctrines [because] there is a general recognition almost everywhere that the two 'ways' that have dominated political thinking since the Second World War have failed or lost their purchase" (2001: 2). The Third Way therefore, according to Giddens, is an alternative public philosophy because it transcends both social democracy's concerns with economic redistribution and neoliberals' concerns with competitiveness by uniting these values in developing a culture that addresses the nature of contemporary societal risks (1994, 2000b,c).

Hombach (2000: 1) similarly describes the Third Way as a public philosophy "that will steer a *third course*, a path between competing ideologies [which overcomes] the extremes of free market economics on the one hand and centralized welfare state on the other."

The Third Way as a political strategy

An alternative interpretation – and one which enjoys widespread support – is that of the Third Way as a political strategy designed to reposition the Left within the political mainstream as a viable alternative to the Right, capable in itself of successfully governing capitalist economies in the age of global capitalism (Reich 1997; Burns and Sorenson 1999; Dionne 1999; Harris 1999; Hay 1999; King and Wickham Jones 1999; Morris 1999; Scanlon 1999; Baer 2000; Campbell and Rockman 2000). Political strategy in this context should simply be understood to mean an electoral tactic designed to win sufficient electoral support from voters for political parties to govern.

According to Dionne (1999, quoted in Temple, M. 2000: 303–4), voters clearly like and want capitalism so that in order to win elections "parties on the left... have to prove they're comfortable with the market [economy] and accept its disciplines; however, voters want capitalism tempered by other values, such as community and compassion." Therefore, New Labour felt it necessary to launch a Third Way which embraced capitalism but also addressed the need for "realism with a heart."

Harris (1999: 52–61) too argues that the Third Way represents the Left's response to the New Right and the "victory" of capitalism over socialism. That is, that the end of socialism as a genuine rival economic system to capitalism renders the debate over the merits of the two systems redundant. Also, the New Right, led by Conservative Prime Minister Thatcher and Republican President Reagan, tightened its grip on political power in the United Kingdom and the United States by developing a new political language to reflect the dominance of capitalism in the popular cultures of those countries. This political language includes expressions such as "privatization" and "the homeowner society," which have since joined the mainstream political lexicon.

According to Harris, if the Left were to persist in the redundant argument of socialism versus capitalism, it would face certain political irrelevance. The Third Way therefore represents the Left's reinvention to enter the mainstream political debate by, first, accepting capitalism as the given economic system and, second, inventing the language of a "New Left" paradigm for "administering" capitalism. Tony Blair succeeded in achieving the former by having Clause IV of the British Labour Party constitution (requiring the socialization of the means of production and distribution) removed and the latter through the language of the Third Way, with terms such as "stakeholder society," "equality of opportunity," and "new social contract." In fact, Blair explicitly acknowledges that a stated political ambition for the Third Way project is as "an attempt to marginalise the free-market Right" (1996b: 13–15).

Hay (1999) too interprets the Third Way as a political strategy, by applying Anthony Downs' framework. In *An Economic Theory of Democracy* (1957: 300), Downs posited that "political parties tend to maintain the ideological positions that are consistent over time unless they suffer drastic defeats, in which case they change their ideologies to resemble that of the party that defeated them." Applying Downs' theory, Hay (1999: 94) argues that Blair's New Labour – having been kept out of office by the Conservative Party for the 18 years to 1997 – recrafted its agenda to more closely resemble that of its opposition, thereby reducing the difference and increasing its electoral appeal. Hay's argument can easily be extended to apply to the US Democratic Party, which had been similarly kept out office for the 12 years to 1992 by its Republican opposition.

Kenneth Baer's comprehensive study *Reinventing Democrats: The Politics of Liberalism from Reagan to Clinton* (2000) examines the modern history of the US Democratic Party and his findings concur with Hay (1999) and Downs (1957). Baer's thesis is that the Third Way project was originally developed by the "New Democrat" faction of the Democratic Party and their most important organizational form, the Democratic Leadership Council (DLC), to reposition the Democratic Party to appeal to the electoral mainstream and thus win elections.

Baer (2000: 68) explains that "those instrumental in the founding of the DLC felt that... its [the Democratic Party's] platform was an amalgam of special-interest concerns and was too far to the left of 'mainstream' America on many issues." The DLC was formed in the aftermath of the 1984 election by a group of elected Democratic officials who believed that the Democratic Party was in danger of marginalization and even extinction unless the party could jettison its image as a party of profligate "tax-and-spenders" appealing only to sectional minority interests – namely labor unions and black Americans – and develop a mainstream public philosophy with wide electoral appeal. Specifically, the DLC thought that the Democratic Party was losing elections because it embraced a public philosophy that repelled "the working-class and middle-class voters," especially "white Southern Democrats," towards the Republican Party – the so-called Reagan Democrats (2000: 12, 32) who voted for and were considered instrumental in electing Republican President Ronald Reagan in 1980.

With the election of their former chairman Bill Clinton to the presidency, the New Democrats saw many of their ideas become national policy and some of their most prominent members enter the presidential cabinet and staff.

There is also consensus that Blair imported Clinton's Third Way simply as a means to reposition the Labour Party to win elections, as it had done for Clinton and the Democratic Party in the US presidential election of 1992 (Adams 1998; Hay 1999; Claven 2000; Fairclough 2000; Foley 2000). Adams (1998: 43) has explained that in reshaping and repositioning New Labour, Blair was strongly influenced by Clinton's performance with the Democratic Party. Secretary of the British Fabian Society, Michael Jacobs (2001a), has also noted that Blair and his Chancellor of the Exchequer, Gordon Brown, have explicitly styled themselves on the US Democrats rather than in the tradition of European social democrats. Foley (2000) goes so far as to speak of Blair's as a "British presidency."

King and Wickham Jones (1999) explain that the "New Democrat" victory in 1992 boosted the British Labour Party's confidence that parties of the Left could win elections. Many leading modernizers and staff of the British Labour Party, most notably Tony Blair and Gordon Brown, spent time in Washington observing and learning from the Clinton Administration. A report on the 1992 Clinton campaign by British Labour Party operatives Patricia Hewett and Phil Gould recommended that in order to win, Labour would need to copy the Democratic campaign. The report was adopted.

Duncan (1999) attributes the political interpretation of the Third Way to Schumpeter's argument, in *Capitalism, Socialism and Democracy* (1942), that if the Left were to govern a capitalist economy they would have to do so according to capitalist not socialist logic:

> Socialists had to govern in an essentially capitalist world...a social and economic system that would not function except on capitalist lines.... If they were to run it, they would have to run it according to its own logic. They would have to "administer" capitalism.
>
> (Duncan 1999: 32)

Morris (1999) argues for an even more explicitly political interpretation of the Third Way. According to Morris, a former political advisor to Clinton, the Third Way is the name he and the Clinton White House gave to the tactic of politically outmaneuvering congressional Republicans by adopting the most central ideological position on issues, in order to appeal to the political center (where the majority of voters are thought to be ideologically located) and in the process make the Republicans appear dogmatic, unreasonable, and therefore politically unappealing. Morris also refers to the Third Way as "triangulation," a metaphor referring to the well-known land surveying technique in which a point in space is accurately located through reference to two other points on either side.

Quirk and Cunion instead refer to Morris' triangulation as "opportunistic centrism" (Campbell and Rockman 2000: 204) and Burns and Sorenson (1999) concur by arguing that the Third Way should be understood as a cynical and manipulative ploy by Clinton and his Democratic Party to capture the political center on issues so as to maximize their voter appeal.

The Third Way as an economic program: a 'New' agenda for globalization

A third interpretation of the Third Way is that of a national economic program for addressing the contemporary demands of globalization. This interpretation is not mutually exclusive to the preceding two but is the one with which this study is concerned. The Third Way economic program begins with the analysis that the world is undergoing unprecedented change in the form of rapid economic and technological globalization. According to Clinton (1996: 37), "the future prospects of average Americans today are being driven by one central force: rapid economic change." Similarly for Blair, the Third Way "is about addressing the concerns of people who [are] undergoing rapid change ... in a world of ever more rapid globalisation" (Blair and Schröeder 1998: 163). The especially important characteristics of globalization for Blair (1998d: 6) are the instantaneous mobility of capital across national frontiers and the emergence of global networks of production and competition, both facilitated by developments in information technology.

The importance of international modes of production is that goods and services are no longer produced and consumed within one country but, facilitated by technology, can be designed in one or more countries, manufactured in others, and exported to yet others for consumption. Thus, competition between countries for employers, and hence for employment, has become as global as the competition between producers for sales.

The implications of the instantaneous mobility of capital across national frontiers are particularly significant for national economic policy. Most importantly, it is understood to mean that national governments that do not observe the economic policy preferences of the international capital markets risk capital flight (Friedman, T. 1999).

The New Economy: the Third Way as a program for economic growth

The Third Way argues that capitalism has entered a new stage of development – the New Economy – in which technological innovation and human capital have become especially important as the factors of economic growth:

> The new economy – like the new politics [the Third Way] is radically different.... Its most valuable assets are knowledge and creativity. The successful economies of the future will excel at generating and disseminating knowledge, and commercially exploiting it. The main source of value and competitive advantage in the modern economy is human and intellectual capital.
>
> (Blair 1998d: 8)

Indeed, for the Third Way, economic growth depends only on technological innovation (Clinton 1991, 1996; Clinton and Gore 1992; Blair 1998d). In turn, technological innovation, it argues, demands higher levels of skills and education, hence the premium it places on high educational standards. According to Blair (1998d: 6), "technological advance and the rise of skills and information as key drivers of employment and new industries ... [are] placing an unprecedented premium on the need for high educational standards." Income in the knowledge economy is dependent on education. As Clinton and Gore (1992: 16) put it: "what you earn depends on what you learn."

The proliferation of information technology, according to Giddens (2001: 183), has led to a declining demand for unskilled workers, whose job opportunities and wages therefore also decline, whilst those with high skills or education can increase their income. In addition, the "Fordist" model of mass industrial production and the long-term employment it offered has been replaced by the rise of the dynamic "information" or "knowledge economy" with an associated increase in workforce fragmentation and employment instability (Reich 1991; Arestis and Sawyer 2001: 38).

Given these developments, a central duty of government, according to Clinton (1996a: 95), is to equip people with what he calls "the basic building blocks of economic opportunity" – the training and skills which will enable them to prosper in the knowledge economy. Indeed, Clinton (1996a: 38) argues that the most important part of his strategy "has been investing in our people and our future – in research and technology, in education and skills." Similarly, Blair (1996b: xii) calls for an "economic strategy based on investment in people, infrastructure and industrial research and development."

The importance of education in the Third Way is difficult to overstate: education and training are explicitly identified as the preferred forms of government intervention. Education is of such importance that Clinton labeled himself the "education governor" during the 1992 presidential election (Burns and Sorenson 1999: 62, 64) and Blair declared his priorities for government were "education, education and education" (Blair 1996a).

As an employment strategy, the Third Way is predicated on the idea that the unemployed can only be helped into the labor market through various supply-side policies (principally education) without a demand-side agenda (Arestis and Sawyer 2001: 26). For this reason, the Third Way considers education a critical economic policy instrument.

'Sound' public finance: the Third Way as a program of public finance

The other component of the Third Way economic program – its program of public finance – promotes the principles of 'sound' public finance. Clinton explains that the central role of government is to create the framework for the economy to grow, and this requires "*reducing the deficit*, bringing interest rates down, holding inflation in check ... expanding opportunities for world trade, supporting research and technology, and increasing educational opportunity ..." (1996a: 95, italics added). He adds that "Government ... doesn't create jobs; that's businesses' responsibility" (1996a: 95).

Employment and prosperity – known as "opportunity" in the Third Way lexicon – can only be achieved, according to Clinton (1996a: 21), through economic growth. Economic growth, in turn, requires that government adopt the principles of 'sound' public finance. This means balanced or surplus budgets. Indeed, Blair and Schröeder (1998: 167) implore that "sound public finance should be a badge of pride for social democrats."

Blair (1998d: 10) warns that due to the demands of global capital, "in macroeconomic policy, medium-sized countries cannot 'go-it-alone': they must be continually sensitive to the international economy and its driving forces"; otherwise they risk losing investment and employment through capital flight. Therefore, in order to attract and retain investment, taxes – both personal and corporate – should be *low* (Blair and Schröeder 1998: 166, italics added).

The Third Way program for public finance favors tight fiscal policy and monetary stability, rejecting Keynesian demand-side stabilization policies as incompatible with the demands of global capital for low taxation and fiscal discipline (Clinton 1996a: 22; Blair 1998d: 10; Giddens 2000b: 73). Government spending should be reduced because, according to Blair and Schröeder (1998: 167), "public expenditure as a proportion of national income has more or less reached the limits of acceptability." Hence the significance they attach to their so-called golden rule: that government should borrow only to finance investment not consumption (Blair and Schröeder 1998: 167).

Clinton (1996: 22), in fact, claims that his highest economic priority was "cutting the [budget] deficit in half [and] bringing interest rates down." Similarly, Blair and Schröeder (1998: 167) argue that "social democrats ... must not tolerate excessive levels of public sector debt."

In summary, the macroeconomic program of the Third Way argues that lower taxation, fiscal discipline, and fiscal and monetary stability lead to lower interest rates, increased investment, and, thus, higher rates of growth (Arestis and Sawyer 2001: 27). It is imperative to note the central logic of this argument: that to attract and retain global investment, taxation and interest rates must be kept low and this requires balanced or surplus budgets.

It should also be noted that a potentially significant conflict may exist between the extensive public investment program (especially with respect to education) that Clinton (1996) and Blair (1996b: xii) claim is a central component of the Third Way program and the requirements of 'sound' public finance for low rates of taxation and balanced or surplus budgets. This study will show that given these two competing demands, Clinton and Blair's Third Way chose to place priority on 'sound' public finance – the distinguishing policy feature of the Third Way – thereby locating it within standard neoclassical theory.

Before proceeding to a detailed examination of policy, a few comments regarding the relationship between economic theory and political program are required. We will see in Chapter 3 that neoclassical economic theory is not a single "church" but permits variations on the basic theme of rational choice by maximizing individuals. We will describe the standard version of neoclassical economics, which extols the virtues of unhindered competition among individuals operating in a "perfect" environment. However, many neoclassical economists see this rarefied model, at best, as a starting point from which to develop a more elaborate model that takes into account real worldly considerations such as imperfect information (Eatwell and Milgate 1983).

This "flexibility" in the theoretical model to which neoclassical economists subscribe provides a similar flexibility to the possibilities of political program that find their intellectual justification in neoclassical economics. The "standard" model, which is explained in Chapter 3, tends to lend weight to the political program of neoliberalism, whereas the elaborations of this model tend to lead into more "social democratic" policy agendas.

Neoclassical economic theory can therefore find expression in at least two different political programs and, for our purposes, these are neoliberalism and social democracy (Adams 1998; De Martino 1998). Whilst both accept the overall neoclassical analysis of the capitalist economy, their primary concerns differ and this manifests itself in their policy practice. Social democracy is primarily concerned with equality and aims "to regulate and socialise the wealth-creating and directionless economic dynamism of capitalism, not replace it" (Pierson 2003) through policies of redistribution, welfare, and public spending (Giddens 1998: 99). Neoliberalism, on the other hand, may sacrifice economic equality and welfare in the pursuit of economic growth through policies that foster wealth creation based on the free market, minimal government, and maximum individual freedom and responsibility (Adams 1998: 28). Thus, to clarify terms, "neoclassical" refers to the body of economic theory and "neoliberal" and "social democratic" to the respective political programs and policy practices. It will be argued that, despite Giddens' (2001: 2) stated aspiration for the Third Way project, the Clinton–Blair Third Way accepted the standard neoclassical economic analysis and expressed it in the form of neoliberal not social democratic policies.

Importantly, it should also be noted that, according to the Third Way, the capitalist market is taken to be the inevitable and most desirable form of economic organization, so that government policies – especially economic policies – must conform to its demands. If prosperity is to be achieved and sustained, this must occur through policies that respect that market. As Blair's Conservative predecessor, Margaret Thatcher, was fond of saying about the market economy: "There is no alternative" (Jenkins 1983).

Finally, it is also worth noting that the Third Way does not make any mention of full employment as a macroeconomic objective. The absence of full employment is closely followed by the absence of an entire demand-side to its economic program: especially the possibility of reducing public debt through economic growth stimulated by such a demand-side program. Alternatively, the requirements of 'sound' public finance for a balanced budget could be achieved through increased tax rates to generate more tax revenue rather than through reduced public spending.

Conclusion

Despite its various labels – the "Third Way" (Clinton 1998c; Blair 1998d), the "Vital Centre" (Clinton 2000c), the "New Centre" (Blair and Schröeder 1998), and the "New Middle" (Blair and Schröeder 1998) – the Third Way program can be understood as a strategy that seeks to reconcile the demands of globalization (and global capital in particular) with individuals' opportunity to prosper, respectively through the twin pillars of 'sound' public finance and a program of supply-side public investment, especially in education and training.

Having noted the potential for conflict between the two pillars of 'sound' public finance and public investment, Chapters 2 and 3 examine theories of economic growth and public finance respectively. They find that the Third Way's economic program is drawn from two very different and potentially conflicting traditions: its program for economic growth is best described as drawing from evolutionary and endogenous growth theories, whilst its program for public finance is from standard neoclassical theory.

Chapters 4 and 5 analyze the Third Way's economic policies in the United States and the United Kingdom respectively. They find that the potential conflict between public investment and 'sound' public finance identified earlier did emerge in practice and was resolved in favor of the latter, locating Clinton and Blair's Third Way within standard neoclassical theory.

Chapter 6 concludes by discussing whether the Third Way could have been a different program. In particular, the Third Way lacks a demand side to its program, such that might have enabled debt reduction through economic growth rather than exclusively depending on reduced public expenditure.

The methodology adopted by this study is to test historical practice against economic theory. It analyzes the economic policy practice of the two-term Clinton Democratic Administration in the United States (1993–2001) and the first term (1997–2001) of the Blair "New" Labour Government in the United Kingdom and tests this against economic theory for the purpose of drawing meaningful conclusions about the economics of the Third Way. The importance of analyzing policy practice in assessing the Third Way's performance is because of the priority both Clinton and Blair place on outcomes over process, and, after all, as the proverb reminds us, "it is by their fruits that we shall know them."

2 The Third Way and economic growth

It is interesting to note that Third Way policy and other documents published before Clinton and Blair entered office do not contain any explicit references to economic theories or theorists. The only explicit reference to theory in that entire time was by Gordon Brown, then Blair's Shadow Chancellor of the Exchequer, who in the autumn of 1994 was lampooned by the media for referring to "post-neoclassical endogenous growth theory" in a speech on economic policy (Crafts 1996: 30). The key documents of the Third Way *program* are identified in Table 2.1.

Despite the lack of explicit references, it will be shown that the Third Way program resonates with two distinct – but not necessarily contradictory – theories of economic growth. These are the evolutionary and the endogenous growth theories, each of which will be discussed in order to show their policy implications.

As discussed in the previous chapter, the Third Way argues that capitalism has entered a new stage of development – the New Economy – in which technological innovation and human capital have become especially important as the determining factors of economic growth.

Indeed, for the Third Way, economic growth depends only on technological innovation (Clinton 1991; Clinton and Gore 1992; Clinton 1996a; Blair 1998d). In turn, technological innovation, it argues, demands higher and higher levels of skills and education – hence the unprecedented premium the Third Way places on high educational standards. According to Blair (1998d: 6), "technological advance and the rise of skills and information as key drivers of employment and new industries . . . [are] placing an unprecedented premium on the need for high educational standards." Income in the knowledge economy is dependent on education. As Clinton and Gore (1992: 16) put it: "what you earn depends on what you learn."

Nye (2001: 251) calls this development "The Third Industrial Revolution" because, he argues, it is as revolutionary in economic terms as the invention of the steam engine in the eighteenth century and the introduction of electricity at the end of the nineteenth. The Third Way program therefore attaches great importance to investment – both public and private – in infrastructure that supports education, research, and innovation and that therefore drives economic growth (Clinton 1996a: 38; Blair 1998d: xii).

Table 2.1 Key documents of the Third Way program

Author(s)	Policy documents	Other (non-policy) publications
Clinton, B. and Gore, A. (1992)	*Putting People First: How We Can All Change America*	
(US) Democratic Party (1992)	*Democratic Party Platform*	
Blair, T. (1996)	*New Britain: My Vision of a Young Country*	
New Labour (1997e)	*New Labour: Because Britain Deserves Better*	
Blair, T. (1998)	*The Third Way: New Politics for the New Century*	
Blair, T. and Schröeder, G. (1998)	"Europe: The Third Way/Die Neue Mitte"	
Giddens, A. (1994)		*Beyond Left and Right: The Future of Radical Politics*
Reich, R. (1992)		"Clintonomics 101: and why it beats Bush–Reagan"

As a program for economic growth, the Third Way draws from both the evolutionary and endogenous (also known as New Growth) theories of economic growth, both of which will be discussed in this chapter. It will be later shown that these theories of economic growth are incompatible with the standard neoclassical theory of public finance practiced by the Third Way. The reason for this incompatibility is simply that these theories of economic growth advocate increased government spending on the provision of certain types of public goods, whilst the standard neoclassical theory of public finance is opposed to public spending generally and to deficit spending in particular.

Economic theories which identify technological innovation and human capital as prime determinants of growth are not at all recent but have an extensive intellectual heritage. According to Rosenberg (1982: 3), the understanding of technical innovation as the means to productivity improvements is common to all economic theories. The Third Way, however, goes further than most in arguing that the emergence of the New Economy places an unprecedented premium on innovation and education as the primary sources of economic growth. Whilst use of the term "human capital" to refer to the productive capacities of the stock of skills and knowledge human beings acquire through education and training is relatively recent (dating from only the mid-twentieth century) (Marginson 1993: 31), the concept itself dates back many hundreds of years (Rosen 1987: 681–2).

Economists of all descriptions have accepted that new products, processes, and knowledge are the main source of dynamism in capitalist growth, but few have examined the origins of such innovation or the consequences of their adoption (Freeman 1987a). Most have preferred, in Rosenberg's (1982) words, not to look inside "the black box" of innovation but to leave that task to technologists and historians (Freeman 1987a). As already noted, however, the Third Way goes further than most, insisting as it does that economic growth is now only dependent on the rate of technological innovation and the skills that that requires.

Evolutionary theory

The economist Joseph Schumpeter is perhaps the most prominent economist to analyze and emphasize the importance of innovation to capitalist economic growth (Coombs *et al*. 1987: 4). In *The Theory of Economic Development* (1934), Schumpeter was concerned with explaining long-term economic development and structural change in capitalist economies, and his theory can be restated as follows.

The internal dynamics of capitalism spring from the continuous competition between firms for profits. Each capitalist seeks to recoup her investment plus a return (in the form of profits) by selling goods to the market against the efforts of other capitalists to do the same.

If all firms produce similar products with similar production costs in a competitive market, then profits cannot exist. Therefore, the means of profitability and the key means of growth in the Schumpeterian view of competition is the search for new processes or products that yield a competitive advantage in the form of more efficient production or new goods. Competition thus reinforces the introduction of technological and organizational change in the accumulation process and these "new combinations mean the competitive elimination of the old" (Schumpeter 1934: 66–7). Competition is therefore critical to the process, but it is competition between entrepreneurs aimed at securing monopoly profits, not competition in the neoclassical sense of perfectly competitive markets (Phillimore 1998: 51). As a consequence, one of the most distinctive attributes of capitalist dynamics has been its constant revolutionizing of the techniques of production – what Schumpeter famously calls the process of "creative destruction" (1942: 84). This idea – the recognition of the critical role innovation plays in economic growth – is Schumpeter's most significant contribution.

As a result of innovation, a flow of income arises that cannot be attributed to the contribution of either labor or capital. The source of this profit is the monopoly rent an entrepreneur receives for achieving a productivity improvement that has not yet diffused to her competitors. Once competitors adopt the innovation, the monopoly rent will cease, profits will vanish, and investment will decline. Economic cycles, according to Schumpeter (1939), can therefore be understood as fluctuations in the development of innovations (Rosenberg 1982: 5; Peet 1999: 37).

Economic growth, for Schumpeter, consists of the discontinuous introduction of "new combinations" of products and methods of production (Schumpeter 1934: 65–6). Note that these occur mostly on the supply-side and are five in number: new products, new methods of production, new markets, new materials, and reorganization of industry (Schumpeter 1934: 66). An enterprise consists of new combinations and an entrepreneur introduces these new combinations, which "leads the means of production into new channels" that can reap a profit (Schumpeter 1934: 88–9). Schumpeter distinguishes between innovations and inventions, and the distinction is a subtle but important one. Schumpeter uses the term "technical development" only for innovations that involve the introduction of new methods of production. Inventions involve new products. Innovations need not depend on inventions and inventions do not necessarily lead to innovations. Rosenberg (1976) is critical of this distinction for placing undue emphasis on innovation at the expense of invention. As a result, argues Rosenberg (1976: 67), "inventive activity itself is never examined as a continuing activity...relevant to the subsequent Schumpeterian stages of innovation...[but as] an activity carried on offstage and out of sight." The principal consequence of Schumpeter's treatment of inventions as exogenous, explains Rosenberg (1976: 68), is that it limits our understanding of the overall process of innovation.

As Schumpeter argued that profits derive from innovation and innovation is by definition a deviation from routine behavior, the economic equilibrium of production, organization, and distribution is continually disrupted so that, contrary to neoclassical theory, capitalist economies are in a constant state of disequilibrium (Nelson and Winter 1982: 41; Archibugi and Michie 1997: 241). In other words, the *static efficiency* of a system that at "every point in time fully utilizes its possibilities" may in the long run be inferior to the *dynamic efficiency* of a system which allocates part of its resources to the generation of new knowledge and innovation (Coombs *et al.* 1987: 15). The essential distinction between static and dynamic efficiency is that the former is achieved by working within a given set of initial conditions while the latter implies the creation of a new set of initial conditions (Klein 1977: 12).

Schumpeter was emphatic that disequilibrium is fundamental to the capitalist dynamic: "Whereas a stationary feudal economy would still be a feudal economy, and a stationary socialist economy would still be a socialist economy, stationary capitalism is a contradiction in terms" (1937, quoted in Rosenberg 1994: 49; Nelson and Winter 2002: 24). Moreover, due to its disequilibrium nature and the fact that economic change for Schumpeter occurs in historical time rather than neoclassical static time (Rosenberg 1994: 60), the changes caused by innovation are regarded as "evolutionary":

> The essential point to grasp is that in dealing with capitalism we are dealing with an evolutionary process.... Capitalism...is by nature a form or method of economic change and not only never is but never can be stationary.
>
> (Schumpeter 1942: 82)

Nelson and Winter (1982: 40) and Rosenberg (1994: 53) point out that Schumpeter also rejects the neoclassical assumption of rational decision-making and replaces it with uncertainty. As Schumpeter explains:

> The assumption that conduct is prompt and rational is in all cases a fiction.... To cling to it, as the traditional [neoclassical] theory does, is to hide an

essential thing and to ignore a fact which ... is theoretically important and the source of the explanation of phenomena which would not exist without it.

(1934: 80)

The "phenomenon" Schumpeter is referring to is innovation, which, he argues, cannot be explained by rationality because firms cannot possibly know all of the costs and possibilities of innovations before they are undertaken, even where innovations have become routine within the firm:

> The assumption that business behavior is ideally rational and prompt, and also that in principle it is the same with all firms ... breaks down as soon as we ... allow the business community under study to be faced by ... new possibilities of business action which are as yet untried and about which the most complete command of routine teaches nothing.

(1939: 98–9)

Kamien and Schwartz (1982), Nelson and Winter (1982), and Rosenberg (1994) distinguish between the form of competition Schumpeter presents in the *Theory of Economic Development* and that in *Capitalism, Socialism and Democracy* (1942), which they label Schumpeter Mark I and Schumpeter Mark II respectively. In Schumpeter Mark I, based on an examination of the typical European industrial structure of the late nineteenth century, the pattern of innovative activity is characterized by technological ease of entry into an industry and by the major role played by individual entrepreneurs and new firms in innovation (Nelson and Winter 2002: 37).

However, in Schumpeter Mark II, based on US industry in the first half of the twentieth century, the pattern of innovative activity comes to be characterized by the prevalence of large established firms and by barriers to entry for new innovators. Large firms that have benefited from economies of scale and have institutionalized (or "routinized") the innovation process with the establishment of research laboratories (Nelson and Winter 1982: 133, 2002: 37) use their accumulated stock of technical knowledge, their advanced competence in large-scale research and development (R&D), production, and distribution, and their financial resources to create barriers to entry by new entrepreneurs and small firms in order to maintain monopolistic advantages (Coombs *et al.* 1987: 95).

The essential difference is that in Schumpeter Mark II, fewer large firms, often oligopolies or monopolies, replace many small firms in competitive markets as the engines of growth (Rosenberg 1994: 52). In both cases, however, Schumpeter considers innovation not only endogenous to the capitalist system but absolutely critical to it, which is once again contrary to the neoclassical view that innovation is an exogenous process (1994: 58).

The label "evolutionary theory" has come to refer to a range of theories relating to economic development which reject the neoclassical concept of equilibrium in favor of a view of capitalist growth as a disequilibrium, cumulative, path-dependent process that occurs in historical time. Especially notable among these are the contributions of Kaldor (1934, 1966, 1972) and Joan Robinson (1962a,b). However, of particular interest for our purposes is the application of evolutionary theory to the study of innovation. Later economists such as Nelson and Winter (1977, 1982) and Rosenberg (1976, 1982, 1994), who have developed Schumpeter's inquiry into the centrality of innovation and competition for economic growth, are often referred to as "neo-Schumpeterian" or "evolutionary" (Freeman 1987a: 858, 1994: 464). As Nelson and Winter explain:

> The influence of Joseph Schumpeter is so pervasive in our work that it requires particular mention.... Indeed the term "neo-Schumpeterian" would be as appropriate a designation for our entire approach as "evolutionary." More precisely, it could reasonably be said that we are evolutionary theorists *for the sake* of being neo-Schumpeterians – that is, because evolutionary ideas provide a workable approach to the problem of elaborating and formalizing the Schumpeterian view of capitalism as an engine of progressive change.
>
> (1982: 39)

Evolutionary theory is so called because, in addition to adopting Schumpeter's view of capitalist growth as an evolutionary process of cumulative and path-dependent innovation, it also adopts the biological theory of evolution as a metaphor with which to explain that "market competition is analogous to biological competition and that business firms must pass a survival test imposed by the market" and that the principal strategy available to firms to do so is innovation (Nelson and Winter 1982: 41; Rosenberg 1994: 15).

Evolutionary theory seeks to explain innovation and economic change and rejects neoclassical theory as unrealistic and inadequate for the purpose (Nelson and Winter 1974, 1977, 1982: 23–4). In particular, it rejects the neoclassical assumptions that firms always behave in a profit-maximizing manner, that the economic system tends towards equilibrium, and that firms are rational actors with costless and unlimited access to perfect information with which they can attain certainty about all possible future courses of action (Nelson and Winter 1982: 3–22).

In their stead, evolutionary theory replaces these assumptions with firms that operate with limited information and bounded rationality, which in turn generate uncertainty within an economic environment which is dynamic rather than static, occurring in historical time, and where change, as with Schumpeter, is a disequilibrium process (Nelson and Winter 1974, 1982). Rationality is bounded in evolutionary theory because economic reality is too complex and information too limited to permit actors to achieve perfect certainty about all possible future courses of action (1982: 35).

According to this view, firms' access to information is limited to their immediate past experience so that they organize and store information through regular and predictable behavioral patterns which become "routine" (Edquist 1997: 203). As Nelson and Winter (1982: 134, 2002: 30) note: "firms may be expected

to behave in future according to the routines they have employed in the past."
In evolutionary theory, these routines play the role that genes play in biological
evolutionary theory because

> they are a persistent feature of the organism and determine its possible
> behavior...they are heritable in the sense that tomorrow's organisms gener-
> ated from today's (for example, building a new plant) have many of the
> same characteristics, and they are selectable in the sense that organisms with
> certain routines may do better than others [so that] their relative importance
> in the population (industry) is augmented over time.
>
> (Nelson and Winter 1982: 14)

Firms' actual selection of innovations is analogous to biological organisms' selection of adaptations that help them to better survive so that, as with Schumpeter,
innovation can be understood as deviations from routine that also disrupt the
equilibrium (Nelson and Winter 1982: 41; Edquist 1997: 6).

A major concern of evolutionary theory is with the dynamic process by which
firms change behavior patterns and innovate over time (Nelson and Winter 1982:
18–19; Edquist 1997: 175–243; Metcalfe 1997: 271). At each point in time, input
and output levels are determined by firms' production techniques (or routines)
and the magnitude of their capital stocks. Together with market supply and
demand conditions that are exogenous to the firms, their decisions determine
market prices of inputs and outputs. The profitability of each individual firm is
thus determined. Profitability operates, through investment, as one major determinant of rates of growth of individual firms. With firms' sizes thus altered,
the same production techniques yield different input and output levels, hence
different prices and profitability. By this process, aggregate input and output and
price levels for the industry undergo dynamic change. Importantly, the production
techniques of firms are subject to change through innovation which disrupts
their routines. Firms therefore "search" for new production techniques or new
products (innovations) with which to achieve monopoly profits armed only with
information limited to their routines. At any time, a diversity of alternative
innovations co-exist, rather than one "optimal" innovation as in neoclassical
theory, about which firms have varying degrees of limited information. Limited
information generates uncertainty about the particular innovation firms actually
select. The search for innovative techniques and the selection of a particular
innovation are therefore cumulative and path-dependent processes, and the
same prices that provide firms with feedback on the selection of innovation
also influence the direction of the search. As noted, the concept of firms'
search for and selection of innovations is the economic counterpart to that of
adaptation in biological evolutionary theory (Edquist 1997: 6). Through the
evolutionary process of search and selection, the firms evolve over time, with
the condition of the industry in each period bearing upon its condition in the
following period.

Nelson and Winter (1982) conclude that firms' routines and their search for and actual selection of innovations are knowledge-intensive processes mainly embedded in the skills and knowledge of their personnel, as most operations of a firm cannot be articulated to the last detail but are a result of what Arrow (1962) calls "learning by doing" (Lundvall 1992: 79; Freeman 1994: 473).

As a result of their evolutionary interpretation of innovation and economic growth, Nelson and Winter (1982) offer two principal policy proposals. The first is that, due to the demands for skills and knowledge required by firms' search for and selection of innovations, government has a central role to play in the provision of education, especially in the retraining of the 'casualties' of unsuccessful selections of innovation (Nelson and Winter 1982: 369; Lundvall 1992: 306).

The second is that, due to the externalities and risks that arise from the inability of innovating firms to exclude other firms from using their innovations, the policies of government institutions play an important role in stimulating, supplementing, and supporting innovation through the provision of education, basic research, and public infrastructure (Nelson and Winter 1982: 387; Metcalfe 1997: 271–2; Phillimore 1998: 65–6).

Metcalfe (1997: 276) argues that as innovation is an evolutionary process of knowledge accumulation (and therefore path-dependent), combined with the positive externalities that characterize knowledge, institutions (including and especially government) have an important role to play in innovation. The incentives to innovate can be significantly influenced, for example, through government intellectual property instruments such as patents, and innovation can be stimulated through the provision of public education and knowledge infrastructure.

From the growing interest among economists in the role of institutions in the evolutionary theory of economic growth has emerged a rich and extensive literature on "national systems of innovation" (Freeman 1987b, 1994; Porter 1990; Reich 1991; Lundvall 1992; Nelson 1993; Edquist 1997).

Friedrich List, who introduced a stages theory of industrial development and economic growth in *The National System of Political Economy* (1841), is the pioneer to whom the concept of national systems of innovation (NSI) is commonly attributed (Lundvall 1992: 16; Archibugi and Michie 1997: 6; Edquist 1997: 157). List distinguishes five stages of economic growth: (a) the savage stage, (b) the pastoral stage, (c) the agricultural stage, (d) the agricultural and manufacturing stage, and finally (e) the agricultural, manufacturing, and commercial stage. List's discussion centers on the transition from stage (c) to stages (d) and (e) and he recognizes that that transition requires industrial innovation based on what he calls "intellectual capital" and learning (Archibugi and Michie 1997: 7; Edquist 1997: 165). In fact, according to Freeman (1997: 24), List (1841) concluded that it is human capital that is decisive for growth and criticized Adam Smith's (1776) emphasis on physical capital. List thus advocates the need for government provision of education and training and for developing institutions and infrastructure that support industrial development (Lundvall 1992: 16; Archibugi and Michie 1997: 8).

Freeman (1987b) and Lundvall (1992) were the first to use the term "national systems of innovation" to refer to "all interrelated, institutional and structural factors in a nation, which generate, select, and diffuse innovation" (Archibugi and Michie 1997: 3; Edquist 1997: 3). Metcalfe defines NSI as:

> that set of distinct institutions which jointly and individually contribute to the development and diffusion of new technologies and which provides the framework within which government forms and implements policies to influence the innovation process. As such, it is a system of interconnected institutions to create, store and transfer the knowledge, skills and artefacts which define new technologies.
>
> (1997: 285)

As innovation is an evolutionary process of knowledge accumulation and learning, the NSI approach stresses the importance of national institutions within that process (Lundvall 1992: 3, 23; Edquist 1997: 15–26). Institutions in the NSI approach can be understood as the formalization of habits and customs which reduce the transaction costs and uncertainty for agents involved in innovation. Veblen (1919: 239, 241) defined institutions as "settled habits of thought common to the generality of man" and therefore suggested they are "an outgrowth of habit." North (1990, 1991) also stresses the importance of the institutional framework to economic growth:

> Institutions are the humanly devised constraints that structure political, economic and social interaction. They consist of both informal constraints (sanctions, taboos, customs, traditions, and codes of conduct), and formal rules (constitutions, laws, property rights).
>
> (1991: 97)

National institutions in the NSI approach are routines for collective action and are therefore similar to the role of routines for the organizational behavior of firms in earlier evolutionary theory. Carlsson and Stankiewicz explain that institutions:

> [A]re the normative structures which promote stable patterns of social interactions/transactions necessary for the performance of vital societal functions.... By the institutional infrastructure of a technological [innovation] system we mean a set of institutional arrangements (both regimes and organizations) which, directly or indirectly, support, stimulate and regulate the process of innovation and diffusion of technology. The range of institutions is very wide. The political system, educational system (including universities), patent legislation, and institutions regulating labor relations are among the many arrangements which can influence the generation, development, transfer and utilization of technologies.
>
> (1995: 45)

Edquist and Johnson (1997: 50) attempt to identify the particular subset of institutions which influence innovation and that may therefore be useful in defining a "system of innovation." They distinguish between institutions that are "formal" (laws such as intellectual property and patent laws) and those that are "informal" (common law, customs, tradition, practices, ethics, and norms of behavior). They find that these institutions can influence innovation by reducing uncertainty by enhancing the transmission of information; managing conflicts; providing incentives to innovate; and directly stimulating innovation (1997: 51–5).

Institutions can reduce uncertainty in the innovation process. For example, evolutionary theory argues that because innovators are unable to appropriate all of the benefits of the knowledge or innovations they create, well-known positive externalities are generated that cannot be appropriated and may therefore discourage innovation (Nelson and Winter 1982: 387; Von Hippel 1982; Lundvall 1992: 316; Metcalfe 1997: 270). In this example, government legal institutions or infrastructure such as patents and other intellectual property laws can reduce innovators' uncertainty about the appropriation possibilities of their innovations.

Equally, legal institutions and infrastructure manage conflicts by creating and enforcing property rights and regulating the kinds of behavior individuals and organizations can engage in. By managing conflicts, such institutions are thought to encourage cooperative behavior not only in the innovation process but throughout society.

A third function of institutions is to provide incentives that influence economic decisions (Lundvall 1992: 303). The taxation system, for example, can affect the intensity and even the direction of innovation efforts through instruments such as taxes, allowances, rebates, and deductions for investments in research and education. Property rights to knowledge and ideas, such as intellectual property laws, are also important forms of incentives as they affect innovators' capacity to appropriate their innovations and the temporary monopoly rents that they generate.

Finally, institutions can also directly stimulate innovations. For example, government can stimulate innovation through the contribution of its network of education and research institutions and public infrastructure, as well as through its role as a major purchaser of innovations.

The contribution of government education and research institutions benefits innovation by producing trained personnel and research that private firms may find uneconomic to do due to uncertainty, risk, economies of scale, and externalities (Coombs *et al.* 1987: 207; Lundvall 1992: 152, 303). Similarly, government has an essential role to play in the provision of public infrastructure, such as energy supply and telecommunications, which is vital as an enabler of many innovation activities but which, yet again, is unlikely to be provided privately due to economies of scale and externalities.

With regard to the role of government as a major purchaser of innovations, a demanding procurement policy can stimulate innovation, and one that favors smaller firms can stimulate competition (Lundvall 1992: 142; Carlsson and Jacobsson 1997: 288). K. Smith (1997: 88) points out that "when we look at the major technological innovations that have shaped the modern world something stands out: most of them...originated or [were] developed in public sector infrastructural organizations."

Still another way in which government can direct innovation is through the regulatory system (Coombs *et al.* 1987: 210; Smith, K. 1997: 90). For example, a government may raise environmental standards, which may then stimulate technological innovations with which to comply with the new standards. This is also a good example of evolutionary theory's concern with dynamic efficiency mentioned earlier.

Dynamic efficiency results from improvements in technical or productive efficiency that arise over a period of time so that a dynamically efficient economy is one which is proficient in improving methods of producing existing products and also at developing and marketing completely new products so that the economy may grow in the future. In both cases, invention, innovation, and R&D can lead to significant improvements in dynamic efficiency. As discussed, Schumpeter (Mark II) made it clear that large firms and oligopolistic markets are more conducive to innovation as entrepreneurs use the advantage of economies of scale to produce innovations that help to secure temporary monopoly profits (Phillimore 1998: 53). It is its central concern with dynamic efficiency that leads evolutionary theory to attribute an important role for government in stimulating and leading innovation.

On the other hand, standard neoclassical theory, as we shall see, is concerned with static efficiency, that is, the most efficient allocation of resources between competing ends at a given point in the present time. This concern with static efficiency rests on the concept of perfectly competitive markets which maximize the allocation of resources without (and indeed precluding) any significant economic role for government (Argyrous 2000; Blaug 2001: 44). This disagreement between the evolutionary and neoclassical theoretical traditions over static versus dynamic efficiency is a key analytical difference with major implications for policy to which we shall return.

Normatively, the NSI approach advocates a central and active role for government institutions in promoting innovation through the provision of and investment in legal and regulatory infrastructure, education and research infrastructure, and physical infrastructure and as major purchasers of innovations themselves (Rosenberg 1982: 235–6; Coombs *et al.* 1987: 206–9; Lundvall 1992: 129–45; Nelson 1993; Archibugi and Michie 1997: 17–18; Edquist and Johnson 1997: 59).

Within the NSI approach, Porter (1990) and Reich (1991) have had a particularly strong influence on the Third Way program and deserve special attention. In his *Competitive Advantage of Nations* (1990), Porter, like List (1841), also develops a historical model of economic development: nations pass through the successive stages of resource-driven, investment-driven, innovation-driven, and wealth-driven economic development within which only the United States and the United Kingdom are mature innovation-driven economies. Using industry sectors firmly located within national boundaries as his unit of analysis, he argues that national economic development is achieved through the competitive advantage of a nation's firms and, contrary to the views of Ohmae (1990) and Chesnais (1994), who argue that globalization is making redundant the role of the nation-state, Porter argues that national government has a vital role to play in developing competitive advantage.

Competitive advantage is of two types: either goods and services that are supplied at a lower cost or those of a superior quality (Porter 1990: 37). Competitive advantage is achieved through innovation, which can be caused by new technologies, changing market demands, the emergence of a new industry, the changing costs of factors of production, or changes in government regulation.

The sustainability of competitive advantage depends on the source of the advantage (Porter 1990: 49–50). The source of competitive advantage can be of a high or a low order. High-order advantages require what Porter (1990: 77) calls "advanced" factors of production; more highly skilled personnel, sophisticated infrastructure, and the ongoing capacity for technical innovation. Low-order advantages are based on "basic" factors of production: low labor costs and low material costs, both of which are relatively easy to replicate and therefore of limited benefit.

Porter concludes that "the central goal of government policy toward the economy is to *deploy a nation's resources (labor and capital) with high and rising levels of productivity*" (1990: 617). The implications for government policy are clear: government should develop an economic environment which fosters competition and innovation, both in physical and human capital, through investment in education, research, and infrastructure (1990: 627). "Nations succeed where the national environment uniquely enables firms to perceive new strategies for competing in an industry [and] where firms are pushed to...compete globally," argues Porter (1990: 68). Acknowledging his intellectual debt to Schumpeter, Porter concludes that the role of the state for growth must ultimately be to stimulate increased competition and innovation (1990: 70).

Another adherent to the NSI approach, Robert Reich, has been especially influential on the Third Way program as he served as Clinton's first Secretary of Labor. In *The Work of Nations*, Reich (1991) argues that the international mobility of capital, the emergence of global networks of production, and the ascendancy of the information economy, all facilitated by developments in information technology, point to the need for a nation to invest in the human capital of its workforce as its most important (and perhaps only) enduring resource in the pursuit of national prosperity.

The significance of the international mobility of capital is that investment can relocate rapidly to any place on the planet in pursuit of maximum returns. The importance of international modes of production is that goods and services are no longer produced and consumed within one country but, facilitated by technology, can be designed in one or more countries, manufactured in others, and exported to yet others for consumption.

As both capital and production processes have become global, labor is the only factor of production which remains set within the nation so that, whilst competition between nations' firms has become meaningless, competition between nations' workers for the best jobs has become paramount (DeMartino 1998: 38).

Where the majority of the NSI literature adopts either the firm (Lundvall 1992; Nelson 1993; Edquist 1997) or industry sector (Porter 1990) as the basic agent of innovation, Reich adopts the individual because, he argues, labor is the only remaining factor of production entirely located within national boundaries and therefore most subject to national policy-making.

Reich further argues that the "Fordist" model of mass industrial production of the twentieth century has been replaced by the new "post-industrial" information economy in which information and knowledge have become the principal source of value. Reich adopts Drucker's (1969) distinction between people who work in the production of physical objects and "knowledge workers": people who work with intangibles such as ideas and information. Consequently, the long-term employment security of the industrial assembly line has been replaced with a growing division between the unskilled, who are left with low-paid jobs, and a new protagonist who is prospering from the information economy – the "symbolic analyst":

> Gone forever are the assembly lines that used to provide lifetime jobs with rising wages and benefits to people straight out of high school, or even the good corporation that promised a lifetime of secure employment to the loyal white collar professional.... The winners in this volatile, new globalized economy are those who can identify and solve problems, manipulate and analyze symbols, create and manage information. Those with a college degree are thus likely ... to end up on the happier side of the great divide.
>
> (Reich 1996: 18)

National prosperity, according to Reich, can therefore only be achieved through a highly skilled labor force producing high value-added goods and services. Reich defines the skills of a nation's workforce as its most important resource in the competition for international investment and high-wage jobs:

> In the politics and economics of the coming [twenty-first] century, there will be no national products or technologies, no national corporations, no national industries. There will no longer be national economies.... All that will remain rooted within national borders are the people who comprise a nation. Each nation's primary assets will be its citizens' skills and insights. Each nation's political task will be to cope with the centrifugal forces of the global economy which tear at the ties binding citizens together – bestowing ever greater wealth on the most skilled and insightful, while consigning the less skilled to a declining standard of living.
>
> (1991: 3)

The path to national prosperity, according to Reich, is to attract and retain international capital by investing in the education and skills of a national workforce so as to produce the most productive "symbolic analysts" in the world. As nations secure investment, a virtuous cycle develops: "well-trained workers attract global corporations, which invest and give workers good jobs; the good jobs, in turn, generate additional training and experience," which attract more global investment (1990: 59).

Based on his 1991 analysis, Reich wrote in 1992 that the Third Way's "centerpiece ... is a major increase in public investment in education, training, and infrastructure" (1992: 1). However, as analysis in Chapter 4 will show, due to the Third Way's commitment to reduced government spending – what Reich calls the "conceptual prison" of deficit reduction (1997: 199) – Clinton was unable to match that rhetoric with actual public investments. As Reich (1999: 3) notes about the Clinton Administration, due to its fiscal discipline it "didn't give [public investment] a chance." Without the all-important public investment agenda, Reich describes the Third Way as not a third way at all but "the Second Way, blazed by Reagan and Thatcher" (1999: 12). This is a central theme to which we shall frequently return. Reich's disappointment with the Third Way *in practice* eventually compelled him to resign from the Clinton Cabinet (1997).

To conclude this section before proceeding to a discussion of neoclassical growth theories, evolutionary theory views capitalist economic growth as driven by innovation which requires, above all, human capital. Thus it advocates, as does the Third Way program, an active role for government in the provision of education, research, and public infrastructure. The policy implications, whilst very general, clearly point to the need for increased public spending in the provision of these public goods. Specifically, they point to the need for government to increase public expenditure on networks of educational and research institutions; infrastructure such as roads, transport, and communications; industrial innovations programs; and government regulation and procurement policies.

Neoclassical theory

The development of the standard neoclassical theory of economic growth is commonly attributed to Ramsey (1928), Solow (1956), Swan (1956), Cass (1965), and Koopmans (1965) (see e.g. McCallum 1996: 12; Barro 1997: 1). It will be argued that this is the model of economic growth that the Third Way adopts *in practice*.

Neoclassical theory assumes that firms possess perfect information and complete rationality, which endows them with foresight and therefore certainty about the future (Nelson and Winter 2002: 29). Armed with these attributes, firms can freely pursue their only motive for existing – the maximization of profits. Moreover, not only is their ability to acquire information perfect, it is also costless (Rosenberg 1994: 5). Firms utilize their perfect information and certainty about the relative profitability of all production possibilities to choose a production function which maximizes profits and is therefore Pareto-optimal (Nelson and Winter 2002: 30).

In neoclassical theory, the prime determinant of economic growth is thrift: the level of saving for capital accumulation determines the level (but not the rate) of growth in output and income through the level of investment in the capital stock needed for production (Grossman and Helpman 1994: 23; Singer 1998: 5;

Cesaratto 1999: 772–6). Therefore, higher levels of national saving correspond to greater stocks of productive capacity and higher levels of output and income (Dowrick 1995: 3). This relation points to an important normative role for government in increasing national savings through fiscal discipline, namely surplus budgets and debt retirement, and low levels of taxation (Grossman and Helpman 1994: 36).

All factors of production in neoclassical theory – whether land, labor, or capital – earn a return exactly equal to their marginal contribution to the value of output and are viewed as perfectly substitutable (Fusfield 1999: 88). Factors of production exhibit diminishing marginal productivity, so that the marginal product of each additional unit of a factor diminishes (Barro 1997). The production system is an equilibrium process in which supply and demand are balanced in all markets and determine the prices at which markets clear.

In neoclassical theory, innovation occurs exogenously and is then adopted by firms seeking to maximize profits, which temporarily disturbs the equilibrium of the production process, but, through competition, innovations are then diffused throughout the industry and competitive equilibrium is restored (Buttrick 1960: 187; Lundvall 1992: 8). Innovation and human capital do matter for growth in standard neoclassical theory, but only to the extent that they can increase the productivity of the factors of production, so that the same outputs can be produced with less factor inputs or, alternatively, more outputs can be produced with the same inputs (Abramovitz 1956; Singer 1998: 6).

The time paths of input, output, and prices are interpreted as the paths generated by profit-maximizing firms in a moving equilibrium driven by changes in product demand, factor supply, and technological conditions (Nelson and Winter 1974: 887). Not only innovation and human capital are exogenous to this system, so are institutions, infrastructure, and consumer tastes (Buttrick 1960: 176; Edquist 1997: 44). The neoclassical production function can thus be formally stated as output (Y) is a function (f) of the rate of capital investment (K) and labor growth (L) so that: $Y = f(K, L)$.

Also important to this discussion of the Third Way is the role of human capital in economic growth. In their *Income from Independent Professional Practice* (1945), economists Friedman and Kuznets considered the role of human capital in neoclassical theory. They defined occupational choice and practice in terms of a free-market system: human capital investments, such as the decision to acquire an education, are a decision for the individual beneficiary because the (pecuniary) benefits accrue to the individual.

Milton Friedman (1955), in his influential essay "The Role of Government in Education," expanded upon his earlier paper with Kuznets to argue that government should not fund education and training because the benefits primarily accrue to the individual and therefore the decision to invest in education should be left to him or her (Marginson 1993: 36; DeMartino 1998: 30). In other words, investment in human capital should be regarded just as investment in any other factor of production. A rational, utility-maximizing individual, the argument goes, will invest in her education and training until the marginal utility – in the form of additional future earning capacity for example – is equal to the marginal cost – which is the income forgone due to study for example. Friedman explains in a definitive statement of the neoclassical position that because the benefits accrue to the individual there is no reason the individual rather than the government should not pay the full cost of the investment in human capital:

> Vocational and professional schooling... is a form of investment precisely analogous to investment in machinery, buildings, or other forms of non-human capital. Its function is to raise the economic productivity of the human being. If it does so, the individual is rewarded in a free enterprise society by receiving a higher return for his services than he would otherwise be able to command. This difference in economic return is the economic incentive to invest in human capital whether in the form of a machine or a human being. In both cases, extra returns must be balanced against the costs of acquiring them. For vocational schooling, the major costs are the income forgone during the period of training, interest lost by postponing the beginning of the earning period, and special expenses of acquiring the training such as tuition fees and expenditure on books and equipment... in both cases, an individual presumably regards the investment as desirable if the extra returns... exceed the extra costs.... If the individual undertakes the investment and if the state neither subsidizes the investment nor taxes the return, the individual... bears all the extra costs and receives all the extra returns: there are no obvious unborne costs or unappropriable returns that tend to make private incentives diverge systematically from those that are socially appropriate.
>
> (1962: 100–1)

Becker (1975: 45) similarly argues that, as with any other form of investment, the rate of return is "the most important single determinant of the amount invested in human capital."

The Solow neoclassical growth model

As a matter of historical interest, EGT emerged from the failure of Solow's neoclassical growth model to adequately explain the role of innovation in economic growth. Solow's (1956) growth model focuses attention on the process of capital formation. Aggregate savings, he argues, finance additions to the national capital stock. An economy with an initially low capital–labor ratio will have a high marginal product of capital. Then, if a constant fraction of the income generated by a new piece of equipment is saved, the gross investment in new capital goods may exceed the amount needed to offset depreciation and to equip new members of the workforce, thus the capital–labor ratio will rise – known as "capital deepening" – and national output and income will increase. Solow's theory is clearly neoclassical because it utilizes an aggregate production function as well as the assumptions of instant market-clearing and general equilibrium

(Jones, C. 1998: 69–70). Swan (1956) contemporaneously developed a similar analysis that was less mathematically explicit (McCallum 1996: 12).

In a famous empirical study, Solow (1957) examined the period 1909 to 1949 in the United States. Solow's conclusion was that over 80 percent of the growth in output per labor hour was due to productivity increases from innovation and not to the growth in the quantity of inputs *per se*. Specifically, Solow found that of the average annual growth of 2.9 percent per annum over that period, 0.32 percentage points was attributable to capital accumulation, 1.09 percentage points due to increases in the input of labor, and the remaining 1.49 percentage points to innovation. This last portion of the growth rate, that portion that cannot be attributed to capital or labor, is known as the "Solow residual" (Coombs *et al.* 1987: 143).

The paradox of Solow's 1957 paper is that he found innovation to be more important for economic growth than capital accumulation (Cesaratto 1999). The reason is that, without innovation, the assumption of diminishing returns to capital means that per capita growth must eventually cease (Barro 1997: 3). Solow's (1960) tenuous solution to the paradox was to argue that investment is the vehicle for innovation since "many if not most innovations need to be embodied in new kinds of durable equipment before they can be made effective" (Solow 1960: 91). Thus Solow sought to protect the integrity of the neoclassical model by substantially redeploying the neoclassical argument that innovation matters to the extent that it increases the productivity of capital. As Phelps (1962: 549) remarks, in Solow's argument "investment has been married to technology." Arrow's (1962) contribution, which Cesaratto (1999: 780) claims may represent the inspiration for EGT, takes Solow's defense a step further in his "learning-by-doing" model with the argument that capital investment is not only the vehicle for innovation but represents its source by linking investment to the increasing returns from learning processes.

Solow's (1957) revision to neoclassical growth theory can be formally stated as output (Y) is a function (f) of capital (K), labor (L), and innovation (A) so that $Y = Af(K, L)$, where A is a given constant. Solow's contribution can be therefore understood as the addition of innovation to the basic neoclassical growth model. Innovation here refers to advances in knowledge and technology and points to the important roles of research, education, and training as sources of growth (Solow 1970).

Like Solow, Denison (1985) found that for the period 1929–82 in the United States, output per labor hour grew at the rate of 1.58 percent per annum, of which 1.02 percentage points were due to technical innovation. Denison's finding thus supports Solow's estimate that most of the output in growth per labor hour is due to innovation. As noted, without innovation, per capita economic growth will eventually cease as diminishing returns to capital set in. Technological progress can offset the tendency for the marginal product to fall, and in the long run countries exhibit per capita growth at the rate of innovation.

However, the problem remained that Solow's model treats technological innovation as exogenous to the production process. Innovation simply occurs and, due to its exogenous treatment, has been famously described as Solow's "black box" (Rosenberg 1982) and "manna from heaven" (Jones, C. 1998: 33). Later economists, such as the endogenous growth theorists, would attempt to unpack, that is, explain, the black box of innovation.

Endogenous growth theory

In response to the failure of neoclassical growth theory to adequately explain the role of innovation within growth, Romer (1990), Aghion and Howitt (1992), Lucas (1988), King and Rebelo (1990), and Grossman and Helpman (1991) have sought to extend neoclassical models so that they incorporate endogenous innovation, hence the name "*endogenous* growth theory" (Dowrick 1995: 3; McCallum 1996: 14).

They begin by expanding the concept of capital in neoclassical theory from physical capital to include human capital (Barro 1997: 2). According to the theory's pioneer, Paul Romer, EGT

> distinguishes itself from neoclassical growth by emphasizing that economic growth is an endogenous outcome of an economic system, not the result of forces that impinge from outside. For this reason, the theoretical work does not invoke exogenous technological change to explain why income per capita has increased by an order of magnitude since the industrial revolution.... It tries instead to uncover the private and public sector choices that cause the rate of growth of the residual to vary across countries.
>
> (1994a: 3)

Romer (1986, 1989, 1994a) argues that innovations are based on ideas and an inherent characteristic of ideas is that they are nonrivalrous. That is, once an idea has been produced, anyone with knowledge of the idea can utilize it. Nonrivalrous goods need to be produced only once because, by definition, more than one consumer can utilize the goods, even simultaneously. Thus, nonrivalrous goods such as ideas involve a fixed cost of production and zero marginal cost. For example, it can cost a great deal to produce the first unit of a software program but, equipped with that knowledge, subsequent units cost very little to reproduce.

Romer's analysis led to a simple but powerful insight: because ideas (and therefore innovations) are nonrivalrous, their producers cannot capture the full benefits or value unless they can capture monopoly rents for their ideas through devices such as patents.

No firm would invest the often vast resources required to develop ideas in a perfectly competitive market because it would not be able to capture the returns required to justify the investment. Therefore, the fact that producers of ideas price their ideas above the marginal cost of production means that they receive increasing rather than constant or diminishing returns to scale. The presence of increasing returns to scale, according to neoclassical canons, indicates imperfect competition. To continue with the software program example: whilst the very first unit of the program is very expensive to produce each additional copy costs very little but is sold at a very high markup. Romer's finding develops Knight's (1944) influential study of the improvements in society's stock of productive knowledge in overcoming the law of diminishing returns in a growing economy.

Furthermore, according to Romer, because ideas can be a classic positive externality, since once they are released their producers may not be able to prevent others from utilizing them, the market will tend to supply a less than socially optimum level of these ideas, as markets tend to do with positive externalities. As the long run rate of economic growth depends entirely on the rate at which innovation and knowledge grow, which the market is thought to under-supply, the public sector has a vital role to play in supplementing the private provision of research and education through policy instruments such as public investment, tax subsidies, and intellectual property rights (Romer 1986, 1994a,b).

Lucas (1988) develops Denison (1962), Schultz (1962), Arrow (1962), Uzawa (1965), and Becker's (1975) models of human capital investment and growth and comes to the same conclusion as Romer, that growth is driven by the rate of investment in human capital (Sinha 2000: 56). In Lucas' model, investment in human capital is more important for economic growth than investment in physical capital. Lucas shows that human capital produces positive externalities to society which the individual is unable to completely appropriate, so that there will be a tendency for individuals to invest less in formal skill enhancement than is socially desirable. He therefore concludes that government policy that results in a permanent increase in the time individuals spend developing their human capital generates a permanent increase in the growth of output per worker and therefore raises economic growth.

As a neoclassical model should, Lucas' establishes a connection between saving and growth "since the higher the discount rate, the lower we would expect saving and investment rates to be in all forms of capital" (Hall, P. 1994: 332). This is why Lucas (1988: 19–20) describes his model as "identical" to Solow's because saving and growth are connected in the rate of human capital investment, and therefore the rate of change of labor efficiency is dependent on the saving and investment decisions of the community. Lucas is substantially redeploying the standard neoclassical argument: that the higher the rate of investment in human capital, the higher will be the efficiency or productivity of labor, and this will increase the efficiency of capital (Fine 2000: 249), thus increasing the growth rate.

Mankiw *et al.* (1992) evaluated the empirical implications of the Solow model and found that it performed well but could be improved by extending the model to include human capital, that is, by recognizing that labor in different economies may possess different levels of education and skills. Their extension of the Solow model found that economic growth is driven by investment in human capital, innovation, investment in physical capital, and low population growth rates. In fact, they suggest factor-shares of one-third each for physical capital, human capital, and raw labor. Furthermore, in the steady state, per capita output grows at the rate of innovation just as in the original (1957) Solow model. Thus they conclude that "the Solow model is consistent with the international evidence if one acknowledges the importance of human as well as physical capital" (Mankiw *et al.* 1992: 433; Grossman and Helpman 1994: 27).

Barro and Sala-I-Martin (1995) collated extensive testing of the impact of investment in human capital on growth and found that educational expenditures by governments have a strong positive impact – an annual rate of return on public education in the order of 20 percent.

EGT can be understood in its formal statement as output (Y) is a function (f) of capital (K), labor (L), innovation (A), and human capital (H) so that $Y = Af(K, H, L)$. The principal contribution therefore is the addition of human capital as a separate form of capital to the Solow (1957) growth model. The decisive difference between standard neoclassical growth theory and EGT, however, is that the latter allows for the possibility of increasing returns, whereby if all inputs are doubled, it is possible for output to more than double. This result obtains because, as Romer (1990) explains, knowledge is not completely excludable, so that a doubling in the amount of knowledge can result in a more than doubling of its productive utilization by firms. Lucas (1988), meanwhile, attributes the increasing returns to human capital rather than to knowledge *per se*.

Unlike standard neoclassical theory but as with evolutionary theorists, EGT theorists argue for public intervention and investment in the provision of basic R&D, education and training, intellectual property rights, and knowledge infrastructure – inputs which the private sector will tend to under-produce (Dowrick 1995). EGT also recommends low rates of taxation on capital as the neoclassical prescription is that taxation should not be levied on capital, the accumulable factor of production, since this will reduce the incentive to save, and hence the level of investment and growth (Fine 2000: 259).

It is imperative to note that whilst EGT reaches similar normative conclusions as evolutionary theory, it does so for very different reasons. Where evolutionary theory recommends government provision of certain public goods due to its unique strategic role in stimulating innovation, EGT does so solely for correcting market failure – the textbook neoclassical rationale for government intervention.

EGT's normative prescriptions have had an influence on the Third Way program. As noted earlier, in the autumn of 1994, the then British Shadow Chancellor, Gordon Brown, was lampooned by the media for referring to "post-neoclassical endogenous growth theory" in a speech on economic policy (Crafts 1996: 30).

Fine (2000: 257) is critical of EGT as a reconstruction of Schumpeter within "mainstream neoclassical economics" and, as evidence, points to the fact that Solow (1991) entitles a section "Formalizing Schumpeter." The evolutionary economist Richard Nelson (1998: 499) also criticizes EGT for attempting to incorporate Schumpeter's innovation model, which is one of disequilibrium, into neoclassical general equilibrium theory. Sinha (2000) notes EGT's failure to deliver on its promise to properly endogenize innovation and human capital within neoclassical growth theory and Kurz and Salvadori (1998) dismiss it as "old wine in a new goatskin." However, perhaps the strongest criticism belongs to

Setterfield (2003), who argues that since endogenous growth theorists can connect capital, labor, innovation, and human capital to the rate of growth, the central problem is that there is very little that it *cannot* connect to growth, which makes it difficult to establish exactly what the determinants of growth are (2003: 24).

Conclusion

Both evolutionary and endogenous growth theories believe the prime determinants of economic growth are innovation and human capital, whilst for standard neoclassical theory it is saving. This analytical disagreement leads to an important divergence over the normative role of government in fostering economic growth.

The evolutionary and endogenous growth theorists advocate active government investment in the NSI: innovation, human capital, and infrastructure. Standard neoclassical theory, on the other hand, advocates fiscal discipline in order to increase savings for capital accumulation, along with low levels of taxation and minimal government intervention. Government spending of any kind is thought to displace private spending through the "crowding-out" effect (see Chapter 3 for a discussion of the crowding-out effect). Investment decisions in innovation and human capital are thought to be best left to individuals and firms to determine and fund. Despite the intellectual debt the Third Way program owes to the normative conclusions of both evolutionary and endogenous growth theories, we shall see that *in practice* it is to the standard neoclassical theory of growth that it most closely adheres.

It is also important to note that both of these approaches to economic growth – the evolutionary and the neoclassical – are principally concerned with the supply side of the economy, that is, with the productive capacity of the economy. This means that both the program and practice of the Third Way lack a demand side, an important issue to which we shall return.

3 The Third Way and public finance

We can now turn to consider the other component of the Third Way program, its program of public finance. In his classic text on the theory of public finance, Musgrave (1959) distinguishes three distinct purposes of public finance: allocation, distribution, and stabilization. Allocation policy is concerned with securing necessary adjustments in the market's allocation of resources between public and private wants. Distribution policy addresses the distribution of resources within the economy. Stabilization policy is concerned with achieving and maintaining full employment, price stability, and economic growth. It is in the context of this last purpose that this chapter reviews the issue of public finance.

There have long been two main intellectual traditions in macroeconomics and they may be broadly defined as either neoclassical or "imperfectionist." The former believes that markets operate most efficiently without interference, whilst the latter believes that government intervention can significantly improve the operation of the markets. However, within these two broad traditions, there are many different theoretical variations, each with its own rationales, mechanisms, and policy prescriptions.

Within the neoclassical tradition alone, for example, "standard" neoclassical theory argues that public sector budget deficits are in all cases detrimental to the growth of the economy because public spending displaces (more productive) private spending, whilst other neoclassical variants argue that public spending can in fact be beneficial for growth as it can increase the productivity of private spending. We will first consider the standard neoclassical proposition that public spending will crowd out private spending and/or create a twin-deficits problem.

Standard neoclassical theory

Neoclassical theory assumes all consumers and firms are rational utility- and profit-maximizing agents respectively who enjoy costless access to perfect information and operate in competitive markets which are characterized by market clearing and equilibrium outcomes (for an overview see O'Hara 1999: 788–9). Consumers decide between the marginal utility and marginal cost of purchasing a good and, similarly, firms decide between the marginal revenue and marginal cost of producing a good. Consumers cease purchasing when marginal utility equals marginal cost and firms cease additional production when marginal revenue equals marginal cost. All markets are assumed to be sufficiently competitive so that all consumers and firms are price-takers, that is, they are individually unable to influence prices. Static efficiency and the optimal allocation of resources are the central concerns, and they are achieved when all markets clear. When this occurs, full employment is also achieved and general equilibrium prevails.

In the standard neoclassical economic system, therefore, there is no danger of recession, other than for brief periods, because of the (microeconomic) laws of supply and demand (Lerner 1977). An excess supply of anything over the demand for it causes the price to fall until the market clears and equilibrium is restored. Unemployment, for example, is an excess supply of labor. It causes the price of labor to fall relative to other prices. At the lower real wage level, the labor market clears and a full employment equilibrium is restored.

As standard neoclassical theory views the economy as always being or tending to be fully employed (Newman 1968: 174), all resources are utilized; therefore goods and services purchased by the government cannot also be purchased by the private sector (Argyrous 1999: 30). Hence, any government expenditure must displace a proportion of private expenditure – so-called real crowding-out. If government expenditure crowds out an equivalent amount of private expenditure, so that the impact on total spending is zero, then it is said to result in "complete crowding-out." Alternatively, crowding-out is considered "partial" if the increased government expenditure reduces private expenditure by a smaller amount. "Overcrowding-out" occurs if the increase in government expenditure displaces a larger amount of private expenditure. (For a qualitative discussion of the process of crowding-out see Arestis 1985: 100.)

There are two distinct mechanisms through which crowding-out occurs. In a closed full employment economy, funds borrowed by the government to purchase goods and services in excess of tax revenue (deficit-finance) cannot also be borrowed by the private sector. The consequent competition for funds raises real interest rates so that government borrowing displaces or crowds out private borrowing for investment – so-called financial crowding-out.

In contrast, in an open economy with internationally mobile capital, net exports rather than domestic investment are crowded out. The reason is that higher real interest rates due to public sector budget deficits attract an inflow of foreign funds which, with flexible exchange rates, cause the currency to appreciate and thereby reduce the affordability (and therefore volume) of exports. This can result in a current account deficit. This argument – that public sector budget deficits also cause trade deficits – is the neoclassical theory of the twin deficits.

Twin-deficits theory relies on an assumption that an increase in government saving will increase national savings, which will, in turn, close the gap between national savings and national investment, thereby lowering the current account deficit as less funds are needed from foreign lenders. This follows the accounting identity whereby the current account (CA) equals investment (*I*) less private saving (S_p) and government saving (S_g):

$$CA = I - (S_p + S_g).$$

(For an extensive discussion of twin-deficits theory see Bernheim 1989; Yellen 1989; Eisner 1991a.)

In a large open economy, like the United States, both mechanisms are likely to operate (Yellen 1989: 18). But regardless of the mechanism through which crowding-out occurs, the implications, according to standard neoclassical theory, are qualitatively identical. In the closed economy scenario, public sector budget deficits reduce domestic investment and move the economy to a growth path with lower per capita output and capital per worker. In the open economy scenario, current account deficits induce growing foreign debt, resulting in a burden of future interest payments which will lower the disposable income of domestic consumers. It is important to bear in mind the critical assumption upon which this argument rests: that markets clear or tend to clear so that resources – including labor – are fully employed. We shall see that without this assumption, this argument cannot hold. Importantly, it will also be shown that the neoclassical theories of crowding-out and the twin deficits exerted a decisive influence on the Third Way's practice of macroeconomic policy. The term "standard" is used throughout this study to distinguish this neoclassical theory from more elaborated versions.

It is of historical interest that the classical economist Adam Smith pioneered the theory of crowding-out as early as 1776 by condemning the transfer of resources from the private sector to the government, whether through taxation or borrowing (Arestis 1985: 102). Adam Smith (1776: 925) argued that "saving is spending" because one person's saving becomes another's investment. Therefore borrowing funds from the public to finance government expenditure, he asserts, involves the "destruction of some capital which had before existed in the country; by the perversion of some portion of the annual produce which had before been destined for the maintenance of productive labour, towards that of unproductive labour." Not only does government expenditure therefore cause real crowding-out of private expenditure but, if it is financed by borrowing, it also causes financial crowding-out of private borrowing (for investment), by raising the interest rates that are required to restore equilibrium between saving and investment (Newman 1968: 15).

For Adam Smith, as with standard neoclassical theory, a nation becomes more wealthy if its citizens and its government all refrain from excessive consumption today and save for the future (Romer 1994b). A high rate of saving will lead to the accumulation of more productive assets. His central concerns are saving and capital accumulation. Excessive spending on current consumption, especially by the government, is the most serious threat to sustained economic growth.

To summarize: the effect of government expenditure in neoclassical theory is to displace either private investment and/or consumption (Musgrave 1959: 556–80). The actual result depends on the type of expenditures the government makes. If the government spends for investment then a portion of private investment will be crowded out. If the government spends for consumption, then a portion of private consumption will be crowded out. If the government borrows, a portion of private borrowing will be crowded out. Finally, if the government debt is financed through foreign borrowing and/or it causes private investment to be financed through foreign borrowing, the currency will appreciate, the volume of exports may decline, and service payments for the debt will leave the country, thus deficits may arise in the current account. Therefore, the budget deficit can result in a current account deficit – the twin deficits.

Normatively, neoclassical theory's concern with government expenditure is two-fold (Rowley 1986). First, increased government expenditure increases the size and scope of the state at the expense of individual liberty. Second, the public sector cannot allocate resources as efficiently as the private sector. Therefore, government expenditure should be kept to a minimum so as to interfere as little as possible with the efficient allocation of resources, and (low) taxation is preferable to government borrowing for the reasons discussed above (Newman 1968: 174).

While standard neoclassical theory concludes that public spending crowds out private spending; theorists have provided a number of (not mutually exclusive) explanations of the *mechanism* through which crowding-out occurs. Of these, monetarism is an important one.

Monetarism began with Milton Friedman's (1956) restatement of the quantity theory of money, and Karl Brunner (1968) – who named the school – added several important hypotheses (Mayer 1990: xi).

The basic tenet of monetarist theory is the quantity theory of money, which states that money is neutral and therefore the price level is proportional to the quantity of money in both the short and the long run. This relation is expressed in the well-known equation of exchange $MV = PQ$: the money stock (M) multiplied by its velocity (V) equals prices (P) multiplied by output (Q).

Monetarism's principal analytical arguments are (1) that the quantity of money is the prime determinant of the level of prices and nominal economic activity; (2) that excessive growth in the money stock is responsible for inflation; and (3) that unstable monetary growth is responsible for economic fluctuations.

Modern monetarists such as Milton Friedman (1968, 1983) and Mayer (1990), however, disagree with the quantity theory's claim that money is neutral in the short run. They distinguish between the short- and long-run effects of changes in money supply. In the short run, they argue, an increase in the money stock can in fact increase the level of aggregate demand and output provided the changes are unanticipated so that inflationary expectations have not fully adapted. Only in the long run do changes in the money stock affect the price level and are therefore neutral with respect to real output and employment.

A central monetarist proposition is that growth in the money stock in excess of the growth in real output results in inflation (Friedman, M. 1956). Milton Friedman (1974: 24) famously expressed this argument as "inflation is always and everywhere a monetary phenomenon." Monetarism's central concern with growth in the money stock and inflation is said to be its distinguishing feature (Laidler 1982: 3–4).

A. W. Phillips (1958) attempted to show through his Phillips curve that there exists an inverse relationship – and therefore always a trade-off – between unemployment and wage inflation. Phelps (1967) and M. Friedman (1968) disagreed, arguing instead that the existence of simultaneous unemployment and inflation (stagflation) negated the Phillips curve relationship in the long run. In the long run, the economy will move to some level of unemployment – which they named the "natural rate of unemployment" – below which inflation accelerates but above which there is no trade-off between unemployment and inflation. Moreover, according to Friedman and Phelps, the Phillips curve ignores the effects of expected inflation on wage setting by employees and employers. They incorporated inflation expectations into the Phillips curve to produce what is known as the "expectations-augmented wage-Phillips curve," which simply states that money wages rise more the higher the expected rate of inflation.

The important implication of Phelps and Friedman's analysis for macroeconomic policy is that using activist fiscal policy to increase aggregate demand cannot reduce unemployment below the natural rate without incurring the cost of accelerating inflation, which may produce a vicious cycle by increasing expected inflation, which in turn increases actual inflation.

Normatively, monetarism prefers policies that minimize variability and uncertainty for the private sector. For this reason, it prefers monetary policy to fiscal policy as the superior instrument of macroeconomic management (Laidler 1982: 3–4; Mayer 1990: 17–18). Monetarism recommends, in particular, a monetary policy of low and constant growth in the money stock *pari passu* with output according to a constant money growth rule rather than at the discretion of the government (Friedman, M. 1983). In this way, inflation is minimized because growth in the money stock does not exceed growth in real output.

Low inflation is seen as essential to providing certainty to consumers and firms' economic planning, thereby avoiding large economic fluctuations. "Our economic system," says Milton Friedman (1968), "will work best when producers and consumers, employers and employees, can proceed with full confidence that the average level of prices will behave in a known way in the future."

Monetarism is opposed to activist fiscal policy, especially when financed by creating money, because it is thought to be inflationary (Stein 1976: 2; Mayer 1990: 39–40). Another reason monetary policy is preferred is because, unlike fiscal policy, it is considered to be relatively free from political pressure, especially when set to a rule (Galbraith 1975: 280). The decisions of the central banks are not subject, like fiscal policy, to the political pressures of the legislature and the executive, where fiscal policy is set, and are therefore considered purer and more immediate in their effect on the economy.

Monetarism views the private sector as inherently stable and more efficient than government because firms are subject to competitive pressures, and therefore it opposes political interference in the marketplace, such as through the imposition of price and wage controls for example (Laidler 1982: 28–9). Another reason monetarism opposes inflation is because it raises the share of the government sector in the economy, with the resulting temptation to increase government expenditures further, resulting in a government spending–inflation spiral. Milton Friedman (1975), for example, is an opponent of big government and favors tax cuts during recessions and public spending cuts during booms, with the net effect of reducing the government's share of the economy.

Milton Friedman (1972) argues that increases in government expenditure displace private expenditure (real crowding-out) and, if deficit-financed, displace private investment by raising interest rates to such a degree as to discourage private investment. The actual extent of the increased government expenditure depends on how the expenditure is financed:

> If...they are financed by creating money, they unquestionably do produce inflationary pressure.... If they are financed by borrowing from the public, at whatever interest rates are necessary, they may still exert some minor inflationary pressure.... However, their major effect will be to make interest rates higher than they would otherwise be.
>
> (1974: 140)

The theory known as the "new classical macroeconomics" attempts to build macroeconomic theory based on explicit neoclassical microeconomic foundations. It also argues that public spending can crowd out private spending and investment. It accepts the standard microeconomic principles of neoclassical theory but makes important additions of its own by replacing the neoclassical assumption of perfect information with Muth's (1961) rational expectations hypothesis and adding its new classical equilibrium (Lucas 1973).

In Muth's rational expectations hypothesis people are thought to be rational utility-maximizing agents who use all available information and their knowledge of the way the economy works to efficiently determine their expectations and modify their behavior rapidly in anticipation of change. Note Muth's important departure from standard neoclassical theory: people use all available information but do not have perfect and complete information. Economic agents therefore do not know the future with certainty and must base their plans and decisions, including price setting, on their forecasts or expectations of the future. Since these expectations are rational, people may make random errors (which are unrelated to previous errors) but they do not make systematic mistakes. For example, if people have information that the money supply will increase and know that this will result in higher prices, then they will alter their behavior accordingly to offset the higher prices. Thus changes in money matter only while they are unexpected, and an increase in money cannot be unexpected for ever.

The second component of the theory, the new classical equilibrium, insists that prices are fully flexible and therefore markets clear immediately. It attempts to explain that economic disturbances and consequent transitory departures from the equilibrium are due to information problems. Lucas presents a neoclassical model with one modification: perfect information is replaced with rational expectations so that some people do not know the aggregate price level but do know the nominal wage or price at which they can buy and sell. If all nominal prices and wages rise in proportion, the real wage remains unchanged, but if workers do not realize that prices have also risen, they will think that the real wage has risen and will supply more labor, so output will rise, until they realize their error.

Similarly, firms know the price of their good in their market but may not know the aggregate price level due to imperfect information. Thus, they form the best expectation they can of the relative price of their good. Firms know there are two types of shocks in the economy: relative shocks which are specific to individual markets and aggregate shocks which raise demand in every market. In the case of an aggregate shock, such as an unexpected increase in the money stock, the aggregate price level will rise. Consider the firm which has an expectation of the aggregate price level and finds that the relative price of its good in the market is high. The firm must then decide whether this is because demand in all markets has increased, raising the aggregate price level, or in just its own market, raising the relative price level. If it is the former, the firm will not want to raise output, but if it is the latter, it will want to increase output. Lucas' key finding is that the firm's rational expectation is to attribute the increased relative price to both sources equally, which means that the firm will increase output in response to an increase in the money stock but only if it is unexpected. Thus, Lucas succeeded in relating higher aggregate prices to higher output as an explanation for transitory deviations from the equilibrium.

The implications of the new classical macroeconomics for policy are remark-able. Any systematic government attempts to stabilize the economy by means of fiscal or monetary policy are bound to be totally ineffective because their effect will be fully discounted by rational expectations. Nor can the government successfully pursue any *ad hoc* measures to offset shocks because the private sector is already anticipating any shocks. Government policy could only assist if its information were better than the private sector's, which is impossible by the definition of the hypothesis as all agents have access to the same information (Modigliani 1977). Under these conditions, government intervention would most likely result in further destabilization.

Based on the hypothesis of rational expectations and the predicted absence of any trade-off between inflation and unemployment in the short and long run, new classical theory concludes with its policy ineffectiveness proposition: that unemployment is insensitive to demand management policies (Stein 1984: 58). Therefore, government should abstain from an active fiscal stabilization policy as its effects would be anticipated and therefore rendered ineffective (Modigliani quoted in Klamer 1984: 123–5). Its effects could only be effective if they were implemented by surprise, which, according to Lucas and Sargeant (1981: 633), "may very well be dangerous" for the economy.

New classical theory recommends fiscal and monetary policy rules which maximize certainty and stability (Lucas 1986). Like monetarism, new classical theory agues for a constant growth rate in the money supply that adheres to a monetary rule and for constant (or smooth) tax rates (Sargeant and Wallace 1976; Lucas and Sargeant 1981: 254, 633). Monetary policy should be considered only as a means of selecting a politically acceptable rate of inflation, and fiscal policy dismissed as an instrument of active stabilization.

The Ricardian equivalence theorem is an extreme extension of the rational expectations hypothesis which also argues that public spending can crowd out private spending and investment. It was originally noted but rejected by the nineteenth-century political economist David Ricardo, for whom it is named, and later refurbished by Barro (1974).

The theorem states that the method of financing government expenditure is irrelevant because taxation and public debt are exactly equivalent in their effect on the economy provided that current and future taxes have no allocative effects; all agents understand that the substitution of current debt issue for current taxation represents the substitution of future taxes for present taxes; and those same agents evaluate future taxes as having exactly the same present value as the current taxes they replace.

The reason that taxation and deficits are equivalent in their effect on the economy is that rational and far-sighted households realize that taxes now are equivalent to taxes later, and since taxes postponed do eventually have to be paid, these households save now to pay for future tax increases, leaving their permanent income unaffected (Barro 1991). Therefore, shifts between taxes and budget deficits do not matter for the rate of consumption, the real interest rate, the quantity of investment, or the current account balance.

The central implication of this argument is that government budget deficits do not affect *total* spending (Barro 1974). This is because when governments run budget deficits, consumers save more to pay for the future tax increases required to repay the deficits; thus consumption declines and total spending remains unchanged. Therefore, government expenditure crowds out an equivalent amount of private expenditure (complete crowding-out).

The ultrarationality hypothesis is the final variant of neoclassical theory, which argues that government spending crowds out private spending. It too is an extreme extension of the rational expectations hypothesis and a close relative of the Ricardian equivalence theorem.

The hypothesis states that government expenditure is a close substitute for private expenditure (David and Scadding 1974). This hypothesis rests on the assumption that the combined savings ratio of the private and public sectors is more stable than that of either alone. Therefore, it follows that an increase in government expenditure would reduce private expenditure by an equivalent amount (complete crowding-out).

The private sector behaves as if government were an extension of it, so that government expenditures are considered as substitutes for private expenditures. Thus crowding-out may take the form of direct substitution independently of any adjustment in the interest rate, inflation, or the exchange rate. Increases in government expenditure not financed by creating money will leave total expenditure unchanged since, like the Ricardian equivalence theorem, the private sector perceives debt-finance as simply deferred tax liabilities.

"Imperfectionist" neoclassical models

The previous section discussed the standard neoclassical propositions of crowding-out and the twin deficits, and the analytical apparatus that has been developed to support them. However, many self-described neoclassical economists would strongly disagree with these propositions. There is a range of views, which we may call "imperfectionist" models of neoclassical theory, which concludes that a market economy does not tend to full employment, which therefore creates scope for active government macroeconomic policy (Eatwell and Milgate 1983). This conclusion is the unifying factor for what I shall term "imperfectionist" neoclassical economics, and I will discuss the various mechanisms by which the conclusion has been reached. The purpose of this section is to show that, even within the neoclassical tradition, there exist a number of theories of public finance that explain, justify, and even prescribe government spending and intervention. Thus, within the neoclassical tradition, there is a wide range of government policy prescriptions available to policy-makers beyond standard fiscal discipline or 'sound' public finance.

The economist David Aschauer shares the neoclassical belief in market clearing, but the importance of his contribution has been to show that crowding-out is not a necessary conclusion of neoclassical theory, contrary to the arguments hitherto reviewed.

In a series of highly influential papers, Aschauer (1988, 1989, 1990) focused attention on public infrastructure by arguing that government capital spending complements private sector productivity and can increase private output *even at full employment*. He even attributes the United States' declining total factor productivity during the 1980s to the reduction in investment in the nonmilitary public capital stock.

In particular, argues Aschauer, expansions in public investment spending have a larger stimulative impact on private output than equal increases in public consumption expenditure. That is, *even at full employment*, government expenditure can still raise aggregate output through its productivity-enhancing effects. Specifically, public investment is argued to induce an increase in the profitability or rate of return to private capital, thereby stimulating private investment expenditure. In other words, public capital expenditure actually *crowds in* private investment. Aschauer (1990: 19) calculates that, in the long run, for every dollar increase in public investment, private investment rises (is crowded in) by approximately 45 cents. Munnel's (1990) reestimates of Aschauer's (1989) original calculations find an even larger marginal productivity of public capital of approximately 60 percent; that is, a $1.00 increase in the public capital stock would raise aggregate output by 60 cents (Munnell 1992: 191).

The extent of Aschauer's conclusions has been challenged by Ford and Poret (1991: 74), who nevertheless conclude that "high infrastructure investments in the post war period have had high productivity growth." Holtz-Eakin (1994: 20) finds that the aggregate data do not reveal a sufficiently large relationship between public sector capital and private production to support Aschauer's claim that government capital spillovers are the source of variations in private productivity. Gramlich (1994: 1193–4) finds the evidence for Aschauer's arguments "decidedly mixed"; he is skeptical of Aschauer's high estimates of public infrastructure's productivity yet argues that it would be more efficient to pay for such investments from user fees rather than general government revenue. K. Smith (1997: 91) finds these studies inconclusive as "they concentrate on relatively simple correlations, they ignore lag structures, and they do not discuss factors... shaping infrastructures [such as] the scientific and technological dimension." Another criticism commonly leveled at Auschauer is that the direction of causation may, in fact, run the other way round: higher levels of output lead to greater public capital investment (Eisner 1991b; Munnell 1992: 194; Gramlich 1994: 1188; Holtz-Eakin 1994: 12).

Within the neoclassical tradition, there is a group of economists which disagrees with the concept of market clearing, believing instead that markets – especially the labor market – do not necessarily clear and that therefore there is a role for active government intervention. These economists attempted to unite Keynesian macroeconomics with neoclassical microeconomic principles in the form of the "neoclassical synthesis," coined by Samuelson in the mid-1950s (Eatwell *et al.* 1991: 504). Modigliani explains that:

> One of the basic themes that has dominated my scientific concern [has been to integrate] the main building blocks of the *General Theory* with the more established [neoclassical] methodology of economics, which rests on the basic postulate of rational maximizing behavior on the part of economic agents...
>
> (1980: xi)

The Neoclassical–Keynesian Synthesis is based on the IS-LM model first introduced by Hicks (1937). The model claims to represent the essence of Keynes' *General Theory* (1936) in the form of a system of simultaneous equations that relate saving, investment, income, and the rate of interest in the goods and money markets. It was later extended by Modigliani (1944), Patinkin (1948), and Hansen (1949, 1953) to relate the goods and money markets to the labor market.

One of the startling results of the IS-LM model is that it failed to obtain the Keynesian case of an "unemployment equilibrium" (Blaug 1980: 678; Snowdon *et al.* 1994: 109). The reason for this failure is known as the Pigou effect after one of the last great classical economists who spoke for the classical school in the 1940s. It argues that, if money wages and prices were flexible, the Keynesian model would not come to rest at less than a full employment equilibrium as falling prices increase real wealth, which in turn increases consumption expenditure. In theory, the economy cannot settle at an unemployment equilibrium but will automatically adjust until full employment is achieved (Pigou 1928, 1943, 1947).

Thus, in order to secure an unemployment equilibrium within the IS-LM framework, neo-Keynesians added rigid money wages and other imperfections to this system. Modigliani (1944) showed that Keynesian results could be derived from an otherwise equilibrium model if the money-wage rate were fixed. Since it was widely believed that wages were "sticky" or less than fully flexible in the short run, Keynesian theory could apply – hence the neo-Keynesian Synthesis, the conclusions of which are neoclassical in the long run but Keynesian in the short run. The synthesis asserts by logical extension that the *General Theory* is in fact a special case of neoclassical general equilibrium theory.

In Keynesian theory, unemployment arises from insufficient demand (Rowthorn 1981). When demand is depressed, firms are forced to sell their output at low prices and, as a result, real wages are high and profits are low. Money wages are high because, due to their rigidity or stickiness, they do not decrease to meet demand in the same manner as the prices of goods. Since profits are low and wages are high, firms refuse to invest and the economy stagnates.

In an important microeconomic development for the theory, Modigliani and Brumberg (1954) formalized the consumption function in the neoclassical terms of utility-maximization. According to the life-cycle theory of consumption and saving (Modigliani and Brumberg 1954; Ando and Modigliani 1963), households decide current consumption and plan future consumption not only on the basis of current income but also based on their wealth, so as to average their consumption over their lifetime. An increase in current wealth then will cause households to increase current as well as future consumption. In turn, this means that increases in current wealth in the form of government bonds will lead to increased current and future consumption and, thus, increased investment and employment.

Keynesian theory argues that, because of market imperfections, the *less-than-full employment* equilibrium that results provides government scope for intervention. The scope consists in supplementing insufficient demand through government expenditure so that firms can raise their prices and generate the profits required to stimulate their investment (Rowthorn 1981). Keynesian theory recommends counter-cyclical fiscal policy so that, in recessions, government may run a budget deficit to stimulate aggregate demand by increasing both public and private investment (Samuelson 1951; Modigliani 1961).

Samuelson and Modigliani's recommendations are based on the neo-Keynesian tenet that there is a fiscal policy multiplier in excess of unity, which itself rests on the view that the economy "normally" operates at less-than-full employment (Stein 1976: 11). Therefore, if tax rates were reduced and the resulting deficits were financed through the sale of bonds, then aggregate income would rise and unemployment would fall. Therefore, contrary to neoclassical theory, government expenditure that is deficit-financed through the sale of bonds need not crowd out private expenditure.

Later theorists, such as Blinder and Solow (1973) and Eisner (1986, 1991a) argue that government expenditure – particularly when deficit-financed – increases net wealth in the form of bonds. Therefore, applying the life-cycle theory of consumption, as households' stocks of bonds rise, their wealth and incomes rise and they will increase both their current and future consumption. The increased consumption should cause private firms to increase investment and, *in conditions of less-than-full employment*, raise employment. Thus, again, government expenditure can increase private expenditure. Tobin and Buiter (1976) similarly find that, in the intermediate run, an increase in government expenditure financed by the issue of bonds achieves a new equilibrium for the economy at a higher rate of interest and a higher level of net national product.

Tobin (1965) and Mundell (1963) add that, through their "Tobin–Mundell effect," because individuals faced with inflation brought on by budget deficits will reduce their holdings in the form of money in favor of real assets, such as land, as the demand for money declines, interest rates fall and investment and capital formation will rise.[1] The importance of their conclusion is to show that within a neoclassical framework, when the economy is at *less-than-full employment*, there is a role for active government intervention and that under certain conditions government budget deficits can be justified.

The important conclusion of all these "imperfectionist" neoclassical models is that a market economy normally operates at *less-than-full employment* (despite their differences over the precise mechanism). This creates the scope for government intervention that need not crowd out private activity. Indeed, it allows for government spending to increase without necessarily leading to an increase in the budget deficit. This conclusion has been formalized by the concept of the balanced budget multiplier. That is, contrary to standard neoclassical views that fiscal discipline and sound public finance are required to keep the budget balanced, "imperfectionist" models allow for government to expand its activities without this necessarily leading to an increase in public debt.

Haavelmo's (1945) balanced budget multiplier theorem states that an increase in government expenditure financed by an equal increase in tax revenue increases the level of income by exactly the amount of the increase in expenditure. The result is that the balanced budget multiplier is exactly unity.

The interesting point is that a dollar change in government expenditure is reflected dollar for dollar in the change in aggregate demand. The multiplier effect of government expenditure is greater than the fall in output implied by an equivalent increase in taxation. Haavelmo's model (1945: 314) assumes that prices remain constant and he warns that at *full employment* an increase in government expenditure would lead to crowding-out of private expenditure. It is only at *less-than-full employment* that increased government expenditure would crowd in or increase aggregate output, and it is this assumption that New Keynesian theory subsequently buttressed.

A multiplier of unity implies that output expands by precisely the amount of the increased government purchases with no induced consumption spending. It is apparent that what must be at work is the effect of higher taxes that exactly offset the effect of the income expansion, thus maintaining disposable income, and hence consumption, constant. With no induced consumption spending, output expands simply by the size of the increased government expenditure.

The balanced budget multiplier result can be formally demonstrated by noting that the change in aggregate demand (ΔAD) is equal to the change in government expenditure plus the change in consumption spending given the level of investment. The latter is equal to the marginal propensity to consume out of disposable income (c), multiplied by the change in disposable income (ΔYD); that is, $\Delta YD \equiv \Delta Y_0 - \Delta TA$, where ΔY_0 is the change in output and ΔTA is the change in tax revenue. Thus,

$$\Delta AD \equiv \Delta \overline{G} + c(\Delta Y_0 - \Delta TA) \tag{3.1}$$

Since the change in aggregate demand must equal the change in output, we have

$$\Delta Y_0 \equiv \Delta \overline{G} + c(\Delta Y_0 - \Delta TA)$$

or

$$\Delta Y_0 \equiv (1/1 - c)\,(\Delta \overline{G} - c\Delta TA) \tag{3.2}$$

Next we note that by assumption the change in government expenditure between the new and the old equilibrium is exactly equal to the change in tax collection, so that $\Delta \overline{G} \equiv \Delta TA$. It follows from this last equality, after substitution in equation (3.2), that with this particular restriction on fiscal policy we have

$$\Delta Y_0 \equiv (1/1 - c)\,(\Delta \overline{G} - c\Delta \overline{G}) \equiv \Delta \overline{G} \equiv \Delta TA \tag{3.3}$$

so that the multiplier is precisely unity.

We can now illustrate the effect of the theorem on aggregate output using equation (3.3). Let us assume the following values: the initial tax rate is $t = 0.1$; the new tax rate is $t' = 0.2$; the initial level of income is $Y_0 = \$100$; the marginal propensity to consume is $c = 0.8$; and the change in government expenditure is $\Delta \overline{G} = +10$.

Inserting our values into the multiplier in equation (3.3) we obtain:

$$\Delta Y_0 \equiv (1/1 - 0.8)\,(10 - 0.8 \times 10) = 5 \times 2 = 10 = \Delta \overline{G} \equiv \Delta TA \tag{3.4}$$

The result is that the change in aggregate income is equal to the change in government spending (see Figure 3.1).

Salant (1966) draws the conclusion that each dollar in government expenditure will have a larger multiplier effect than a dollar of reduction in taxes and that therefore it is more productive for government to spend a dollar than to give that dollar to the private sector to spend in the form of a tax cut. It follows that government expenditure can induce a higher increase in demand than private sector expenditure.

The balanced budget multiplier is critical because if one accepts that the economy can rest at *less-than-full* employment then the government is not locked into contractionary public finance policy.

More recently, there has emerged a response to monetarism and new classical economics that attempts to reach the earlier Keynesian conclusions through new mechanisms. It accepts the standard neoclassical microeconomic principles to

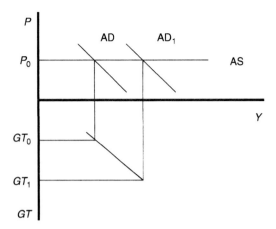

Figure 3.1 The balanced budget multiplier.

develop its own explanation of disequilibrium and wage and price stickiness and arrives at the Keynesian conclusion that markets do not clear in the long run, which creates scope for government intervention in the markets, especially in the labor market (for an overview see Gordon 1990). "New Keynesian" theory should therefore be understood not as a new theory but as a development that provides microeconomic foundations to the conclusions reached by earlier Keynesian theory.

Keynes (1936) assumed that nominal wages are fixed and that, in any event, flexible wages would not succeed in stabilizing output and employment so that the active use of fiscal policy is a preferable means of maintaining full employment. New Keynesian theory argues that wages and prices are not fixed but very slow to adjust to changes in demand. Its attention is focused mainly on wages and the adjustment process to explain why adjustment is not immediate or at least not very fast so as to enable markets to clear and equilibrium to be achieved. New Keynesian theory suggests six possible reasons to account for wage and price stickiness which may result in fluctuations in output and employment.

1   Wages are slow to change because they are fixed in long-term contracts. These contracts may be explicit, as with union contracts, and fixed for a number of years. Or they may be implicit, an unwritten agreement between firm and employee that the wage will remain fixed for a period of time.

   If wages (and prices) are adjusted at different times for different firms and industries, then the economy-wide average wage and the aggregate price levels adjust only slowly to changes in demand and may result in disequilibrium.

2   Menu cost theory argues that the small costs of changing prices can have large effects (Akerlof and Yellen 1985; Mankiw 1985). If it is costly for firms to change the prices they charge and the wages they pay, the changes will be infrequent; but if all firms adjust prices and wages infrequently, the

economy-wide level of wages and prices may not be flexible enough to avoid occasional periods of even high unemployment.

The argument asserts that when firms set prices optimally, they lose very little by meeting increases or decreases in demand by producing more or less without changing prices. Then if there is some small cost for the firm of changing its prices or wages, a small change in demand will not precipitate a price or wage change. But if firms do not change prices in response to changes in demand, then the economy exhibits price (and/or wage) stickiness. Thus, even extremely small costs of changing prices can generate sufficient wage and price stickiness to give changes in the money stock substantial real effects.

It is essential to this result that firms be monopolistic competitors that set wages and prices, rather than taking them as given by the market. The key to the small menu cost argument is that for a monopolist or monopolistic competitor, price is always above marginal cost. If offered the opportunity to sell more at the current price, a monopolist is willing to do so. Thus monopolistic competitors that find the menu costs of changing prices too high will nonetheless willingly sell more when demand increases, perhaps as a result of an increase in the money stock. Further, because the price (which is equal to the marginal value of the good to the consumer) exceeds marginal cost by definition, society benefits from the increase in output.

If firms were competitive, price would be equal to marginal cost, and firms would not be willing to increase output if price remained constant, even if demand increased. Thus New Keynesian theory demonstrates a close relationship between imperfect competition and Keynesian macroeconomic policy prescriptions – particularly that an increase in aggregate demand will lead to an increase in output (Blanchard and Kiyotake 1987).

3   Under conditions of imperfect competition, the profits of each firm depend on the actions of other firms but, at the same time, each firm must decide its prices and output without perfect knowledge of what other firms will do. The actions of other firms are a matter of expectations. These facts have extremely important implications. First, there is inevitably interdependence among firms because they must form expectations about each others' behavior. Second, depending on what firms assume about other firms' actions, the economy may reach different equilibria.

One difficulty raised by the possibility of multiple equilibria is that coordinating responses to economic shocks may produce slow adjustment of wages and prices. Thus, the problem of coordination prevents an instant return to a full-employment equilibrium.

4   Efficiency wage theory focuses on the wage as a means of motivating labor (Akerlof and Yellen 1986; Lindbeck and Snower 1989). The amount of effort workers commit to the job is related to how well the job pays relative to alternatives. Firms may want to pay employees wages above the market-clearing wage to ensure that they work hard in order not to lose their "good" jobs. By the same token, firms are reluctant to cut wages because that affects worker morale and output.

Efficiency wage theory suggests there may be two types of labor markets: one for desirable above-market-wage jobs and another for lower-wage jobs. This is the dual labor market hypothesis. Unemployment can then be explained as persons waiting for above-market-wage jobs and refusing to accept lower-wage jobs (Akerlof *et al.* 1988).

5 The theory of imperfect information in its simplest form argues that individuals' information is always less than perfect and that this leads to actions which are of less than optimum efficiency, resulting in disequilibrium. Specifically, the lack of perfect information creates a distortion called "asymmetrical information" whereby purchasers are at a relative disadvantage to vendors because the former have access to information of inferior quality and quantity (Stiglitz 2000). Due to asymmetrical information, purchasers cannot distinguish between good quality and poor quality purchases as efficiently as vendors, so that poor quality goods can displace those of high quality, resulting in a market failure called "adverse selection." Akerlof (1970) shows, for example, that asymmetrical information could lead to adverse selection in the used car market.

Stiglitz (2000) argues that asymmetrical information and adverse selection interfere with the optimum allocation of resources and prevent equilibrium from being achieved. Indeed, equilibrium may never be achieved in any market because of the cost or difficulty or even impossibility of achieving perfect information. Thus, asymmetrical information and adverse selection can be used to explain disequilibrium in the goods, capital, and even labor markets.

Applying asymmetrical information, Akerlof (1970) argues that employers may not hire applicants from minorities, for example, because imperfect information about a specific applicant leads the employer to apply generalized information about that minority to the applicant. Similarly, imperfect information prevents job seekers from making optimum decisions because they cannot know the future inflation rate and therefore the real wage.

Greenwald and Stiglitz (1986) show that whenever information is imperfect – which they argue is essentially always – then a market is in disequilibrium. Through their Fundamental Non-decentralizability Theorem, they establish that, in general, due to imperfect information, efficient market allocations cannot be attained without government intervention.

6 A simple yet elegant explanation for wage stickiness and unemployment is Lindbeck and Snower's (1989) "insider–outsider" theory. The theory argues that employees who hold jobs are "insiders" and the unemployed are "outsiders." Firms negotiate with the insiders and the insiders have no rational reason to cut their own wages to create jobs for the outsiders.

As noted, New Keynesian theory should be understood not as a new theory of macroeconomics but as an attempt to provide a neoclassical microeconomic foundation to existing Keynesian macroeconomics. Therefore, its policy recommendations are the same as those of Keynesian theory. As wage and price rigidities do prevent markets from clearing and result in unemployment, activist government policy can and should be used to try to stabilize the economy. It differs only from Keynesian theory in attempting to provide a theoretical explanation for the slow adjustment of wages and prices on which the effectiveness of activist stabilization policy is based.

The changing focus of neoclassical theory

As we have seen, neoclassical theories are united by their belief that consumers and firms are utility- and profit-maximizing agents respectively operating in markets with equilibrium outcomes. The neoclassical theories reviewed have been concerned with and divided over the effects of government expenditure as a whole on the economy. In more recent times, however, the focus of economists, neoclassical and otherwise (e.g. Currie 1981; Eisner 1986; Bernheim 1989; Yellen 1989; Rock 1991), has shifted from government expenditure to a narrower preoccupation with the effects of budget deficits, in particular the effects on the economy of the twin-deficits theory. As discussion in following chapters will show, the macroeconomic practice of the Third Way, with its central focus on public debt reduction, shares this concern.

Those economists who oppose budget deficits (e.g. Bernheim 1989 and Friedman, B. 1991) employ neoclassical twin-deficits theory to argue that government expenditure crowds out private expenditure and budget deficits result in current account deficits, thus threatening the growth path of the economy. It will be shown that so too does the practice of the Third Way.

Conclusion

This section has shown that within the neoclassical tradition there exists an extensive range of competing theories of public finance, with a wide range of analyses and policy recommendations.

According to standard neoclassical theory, government expenditure displaces or crowds out private expenditure. If the public expenditure is deficit-financed, interest rates rise and private borrowing is crowded out. If the deficit is financed through foreign borrowing, service payments on the debt will leave the country, which, combined with a stronger currency and lower exports, will result in a current account deficit. Therefore, the public budget should be balanced and government expenditure kept to a minimum.

This section has also shown that there are a number of different mechanisms through which crowding-out actually occurs and these include monetarism, the Ricardian equivalence theorem, and the ultrarationality hypothesis.

At *less-than-full employment*, however, "imperfectionist" neoclassical theories argue that government spending stimulates aggregate demand, thereby increasing investment and employment and can actually crowd in private spending, especially by running a budget deficit. Aschauer argues that *even at full employment*, government investment spending can crowd in private spending.

This chapter finds that the Third Way's program for economic growth is from a very different theoretical tradition to that of 'sound' public finance. In fact, evolutionary and endogenous growth theories' advocacy for increased public investment may be in direct conflict with standard neoclassical theory's requirement for fiscal discipline. Discussion of the Third Way's economic policy practice in the chapters that follow will show that this conflict did emerge and that the Third Way addressed it by sacrificing its program for economic growth, namely its public investments, in favor of the fiscal discipline required by standard neoclassical theory.

4 The Third Way in the United States

This chapter analyzes the historical practice of Clinton's management of economic policy. Before proceeding to assess the policies, however, a word on the different political systems is warranted. In the US political system, presidents alone do not control outcomes. The Constitution separates power between the three discrete branches of government: the president (executive), the Congress (legislature), and the judiciary. Policy is principally developed within the executive and congressional branches. The judiciary can affect the legality of policy. Some scholars insist that all policy in the United States originates from the president (such as Kingdon and Mayhew, quoted in Campbell and Rockman 2000: 51), but, as we shall see with the case of the Congress elected in November 1994, this is not an accurate view.

Meanwhile, under the United Kingdom's political system the Cabinet (executive) is led by the prime minister, who must by definition be the leader of the party (or coalition of parties) which holds the majority of seats in the House of Commons. The most evident difference is the operating environment. The president operates within an environment requiring compromise and negotiation with Congress, especially but not only during periods of divided government, when the presidency and the Congress are controlled by different political parties, as was the case for most of Clinton's two terms: between the congressional elections of November 1994 and the end of his presidency in January 2001. On the other hand, the prime minister of the United Kingdom controls the legislature and therefore the passage of legislation, generating fewer demands for compromise.

In previous chapters it was shown that the two components of the Third Way program are its program for economic growth, which advocates increased public investment in the provision of NSI and infrastructure, and its program of 'sound' public finance, which advocates fiscal discipline. This chapter will argue, first, that the overall macroeconomic framework of the Clinton Administration was contractionary – based on the twin-deficits proposition of standard neoclassical theory – and, second, this constrained the key public investment elements of the Third Way program to such an extent that Clinton effectively abandoned them in favor of fiscal discipline. This will be shown through a detailed examination of public spending in the key areas of fiscal policy, investment policy, and education policy.

Fiscal policy

Despite the fact that Clinton had campaigned on a platform of economic growth consisting of, first, an economic stimulus package composed of "middle-class" tax cuts and public investment and, only second, a commitment to deficit reduction (Clinton and Gore 1992; Clinton 1993a), fiscal discipline came to be the defining feature of his fiscal policy.

The "stimulus package"

Upon assuming office in 1993, Clinton initially chose to concentrate his attention on the economic stimulus package (over deficit reduction) as his first priority (Woodward 1994: 172–3). Clinton told the Congress in his first *State of the Union Address* in 1993:

> Our immediate priority is to create jobs, now.... To create jobs and guarantee a strong recovery, I call on Congress to enact an immediate jobs package of over 30 billion dollars. We will...create half a million jobs: jobs that will rebuild our highways and airports, renovate housing, bring new life to our rural towns, and spread hope and opportunity among our nation's youth with almost 700,000 jobs for them this summer alone.
>
> (1993d)

The package he eventually sent to Congress, however, had been pared back by deficit reduction measures and only proposed $16.3 billion in spending and $12 billion in business tax incentives to stimulate economic growth in the fiscal year 1994 (Weatherford and McDonnell 1996). Specific proposals included $4 billion in extended unemployment benefits, $1 billion for job training and employment, summer jobs, highway construction, and community-development block grants. Burns and Sorenson (1999: 105) describe the package as "a grab bag of items, ranging from boosted Head Start funding and free immunization for children to community-development grants to the kind of boondoggles that Republicans still associate with the New Deal."

In the end, the Democrat-controlled Congress only approved $4 billion of extended unemployment benefits and negated the rest. Senate Republicans and "New" Democrat senators such as John Breaux and David Boren opposed the bill. Reich claims that the congressional cuts were more dramatic: the five-year package of $231 billion in new investments had been reduced to $1 billion in fiscal 1994 and $6 billion in fiscal 1995 (Reich 1997: 104). On April 21, 1993, Clinton angrily surrendered the package, saying "I'm very disappointed about this" (Woodward 1994: 173).

The other major commitment that Clinton had campaigned on – the "middle-class" tax cut – was also a casualty. Clinton quickly came to consider the tax cut too expensive and abandoned it in favor of deficit reduction (Woodward 1994: 34, 97; Weatherford and McDonnell 1996; Stephanopoulos 1999: 136).

It is also worth examining Clinton's fiscal performance in his management of discretionary spending compared with his presidential predecessors. The United States budgetary system distinguishes between two types of government expenditure: mandatory and discretionary (OMB 2002). Mandatory spending accounts for two-thirds of all federal government spending and consists of entitlement programs – such as Social Security, Medicare, Medicaid, and Food Stamps – as well as interest on the national debt. Mandatory spending is called so because it is mandated, that is, automatically appropriated by permanent laws, unless the president and the Congress amend the laws that govern it. The balance of government spending is discretionary spending, which requires the congressional passage and presidential signature of 13 appropriation laws. The president and the Congress retain much more control over discretionary spending than they do mandatory.

Traditionally, the Democratic Party is more closely associated with domestic spending through its customary support of social welfare programs and public works projects, whereas the Republicans have been more vocal in opposing increases in government spending (Hibbs 1987). Chart 4.1 shows discretionary spending by administration since 1962 and reveals two features: first, Democratic administrations have generally had higher levels of discretionary spending, and second, Clinton's discretionary spending is significantly lower than his Democratic predecessors' and even lower than his Republican predecessors'. Thus, in relation to discretionary spending, Clinton's performance resembled that of a Republican president rather than a Democrat.

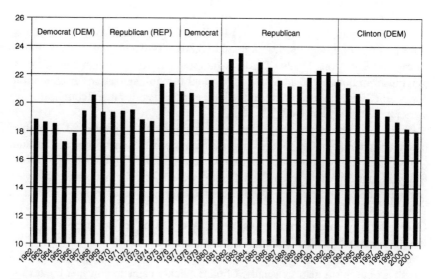

Chart 4.1 US federal discretionary spending (% of GDP) 1962–2001.

Source: OMB 2002: table 8.4.

The "Deficit Reduction Plan"

As noted earlier, deficit reduction was of only secondary importance on Clinton's campaign agenda, yet in August 1993, he implemented his "Deficit Reduction Plan" in the form of the Omnibus Budget Reconciliation Act 1993 (OBRA93). OBRA93 was designed to reduce the deficit over the five fiscal years between 1994 and 1998 by $496 billion, composed of $255 billion in spending cuts and $241 billion in tax increases ("Clinton's Five-Year Economic Plan," *Historic Documents of 1993*: 182).

The $255 billion in spending cuts would come from reducing defense expenditure ($77 billion) and Medicare payments ($55.8 billion), transferring a share of the federal government's Medicaid administrative costs to the states, a reduction in the federal workforce of 100,000 full-time-equivalent positions, and a decrease in agricultural crop subsidies ("Clinton's Five-Year Economic Plan," *Historic Documents of 1993*: 182; Woodward 1994: 34; Weatherford and McDonnell 1996; Stephanopoulos 1999: 136).

The $241 billion in tax increases would come from two new income tax brackets – 36 percent on annual incomes above $115,000 for individuals and $140,000 for couples and a tax surcharge of 10 percent (a 39.6 percent marginal rate) on annual incomes above $250,000; increasing the tax rate for firms with annual taxable incomes over $10 million from 34 to 36 percent; a tax on gasoline and diesel fuel of 4.3 cents per gallon; raising the taxable portion of Social Security benefits from 50 to 85 percent for individuals with an annual income above $34,000 and for couples above $44,000; and eliminating the tax deductibility of lobbying expenses (Clinton 1993a; "Clinton's Five-Year Economic Plan," *Historic Documents of 1993*: 183; Burns and Sorenson 1999: 111).

An important component of OBRA93 is the significant expansion of the earned income tax credit (EITC) for low-income earners which Clinton had campaigned on (Clinton and Gore 1992: 165–6) and had re-iterated in his first *State of the Union Address* in 1993:

> We believe in jobs, we believe in learning, and we believe in rewarding work. We believe in restoring the values that make America special. There is dignity in all work, and there must be dignity for all workers...our new direction makes this solemn commitment: By expanding the Earned Income Tax Credit, we will make history: We will help reward work for millions of working poor Americans. Our new direction aims to realize a principle as powerful as it is simple: If you work full-time, you should not be poor.
>
> (Clinton 1993d)

The EITC provides a tax incentive to engage in paid work by providing a dollar for dollar reduction in the taxes which eligible low-wage earners owe the federal government (Burns and Sorenson 1999: 113; Coates and Lawler 2000: 42). If the credit exceeds the worker's tax liability, the government refunds the difference. By effectively increasing the wage rate, the EITC offers those eligible an added incentive to work. Importantly, the EITC benefits only the working poor, not welfare recipients.

The tax credits paid under the EITC program increased from $15.5 billion in 1993 to $31 billion in fiscal 1999 (CEA 2001: 200). According to one National Economic Council (NEC) official, it would benefit 5 million full-time workers receiving the minimum wage and 10 million more would receive additional benefits, so that every family with a full-time working parent would have an income above the poverty line (Woodward 1994: 127, 310). The Republicans first developed the EITC and Reagan called it "the most important anti-poverty policy in America" (Reich 1997: 88) and increased it as a means of raising the working poor out of poverty (Weatherford and McDonnell 1996). Table 4.1 illustrates Clinton's expansion of the EITC: the inclusion of workers without children for the first time and an increase in benefit of over double for families with two or more children.

Clinton proposed in his final budget (2001) that the EITC be expanded again with a ten-year $23.6 billion proposal to increase the maximum credit for families with three or more children by approximately $500, and for married two-earner couples by $250 by allowing them higher combined earnings (OMB 2001: 58).

Clinton claimed that 70 percent of the new taxes he introduced would be paid by those who earn more than $100,000 a year and that the increases in tax rates affected only the 1.2 percent highest income earners (Clinton 1993h). Media commentators labeled this a "massive tax hike" and a "soak-the-rich plan" designed to make up for the tax inequities of the 1980s "decade of greed" (*The Washington Times* April 15, 1994). Yet Stephanopoulos (1999: 395) recalls that Clinton later proclaimed to a roomful of wealthy contributors, "It might surprise you to know that I think I raised [taxes] too much."

OBRA93 actually delivered a total deficit reduction of $1,200 billion – more than twice as much as planned – over the period because of the higher than expected growth in tax receipts from a long-lasting economic expansion (OMB 2001: 14).

In his 1997 *State of the Union Address*, Clinton announced his plan to balance the budget. In August 1997, he signed the Balanced Budget Act (BBA97) to balance the budget with $247 billion in savings between 1997 through 2002. But in 1998, the budget result was an earlier than expected $69 billion surplus – the first

Table 4.1 Clinton's 1993 expansion of the EITC

		1993 EITC (pre-Clinton)	Clinton original EITC proposal	New EITC 1993
Family with 2+ children	Income ceiling	$23,070	$30,000	$28,000
	Maximum benefit	$1,513	$3,371	$3,371
Low-income worker without children	Income ceiling	Ineligible	$9,000	$9,000
	Maximum benefit	Ineligible	$306	$306

Source: Adapted from Coates and Lawler 2000: 42.

surplus since 1969 – due, once again, to the higher than projected tax receipts generated by economic growth (OMB 2000: 27–8, 2002: table 1.1).

As part of the BBA97, Clinton's Taxpayer Relief Act established a tax credit of $500 for each dependent child under 17 years of age, created education tax credits for postsecondary school costs, made interest on student loans deductible, and reduced the tax rate on long-term capital gains (CBO 2000: 4). The net effect of the Act was to reduce the impact of federal income taxes by approximately 1 percent overall (CBO 2000: 5). The 1997 budget delivered the tax cuts the Republicans had long sought by reducing the capital gains tax, raising the tax exemption threshold on estates to over $1 million, and giving 68 percent of the total tax cut, amounting to $7,135 per person, to the top 1 percent of taxpayers (those earning over $246,000 per annum), while those earning under $59,000 a year received an average cut of $6.00 (Berman 2001: 74).

According to the Congressional Budget Office (CBO), between 1979 and 1997 effective federal income tax rates declined for every quintile of income distribution (CBO 2001: xiii). Despite the OBRA93 legislation, which raised the top income tax rate to 39.6 percent, Clinton did not significantly alter the overall tax burden, and his performance in this respect is described as most closely resembling that of Reagan and Bush (senior), because the highest income quintile has paid more of the total tax receipts but only commensurately with the growth in its overall share of national income (Wildavsky 1998).

Chart 4.2 shows that between 1993 and 2001 growth in tax receipts far outpaced that in outlays. In that time, federal tax receipts increased by 52 percent whilst outlays increased by only 10 percent in constant 1996 dollars (OMB 2002: table 1.3). Moreover, as a share of gross domestic product (GDP), federal tax receipts rose from 17.6 to 20.6 percent but government outlays actually declined

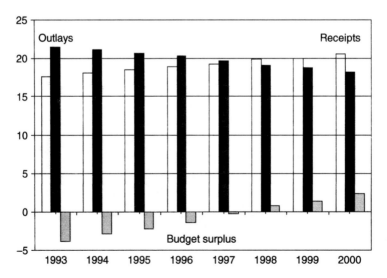

Chart 4.2 US federal receipts, outlays, and budget surplus (% of GDP) 1993–2000.
Source: OMB 2002: table 1.3.

from 21.5 to 18.2 percent – the lowest level of expenditure since 1966 (OMB 2002: table 1.3).

The cumulative effect of Clinton's fiscal discipline policy was to reduce the budget deficit every year, from 3.9 percent of GDP in 1993 to a surplus of 2.4 percent in 2000 (OMB 2002: table 1.3). In the process, of course, he also reduced federal net debt (held by the public) from 49.5 percent in 1994 to 34.7 percent of GDP in 2000, the lowest level since 1984 (OMB 2002: table 7.1). The difference between the pre-OBRA93 deficit path and after is striking: before OBRA93 the national debt was expected to exceed GDP by 2009, yet by 2001 Clinton's Council of Economic Advisers (CEA) (2001: 81) were projecting its elimination by 2011.

Clinton told the Congress in his 1998 *State of the Union Address*:

> Americans in this chamber and across our nation have pursued a new strategy for prosperity: fiscal discipline to cut interest rates and spur growth.... Tonight, I come before you to announce that the federal deficit – once so incomprehensibly large that it had eleven zeroes – will be simply...zero.... And if we maintain our resolve, we will produce balanced budgets as far as the eye can see. We must not go back to unwise spending, or untargeted tax cuts, that risk reopening the deficit.... I ask all of you to meet this test: approve only those priorities that can actually be accomplished without adding a dime to the deficit.
>
> (1998c)

Chart 4.4 shows that Clinton's fiscal discipline distinguishes him from previous Democratic presidents and his fiscal performance resembles that of Republican presidents more than Democratic. As a share of GDP, Clinton can lay claim to the lowest level of total federal spending since 1966, the first budget surplus since 1969, and the lowest level of federal debt since 1984 (OMB 2002: tables 1.2 and 7.1). In fact, despite the strength of Republican opposition to growth in

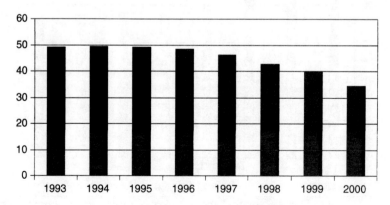

Chart 4.3 US federal government debt (% of GDP) 1993–2000.
Source: OMB 2002: tables 1.3 and 7.1.

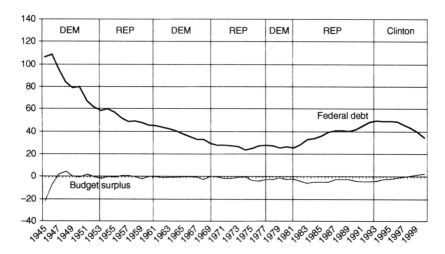

Chart 4.4 US federal budget surpluses and federal debt (% of GDP) 1945–2000.
Source: OMB 2002: tables 1.2 and 7.1.

government spending, Clinton's performance in this regard has been more fiscally stringent, particularly when compared with the Reagan and Bush (senior) administrations.

The fact that Clinton should distinguish himself through deficit reduction is surprising given its secondary importance on his original agenda. Clinton's 1992 campaign manifesto, *Putting People First*, mentions it only once in passing. The centerpiece of Clinton's 1992 presidential election platform was economic stimulus and growth, famously summed up in his campaign slogan: "[It's] the economy, stupid!" (Woodward 1994: 54; Burns and Sorenson 1999: 75; Stephanopoulos 1999: 88). Deficit reduction did not at that point attract Clinton's attention and, according to Woodward (1994), he turned to it only when rival presidential contenders raised the issue's profile:

> Clinton was only vaguely focused on the federal deficit that [Democratic rival Paul] Tsongas was always harping about...[Independent presidential nominee Ross] Perot had elevated deficit reduction to topic A.... Balanced budget mania was now sweeping the country. The deficit problem had never been central to Clinton's vision, but the Clinton team now realized they were obliged to include specific deficit reduction goals in their overall plan. Unfortunately, Clinton's campaign pledges – new investments, a middle class tax cut, a stimulus of fast-track spending to jump start the economy, and health care reform – were expensive and could increase the deficit.
>
> (1994: 32, 41–2)

On January 27, 1993, one week after his inauguration, Clinton met with Alan Greenspan, the Reagan-appointed chairman of the Federal Reserve System. Greenspan warned Clinton that after 1996 the deficit would grow precipitously, as would the interest on the debt. Greenspan argued that by reducing the deficit, interest rates would fall, thereby encouraging investment and jobs – the standard neoclassical argument. In addition, Greenspan argued that Clinton should abandon the stimulus package as "it was impossible to jump-start the economy with a short-term stimulus package" (Woodward 1994: 70).

In the end, Greenspan converted Clinton to the cause of deficit reduction, privately recommending a target reduction in the deficit of $140 billion by 1997 – the very figure Clinton used in his first *State of the Union Address* (1993d) the following month (Woodward 1994: 68–71; Burns and Sorenson 1999: 101). Greenspan also later urged Clinton and the Congress to pass the $500 billion target for overall debt reduction (Woodward 1994: 266). Woodward (1994: 135) even suggests that Greenspan was "the ghost writer of the Clinton [economic] plan." Woodward remarks that "with the stimulus killed... and the middle class tax cut abandoned, *all that remained of [Clinton's] economic plan seemed to be deficit reduction*" (1994: 211, italics added).

Woodward (1994) also points out that much of Clinton's thinking during the development of the deficit reduction legislation in 1993 came, with Greenspan's help, to be directed at pleasing the bond market and so drive down interest rates. Greenspan played the central role in converting Clinton to the cause of deficit reduction with warnings that "if [Clinton] appeared to be backing off [deficit reduction]... the markets would react, appropriately, negatively" (Woodward 1994: 266). Secretary of the Treasury Lloyd Bentsen also warned Clinton "that Wall Street is watching. The market needs to believe that you're serious about reducing the deficit" (Reich 1997: 61). But the self-described "liberals" in the Administration complained, "deficit reduction is the only game in town" (Reich 1997: 157).

Clinton derisively dubbed his deficit reduction effort "the financial markets strategy" (Woodward 1994: 266). Woodward (1994: 277) further recounts that Clinton was especially upset by an editorial in *The New York Times* headlined "A Budget Worthy of Mr. Bush" which described Clinton's budget package as "much like the one George Bush signed three years ago," referring to the 1990 budget deal that had also contained about $500 billion in deficit reduction over five years. Woodward graphically describes Clinton's displeasure at replacing his spending program with deficit reduction:

> "I hope you're all aware we're all Eisenhower Republicans," [Clinton] said, his voice dripping with sarcasm...."We stand for lower deficits and free trade and the bond market. Isn't that great?"... He erupted again, his voice severe and loud. "I don't have a goddamn Democratic budget.... None of the investments, none of the things I campaigned on."
>
> (1994: 165)

Yet Clinton later, towards the end of his presidency, explains the logic of his deficit reduction plan as vital to the health of the economy:

> Our strategy has been based, first and foremost, on a commitment to fiscal discipline. By first cutting and then eliminating the deficit, we have helped to create a virtuous cycle of lower interest rates, greater investment, more jobs, higher productivity, and higher wage.... The result has been a virtuous cycle, in which the right policies in 1993 kicked off a chain reaction of smaller deficits, lower costs of capital, higher investment, increased technology in the workplace, and faster economic growth. As the deficit became a surplus, the virtuous cycle kept turning... mounting surpluses mean that the government, rather than draining resources away from private investment, is now freeing them up. And indeed the last 8 years have seen a dramatic increase in investment.
>
> (CEA 2001: 3, 43, 249)

When launching the last *Economic Report of the President* (2001) of his presidency, Clinton (2001c) again emphasized the central importance of fiscal discipline to his economic strategy. "The evidence... shows that maintaining the path of fiscal discipline is critical to... economic progress. Fiscal discipline has allowed... people to increase investment, productivity, and living standards [through] lower interest rates."

As discussed in Chapter 3, Clinton's argument is a precise restatement of the neoclassical theory of crowding-out and is repeated throughout his economic policy documents (OMB 1996: 10, 1997: 25, 1998: 23, 1999: 23, 2000: 24, 2001; CEA 1999: 43, 2000: 33, 2001: 43):

> Budget deficits force the Government to borrow money in the private capital markets. That borrowing competes with (1) borrowing by businesses that want to build factories and machines that make workers more productive and raise incomes, and (2) borrowing by families who hope to buy new homes, cars, and other goods. The competition for funds tends to produce higher interest rates.
>
> (CEA 2001: 43)

Whilst acknowledging the role of Greenspan and the Federal Open Market Committee in controlling interest rates, Clinton takes credit for the economic growth, arguing that "though the Federal Reserve has played a crucial role in this economic expansion, monetary policy was able to do its job better and more easily because of the sound fiscal policy of this Administration, as Fed members have acknowledged" (OMB 2001: 18).

It is not coincidental that fiscal responsibility also formed the centerpiece of the congressional Republicans' policy document *Contract with America* (1994). The Republicans, led by House Speaker Newt Gingrich, proposed a ten-point plan which placed a Fiscal Responsibility Act first. The act would contain requirements for a balanced budget and limitations on tax as well as a line-item veto for the president. Following the Republicans' landslide victories in the congressional elections of 1994, fiscal discipline, amongst other policies, was to become the new battleground between Congress and the White House, and in what would become a theme of the Clinton presidency, the unfolding drama of policy battles would follow the script spelled out in the *Contract with America* (Woodward 1994).

"Reinventing Government"

Clinton's strategy to improve overall government performance consisted, principally, in the National Performance Review, complemented by the Government Performance and Results Act of 1993 and the Government Management Reform Act of 1994.

The Government Performance and Results Act of 1993 requires all Cabinet departments and agencies to prepare individual performance plans that must be transmitted to Congress with the performance goals they plan to meet that year. By the end of 2000, all 14 Cabinet departments and approximately 85 independent agencies had prepared two cycles of strategic plans, four annual plans, and had completed the first set of annual reports that compare actual corporate performance against goals set in the annual plans (OMB 2001). These plans provided the basis for the second Government-wide Performance Plan, which was contained in the fiscal 2000 budget (OMB 2000: 33–4). The Government Management Reform Act of 1994 introduced the requirement for a consolidated financial report for the government as a whole (Clinton 1994e).

In March 1993, Clinton launched the National Performance Review, commonly referred to as the "Reinventing Government Initiative (REGO)" (DLC 2001a), in which he asked Vice President Gore

> to make the entire federal government both *less expensive* and more efficient to change the culture of our national bureaucracy away from complacency and entitlement toward initiative and empowerment... [and that] *cutting spending will be a priority* [as] there are many things the states or the private sector could do better.
>
> (1993f, italics added)

Gore added the additional term of reference: "a federal government that treats its taxpayers as if they were customers" (1993: 7). In 1996 the National Performance Review was renamed the National Partnership for Reinventing Government.

Gore's final report, *From Red Tape to Results: Creating a Government That Works Better and Costs Less: Report of the National Performance Review* (1993), found that the "root problem" was that government was composed of centralized bureaucracies that delivered "one size fits all" solutions suited to the industrial era but not to the information age; that government regulation was excessive and stifling innovation; that consumers of government services were not treated like customers; that procedures stifled individual employees from developing innovative solutions; and that the monopoly power of many public organizations discouraged them from innovation.

The Office of Management and Budget (OMB) (2001) credits the National Performance Review and the National Partnership for Reinventing Government with abolishing an estimated 377,000 full-time-equivalent federal civilian positions, reducing the total number to the lowest level since 1960; eliminating 250 federal government programs; creating over 4,000 customer service standards and introducing private sector customer satisfaction measures to the public sector; and reducing 640,000 pages of internal rules.

Monetary policy

In the United States, the president does not directly control interest rates; they are set independently by the Federal Open Market Committee of the central bank, the Federal Reserve System. However, social scientists have discovered considerable presidential influence on monetary policy processes and outcomes. Such influence is expressed through both the appointment of members of the Federal Open Market Committee and direct lobbying of the central bank (Chappell 1993; Krause 1994; Havrilesky 1995). Moreover, it has been argued that Democrats and Republicans have different preferences with regard to monetary policy (Alesina and Sachs 1988; Grier 1991). Periods of Republican administration appear to have lower rates of inflation. In addition, they are more inclined to higher interest rates and slower growth in the money supply than Democrats (Woolley 1984; Hibbs 1987). An assessment of Clinton's monetary policy, both of interest rates and money supply, should reveal whether his performance more closely resembles that of previous Democrats or Republicans.

Inflation

Since the end of the Second World War, Democratic administrations have been characterized by higher levels of inflation than their Republican counterparts (Tufte 1978; Hibbs 1987; Quinn and Shapiro 1991; Coleman, J. J. 1996). One potential benchmark with which to assess Clinton is his performance with respect to inflation: Burns and Taylor (2001) argue that if Clinton is not a traditional Democrat he should tolerate less inflation than have previous Democratic administrations.

Chart 4.5 shows the annual percentage change in the Consumer Price Index from 1945 to 2000. The years when Clinton's Democratic predecessors occupied the White House (1945–53, 1961–9, and 1977–81) generally exhibit higher rates of inflation than those when Republicans controlled the presidency. As Chart 4.5 shows and Burns and Taylor (2001: 389) note, the Clinton Administration "breaks with this general pattern: the mean inflation rate under Clinton stands at 2.3 percent, about half that achieved by Democratic administrations and even lower than the [4 percent] post-war Republican average." It is important to also note, however, that inflation in most countries was lower in the 1990s and that therefore the role of policy in controlling inflation should not be exaggerated.

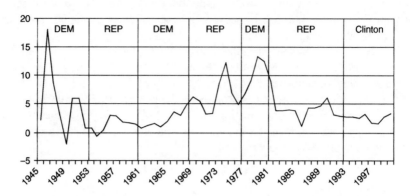

Chart 4.5 Annual percentage change in the US consumer price index 1945–2000.
Source: US Bureau of Labor Statistics 2001.

Money supply

Chart 4.6 examines the annual percentage change in the United States' money supply between 1959 and 2000, defined as "M3." M3 consists of deposits with all savings banks plus fixed deposits and certificates of deposits with all trading banks as well as the sum of currency and checks in the hands of the public.

Chart 4.6 reveals that Clinton's performance in the supply of money also more closely resembled that of Republican administrations rather than Democratic. The average annual rate of change in the money supply during the Clinton Administration is 6.5 percent, much lower than previous Democratic administrations since 1959 (with an average of 9.4 percent) and lower too than Republican administrations (with 7.8 percent). In dollar terms, between 1993 and November 2000, the money supply increased by 62.6 percent (CEA 2001: 355).

Burns and Taylor (2001: 396) employ Friedman and Schwarz's "high-powered" money measure of money supply in examining Clinton's performance. High-powered money is defined as money in circulation plus vault cash plus deposit liabilities of the Federal Reserve to banks. They also find the "annual average money-supply expansion [of 7.0 percent was] not particularly extraordinary" (Burns and Taylor 2001: 397).

Interest rates

Chart 4.7 shows the monthly US federal funds interest rate between 1954 and 2001. The federal funds interest rate is the rate at which banks lend reserves to each other overnight. It shows that the difference in average federal funds rate between administrations of different parties is not significant: for previous Democratic administrations the rate is 5.7 percent, for Republican administrations 6.55 percent, and for Clinton 5.0 percent. It is worth noting that the average rate for Clinton's predecessor, Bush (senior), is a low 2.6 percent.

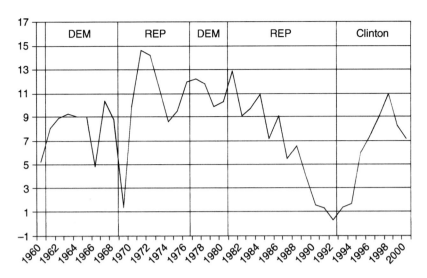

Chart 4.6 Annual percentage change in the US money supply (M3) 1959–2000.
Source: CEA 2001: table B-69.

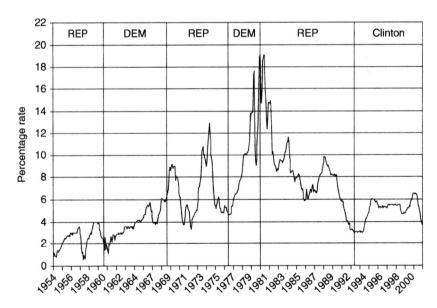

Chart 4.7 Annualized average monthly US federal funds rate 1954–2001.
Source: US Federal Reserve Bank 2001.

Table 4.2 US interest rates

Type of rate	1993 rate (%)	2000 rate (%)	Percentage point change
Federal funds rate	3.02	6.51	+3.49
3-month Treasury bills	3.02	6.19	+3.17
10-year Treasury bonds	5.87	5.78	−0.09
30-year Treasury bonds	6.59	5.78	−0.81
New home mortgage yields	7.20	7.53	+0.33

Source: CEA 2001: 360–1.

Burns and Taylor's examination (2001: 398) of the annualized average monthly real federal funds rate between 1949 and 1999 finds that Clinton's performance is closer to that of Republican than Democratic administrations: Clinton's average annual score is 3.0 percent, whereas for all other Democrats it is 1.2 percent, and for Republicans 2.3 percent.

In July 2000, the three-month Treasury bills rate overtook the 30-year Treasury bonds rate. This means that, for the first time since 1981, yields on longer-term securities fell below those on shorter-term securities. This development appears to have been determined mostly by diminishing government debt resulting in recognition in the market that the stock of Treasury securities would decline. This perception was reinforced in January 2000, when the Treasury detailed plans for buying back federal debt (CEA 2001: 67).

As noted, the neoclassical argument for deficit reduction – that it prevents crowding-out of private investment – is repeated throughout Clinton's economic documents, such as the budget papers and economic reports (OMB 1996: 10, 1997: 25, 1998: 23, 1999: 23, 2000: 24, 2001: 27; CEA 1999: 43, 2000: 33, 2001: 43).

Many economists agree that Clinton's interest rate containment is the direct product of the declining deficit (Miller and Russek 1996 quoted in Burns and Taylor 2001: 398; Blinder and Yellen 2001). Others, such as Meeropol (2000: 276) and Berman (2001: 51), contend that interest rates were kept low because in mid-1995 Greenspan paid less attention to the popular theory of the Non-Accelerating Inflation Rate of Unemployment (NAIRU). This argues that when unemployment falls below a "natural" minimum rate, inflation accelerates exponentially. In order to fight inflation, then, interest rates should be raised preemptively when unemployment is deemed to be approaching that minimum rate. The Full Employment Act 1946 identifies that minimum rate as 6 percent. Instead of targeting unemployment in this manner, Greenspan chose to target inflation much more directly. As accelerating inflation did not materialize, despite very low unemployment rates, Greenspan did not raise interest rates to the level that the NAIRU theory might have warranted (Bernstein and Baker 2003: 2).

Investment policy

This section analyses Clinton's performance in investment policy in two subsections: public investment and private investment. Public investment consists of direct federal government capital expenditure in NSI and infrastructure. The next subsection examines those policies designed to stimulate private investment.

We have shown that the overall macroeconomic settings of the Clinton Administration were contractionary. This prevented Clinton from pursuing his Third Way program in the key policy areas of public investment in infrastructure, education, and R&D.

Public investment

The Clinton Administration claims to have complemented its strategy of fiscal discipline – which, as we have seen, it credits as the lynchpin for creating an economic climate conducive to private investment through lower interest rates – with a supply-side strategy of public investment in infrastructure to improve the productive capacity of the workforce and the economy:

> If fiscal discipline had been achieved through cutbacks in education, training, and technological development, it probably would have failed. At the least it would have undermined the potential for long-term growth. But the Administration did not make this mistake; instead its budget proposals consistently pushed for increased spending for growth-oriented programs while reducing total outlays....
>
> The most effective fiscal strategy to prepare for the future is to pursue policies that boost the productive capacity [supply side] of the economy. These include encouraging productive public investments in infrastructure and human capital – as well as maintaining fiscal discipline, to encourage public saving and private investment. Productive public investment complements private investment in raising the economy's capacity to produce goods and services.
>
> (CEA 2001: 43, 91)

Clinton placed a high importance on his investment-spending program early in office; indeed he frequently described public investments as "the things I got elected for" (Woodward 1994: 90). Similarly, Clinton's Labor Secretary and close adviser, Robert Reich, argues that the public investments, especially in education and training, are the distinguishing feature of the Third Way, without which "the Third Way wouldn't be a third way at all [but] the Second Way, blazed by Reagan and Thatcher" (1999).

Despite Clinton's pro-public investment rhetoric, Chart 4.8 shows that total public investment outlays for major physical capital, R&D, and education and training in fact declined during his presidency. Instead of the additional "$50 billion each year" promised in his election manifesto (Clinton and Gore 1992: 3), in constant (1996) dollars, investment spending declined by a total of

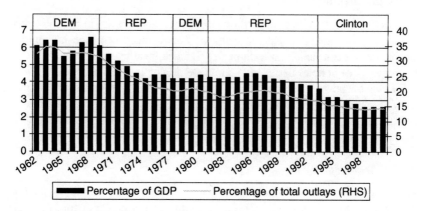

Chart 4.8 US total public investment for physical capital, R&D, and education and training 1962–2000.

Source: OMB 2001: table 9.1.

$25.6 billion by 1996 and by a total of $11.5 billion by 2000 (OMB 2001: table 9.1).

Also noteworthy is that Clinton's level of investment does not in any year exceed the 1992 level, in either constant dollars or as a percentage of total outlays or as a percentage of GDP. The decline in investment spending as a percentage of total outlays is particularly striking because it occurred in a period when federal revenue increased by 85 percent (OMB 2001: tables 1.2 and 9.1). The decline in public investment as a percentage of GDP from 3.8 percent in 1992 to an estimated 2.6 percent in 2001 is also striking because GDP grew by 58.9 percent in the same period (CEA 2001: table B-1; OMB 2001: table 9.1).

Reich claims that the cuts to new investments were even more severe: the five-year package of $231 billion had been reduced to $1 billion in fiscal 1994 and $6 billion in fiscal 1995 (1997: 104). By either measure, it is clear that Clinton sacrificed public investment in favor of fiscal discipline.

Chart 4.8 shows total investment outlays in major public physical capital, R&D, and education and training for the years 1962–2000. It reveals that Clinton's is the only Democratic administration to reduce investment expenditure in that time and that his pattern of reductions resembles that of the Republican Nixon/Ford administrations (1969–77).

Chart 4.9 shows US federal government infrastructure spending between 1956 and 1998 both as a percentage of total federal spending and as a percentage of GDP. The CBO defines infrastructure as highways, mass transit, rail, aviation, water transportation, water resources, water supply, and wastewater facilities (CBO 1999). It reveals that Clinton's spending is significantly less than previous administrations, particularly Democratic. In fact, quantitatively, Clinton's performance most closely resembles that of the Reagan Administration. Reagan affected the largest decline in spending and Clinton has continued to maintain spending at that lower level. This is noteworthy because traditionally the Democratic Party is

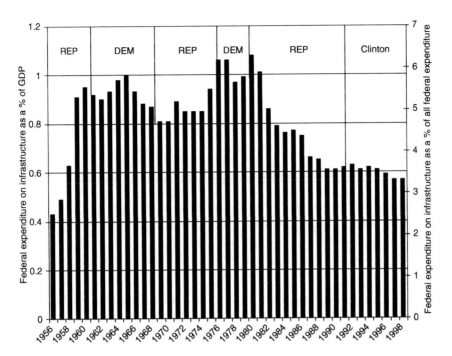

Chart 4.9 US federal expenditure for infrastructure 1956–98.

Source: CBO 1999: 19, 21.

more closely associated with domestic spending, through social welfare programs and public works, whereas the Republicans have been more vocal in opposing increases in government spending (Hibbs 1987).

As noted, the reason for the reduction in investment spending is to be found in deficit reduction. Investments became, along with the stimulus package and the "middle-class" tax cut discussed earlier, another casualty of the all-important deficit reduction plan, which Reich condemns as a "conceptual prison" (1997: 119). It shows that Clinton's priority had shifted from public investment to fiscal discipline. In fact, investments rapidly went from being "the things [Clinton] got elected for" to barely worthy of a passing mention by his first *State of the Union Address* (Clinton 1993d; Woodward 1994: 90).

Many commentators agree with Clinton's assertions about the importance of public investments but are disappointed with his performance in this regard (Davis *et al.* 1996; *The Nation* May 26, 1997: 3; Reich 1997, 1999; Leighninger 2000). Clinton is accused of having sacrificed public investment for deficit reduction and tax cuts for private investment and the wealthy. In December 1998, the heads of 33 scientific and engineering organizations called on Clinton to at least double federal research investment over the following 12 years, pointing out that it had reduced to half that of 30 years earlier as a percentage of GDP (*Sea Technology* December 1998: 12).

One national magazine criticized the BBA97 for ignoring the exigency of public investments: "the real threat is the 'investment deficit', which will worsen under the accord...the agreement cuts expenditures to pay for tax cuts for the affluent, in capital gains and estate taxes [and] $1.2 billion in business tax breaks and incentives" (*The Nation* May 26, 1997). Reich claims that the BBA97 would require cutting another 25 percent from the "modest" domestic spending that had been planned between 1997 and 2002:

> We're now well beyond cutting fat. Critical bones are being sacrificed. Forget new investments. Even to hold education and training steady with their level in the Bush Administration (adjusted for inflation and a growing population) would require that everything *else* [sic] in the domestic discretionary budget be hacked by over a third. Since corporations will holler before giving up their welfare, and middle- and upper-income voters won't part with their Medicare (especially now that B[ill Clinton] has vowed to protect it), what's left to cut? Public welfare, food stamps, low-income housing, nutrition for poor children, mass transit, and everything else that keeps the bottom ten percent afloat.
>
> (1997: 291)

Some scholars find Clinton's performance a clear repudiation of a Keynesian "consumption-led" approach that has been the hallmark of Democrats and more like the Republicans' private "investment-led" philosophy (Quinn and Shapiro quoted in Burns and Taylor 2001: 399). Reich (1997: 306) rather bitterly describes Clinton's approach as "standing Keynes on his head."

Privatization

In the 1980s, the Reagan Administration introduced the newly coined term "privatization" to the United States from Margaret Thatcher's Britain (Yergin and Stanislaw 1998: 364). Privatization has since become part of the lexicon of Democrats as well as Republicans (Baer 2000: 167). Indeed, when Clinton announced the National Performance Review on March 3, 1993, he remarked, "the Federal Government simply can't do everything and there are many things... the private sector could do better" (Clinton 1993f). One of the principal recommendations of the review was privatization or, in Vice President Gore's words, "spinning off functions to the private sector that are better accomplished there" (Gore 1995: 117). Shoop (1995) observes that when Vice President Gore launched the second phase of the Clinton Administration's REGO in December 1994 "he dusted off a term [privatization] that hadn't been heard much since the Reagan Administration, and which Democrats have almost never dared speak." In fact, Gore told a press conference "REGO I (Reinventing Government Phase I) had set out to make government work better and *cost* less. Now we are going make government work better and *do* less" by ordering the executive to identify programs suitable for privatization "to the private sector where they belong" (Shoop 1995, italics added). It should be emphasized that privatization is a policy at the extreme end of a continuum that includes the neoclassical prescription for reduced public expenditure. It is at the extreme end because it goes beyond simply reducing government spending and actually divests government of its assets, thereby reducing the size of government overall.

Privatization has over time expanded to mean not only the sale of government assets but also the increasing participation of the private and not-for-profit sectors in the provision of government services, even those previously thought of as exclusively public (Yergin and Stanislaw 1998: 366). The express purpose is to bring market forces to bear: to increase efficiency, to reduce costs and the burden on public budgets, and to improve the quality and effectiveness of services. Clinton Administration official and head of Vice President Gore's National Performance Review, Elaine Karmack, interprets privatization as broadly "divesting the government function" (Karmack quoted in Shoop 1995). Kittower (1997) notes that due to opposition from labor unions and other quarters, some avoid using the "P-word" (privatization) and talk of out-sourcing, competitive bidding, or partnerships, yet they are all forms of privatization.

Privatization of government goods and services has been occurring in many countries since about 1980, yet the United States was "the last country in the world to adopt [it] as an important component of its management and budget strategy" (Shoop 1995). The reason may be that, traditionally, there has been much less public ownership in the United States than in other countries, so the relative volume of public assets and services available to privatize is smaller (Shoop 1995; Yergin and Stanislaw 1998: 364). It should be noted that in the United States, unlike the United Kingdom, most government assets and services are owned and delivered by state, county, and city, not federal governments.

Privatization proliferated in a wide range of government activities during the Clinton Administration (Reason Public Policy Institute 1999, 2001: 13). Some of the privatization highlights of its fiscal 1996 budget, for example, include distributing rental vouchers to eligible recipients to purchase private rental accommodation; selling four of the Energy Department's power marketing administrations for an estimated \$3.7 billion; selling the Naval Petroleum Reserve for an estimated \$1.6 billion; selling excess uranium for an estimated \$400 million; inviting the private sector to build-own-operate three federal prisons and one detention centre; allowing employees to purchase commercial functions of the General Service Administration through employee stock ownership plans; and corporatizing a fifth of the Bonneville Power Administration. In fact, Clinton set an ambitious agenda to sell off as many electricity utilities as possible but abandoned another proposal to privatize the Social Security disability claims process in the face of labor union opposition (Shoop 1995). Private correctional facilities were a growth industry in the 1990s. By the end of 1996, 132 private prisons were in operation, with another 39 under construction. The growth in the number of "charter schools" – public schools that secede from local school districts and set their own curricula – is another example (Reason Public Policy Institute 1999).

Despite their application in the United States since at least the 1970s, public–private partnerships (PPPs) became especially fashionable during the Clinton Administration as "the epitome of a new generation of management reforms"

(Linder 1999: 35; Stiglitz and Wallsten 1999). PPPs were rediscovered by David Osborne (a fellow at the New Democrats' Progressive Policy Institute) and Ted Gaebler in their influential 1992 publication *Reinventing Government: How the Entrepreneurial Spirit Is Transforming the Public Sector*, in which they advocate that above all the state should "steer, not row," that is, set policy and regulate but not necessarily provide public services which could be provided by the private sector.

The Clean Car Initiative Clinton launched on September 29, 1993, is an example of a PPP. Under the terms of the partnership, the long-term goal was to triple the fuel efficiency of motor vehicles through the collaboration of industry and government engineers, and the government would bear the greater share of the risk identified by the project steering group. Clinton remarked that the partnership

> brings together a number of things we are trying to do in this administration.... Government can't do these things by itself, but there are a lot of things we need to be working on that market forces alone can't do. So *the third way*, a partnership between Government and the private sector...
>
> (1993j, italics added)

From this first instance, PPPs grew throughout the 1990s to become a central vehicle for service delivery in many policy areas, from health care (Sparer 1999) to welfare (Rom 1999) to urban renewal (USDHUD 2001a) to technological research (Stiglitz and Wallsten 1999). Linder suggests that the popularity of PPP can in part be explained by its linguistic appeal to the traditional virtue of cooperation as opposed to the privatization fashionable in the 1980s:

> [T]he hallmark of partnerships is co-operation not competition; the disciplining mechanism is not customer exit or thin profit margins, but a joint venture that spreads financial risks between public and private sectors.... The idea of government and business partnering for some common [public] purpose evokes images of wartime solidarity and memories of small town life in America, where business and local government shared talent and community responsibilities.
>
> (1999: 36)

To facilitate this form of delivering public services, in 1997 the Internal Revenue Service extended from 10 to 20 years the permissible time span for public agencies to allow private sector providers to operate, maintain, and manage contracts, thereby increasing the size of the private equity that can be invested (Kittower 1997).

According to its proponents, partnerships require a meeting of the minds between public and private parties: government parties embrace entrepreneurship and, reciprocally, business actors embrace public interest and greater accountability (Linder 1999: 36–7). The central problem, according to this interpretation, is that government bureaucracies are slow, rigid, and uniform while private firms, in contrast, are seen as nimble, innovative, and flexible (Rom 1999: 159).

There is agreement that the principal reason governments privatize is fiscal stringency, that is, when governments perceive that they do not have access to the financial resources required to deliver the services expected without driving budgets into deficit, and thus turn to the private sector for efficiency improvements, cost savings, and financial equity (Kittower 1997; Linder 1999: 46; Sparer 1999: 152). In one survey of US public officials' principal reason for considering privatization, "internal financial pressure" was nominated by 55.2 percent of respondents and "external financial pressure" by 41.4 percent (Reason Public Policy Institute 1999).

In addition to budget savings, argue the proponents, partnerships offer the advantage of deregulating employment relations by transferring public projects from a public to a private workforce, and the application of market forces that implies (Linder 1999: 47). Linder (1999: 48) notes that another perceived benefit of partnerships is that they privatize government functions without reducing its legitimacy, unlike outright asset sales.

Rosenau (1999) meanwhile laments that despite the billions of public dollars committed in PPPs during the Clinton Administration, not much is known about their success.

Private investment

Clinton's policy for encouraging private investment contained two components: lower interest rates and tax incentives. We have already seen that Clinton sought to induce lower interest rates by reducing the budget deficit, thereby reducing the financial crowding-out of private borrowing (OMB 1996: 10, 1997: 25, 1998: 23, 1999: 23, 2000: 24, 2001: 27; CEA 1999: 43, 2000: 33, 2001: 43).

Besides interest rates, the other instrument Clinton adopted to stimulate private investment was tax incentives. As part of the 1993 budget package, Clinton (1993h) implemented a range of tax incentives; in his own words "over 90 percent of small businesses would be eligible for tax reductions if they invest in their businesses" and investors who kept investments in new firms, especially new high-technology firms, capitalized up to $50 million for five or more years were given a capital gains tax break of 50 percent.

Chart 4.10 shows that private investment increased significantly during the Clinton presidency. As a percentage of GDP, between 1992 and 2000 private fixed investment increased from 13.4 to 17.9 percent and investment in equipment and software increased from 7.1 to 10.5 percent (CEA 2001: 274, 296).

Despite the apparent effectiveness of tax incentives in generating investment, Clinton insists, nevertheless, that the key was to reduce interest rates through reduction of the budget deficit:

> The most direct link between fiscal discipline and growth is that through low interest rates, which encourage investment. As interest rates fall, financing of all kinds of activities becomes less costly. In addition, low interest rates keep the stock market strong, allowing companies both old and new to lower their cost of capital. Strong investment is essential to rapid growth, and by

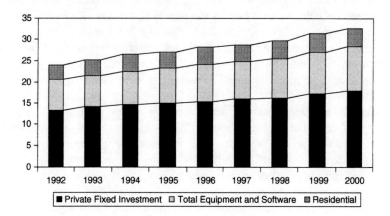

Chart 4.10 US private investment (% of GDP) 1992–2000.
Source: CEA 2001: 274, 296.

> reducing the amount of saving that must go to finance the public debt, fiscal
> discipline has made room for strong investment. The result has been a
> virtuous cycle.
>
> (CEA 2001: 43)

The argument contained in the above passage is particularly important as it is
repeated so often throughout Clinton's economic policy as to acquire the status of
a mantra. Thus, it would seem that for Clinton all economic policies – if indeed
not all policies – rest on the cornerstone of fiscal discipline. See Chart 4.11.

As noted, Clinton's deficit reduction effort, which he dubbed the "financial
markets strategy," was designed to please the bond and equity markets into reducing interest rates and thereby encouraging investment (Woodward 1994: 266).
Clearly, the US equity markets appreciated his efforts. Between January 1993 and
2000 the Dow Jones Industrial Average increased from 3,255.99 to 11,500 points
and the broader Standard and Poor's 500 Index from 435.13 to 1,500. The average annual return for both measures was just over 26 percent in that period, the
best annualized returns for both measures since the Second World War (Burns and
Taylor 2001: 399). In fact, Clinton, in first place for annualized returns for the
Dow Jones Industrial Average, is the only Democrat in the top five, followed
by Reagan with 16 percent, Bush 13 percent, Eisenhower 13 percent, and Ford
12 percent.

The "New Economy"

The Clinton Administration credits investment in new technology with leading to
the emergence of what has become known as the New Economy (CEA 2001: 19).
The New Economy is the name used to refer to a high rate of economic growth
characterized by high productivity growth, low unemployment, and moderate

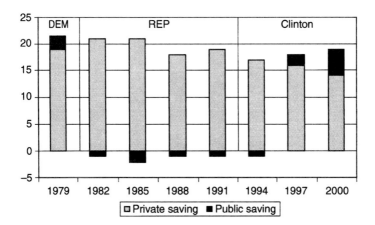

Chart 4.11 US national saving (% of GDP) 1979–2000.
Source: CEA 2001: 82.

inflation that are claimed to have resulted from improvements in information and communication technologies and business practices. Some of the more enthusiastic commentators have gone so far as to claim that in the New Economy, the traditional relationship between employment and inflation, whereby growth in employment is thought to fuel growth in inflation, is broken, thereby signaling the end of the traditional business cycle (Martin 2001).

From the first quarter of 1993 to the third quarter of 2000, real GDP grew at an average annual rate of 4.0 percent – 46 percent higher than the average between 1972 and 1993 (CEA 2001: 19). In that period, US output per hour in the non-farm business sector grew at a high average rate of 2.3 percent, compared with an average of 1.4 percent for the previous 20 years and, from the fourth quarter of 1995, an average rate of 3 percent per annum (CEA 2001: 20).

The measured unemployment rate decreased markedly from 6.9 percent in 1993 to 4 percent in 2000, and it remained below 5 percent between 1997 and 2001 (CEA 2001: 324). Such low levels of unemployment in the past have meant rising levels of inflation (CEA 2001: 324; USDL 2001). Yet inflation averaged only 2.5 percent between 1993 and 2000, ranging between 3.4 and 1.7 percent (USDL 2001). Chart 4.12 shows that the 1990s saw a new development: low levels of unemployment contemporaneous with low levels of inflation. It is thought that what makes this new development possible is high productivity growth, especially through the application of technology to production (CEA 2001: 22). This is the defining feature of the New Economy.

Although the information technology sector accounts for only 8.3 percent of GDP, it accounted for almost one-third of output growth between 1995 and 1999 and 11 percentage points of the 14 percent real growth in total equipment and software spending by business (CEA 2001: 25).

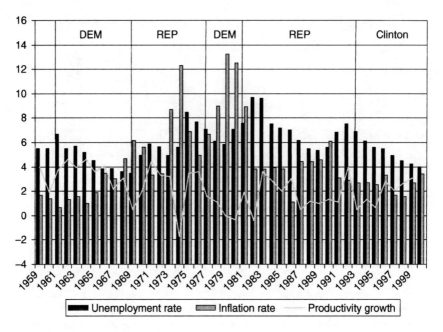

Chart 4.12 US unemployment, inflation, and productivity 1959–2000.
Source: CEA 2001.

According to the CEA in yet another restatement of standard neoclassical theory:

> The increased growth prompted by the new technologies has helped the
> Federal Government restrain its spending growth and boosted its revenue;
> the resulting smaller budget deficits (and later surpluses) have helped keep
> interest rates down, encouraging further investment in new technologies.
> Economic policies directed toward promoting competition have prodded
> firms to adopt the new technologies [and] policies aimed at opening foreign
> markets have increased earnings in the U.S. technology sector.
>
> (2001: 23)

Education policy

Education policy held a special place on Clinton's policy agenda as, according to
Burns and Sorenson (1999: 62, 64), early in his political career Clinton had
resolved to become the "education governor" of Arkansas and had used the issue
as a "springboard to the presidency." In his 1997 *State of the Union Address*,
Clinton (1997) declared "my number one priority for the next four years, is to
ensure that all Americans have the best education in the world." Clinton ele-
vated education and its funding issues to a high priority on the national agenda by
focusing on access, enforcement of national standards, devolution to states and

school districts, accountability, teacher quality, class-size reduction, literacy, after-school programs, public school choice, disadvantaged schools, and bilingual education (*What Works in Teaching and Learning* January 24, 2001). However, even in education policy – a policy area which Clinton claimed to hold dear – deficit reduction came to dominate in the form of real funding cuts.

Funding

Despite the creation of a range of new programs and his aspiration for universal college education and physical school improvements, Clinton provided only modest funding increases (Hardi 2001). Table 4.3 summarizes changes to funding for new and pre-existing student financial assistance programs.

According to Hardi (2001), Pell Grant funding has barely outpaced inflation since fiscal 1993 and even then only because of a $1 billion increase in fiscal 2001. Pell Grant funding was only embraced by the Clinton Administration after the Republicans captured the Congress in 1994 (Hardi 2001). Taken together, Pell Grants, TRIO, GEAR UP, the HOPE, and lifetime learning credits and the campus-based programs have only just kept pace with college costs, which have risen faster than inflation, although almost half of the total increase comes from the tax credits, which do nothing for the poorest students. Complying with the rationale of the "user-pays" system, increased access to college has come at the price of increased student indebtedness.

Table 4.3 Student financial assistance under the Clinton Administration

	1993	2001	2001 (inflation-adjusted)	Change (inflation-adjusted) (%)
Pre-existing student aid programs				
Pell Grant total cost	$6.5 billion	$8.8 billion	$7.2 billion	11
Pell Grants maximum grant	$2,300	$3,750	$3,060	33
Work–study total cost	$617 million	$1.0 billion	$824 million	34
SEOG total cost	$583 million	$780 million	$564 million	−3
Perkins Loans total cost	$181 million	$160 million	$130 million	−28
TRIO	$388 million	$780 million	$636 million	64
Student loans program total costs	$6.9 billion	$3.1 billion	$2.5 billion	−64
FFEL Program	$6.9 billion	$3.7 billion	$3.0 billion	−57
Direct Loan Program	0	−$646 million	−$527 million	−100
New student aid-related programs				
Americorps (excluding VISTA)	Begun 1993	$252 million		
GEAR UP	Begun 1998	$295 million		
College tax credits	Begun 1997	$7.9 billion		
Loan interest deduction	Begun 1997	$333 million		

Source: Adapted from US Department of Education in Hardi 2001.

McPherson and Schapiro (1997) find that the government's share – both federal and state – of student aid funding has been declining since the 1980s and has been offset by increasing tuition payments from students and families, discouraging students from lower-income families from enrolling in colleges at all; that student aid programs have failed to keep pace with inflation in college costs; and that Clinton's policy proposals seem focused principally on assisting the middle- and upper-income families by offering tax credits, rather than grants, which are of benefit only when income reaches a certain level; in this case families in the $60,000–80,000 income bracket will benefit most. They also find that schools increased their own aid spending when Pell spending increased, absorbing much of the benefit of the tax cuts themselves. Brainard *et al*. (2000) similarly find that "under Clinton, there has been a massive expansion of assistance to middle-income [but not low-income] students."

In his 1997 *State of the Union Address*, Clinton (1997) proposed a new school upgrade initiative of $5 billion to help communities finance $20 billion in school construction over the following four years. In early 1998, the Clinton Administration proposed to underwrite approximately $22 billion in zero-interest school construction bonds (Temple, J. 1998: 221). Instead of receiving interest payments financed by the local schools, individual and corporate bondholders would receive tax credits from the federal government (US Department of the Treasury in Temple, J. 1998). In the 2001 budget, Clinton reserved $1.2 billion for a program to support renovation of dilapidated school facilities yet conceded that the net need for school repair would cost over $100 billion (Clinton 2001a).

The *Statistical Abstract of the United States* (2000a) reveals that federal funding to schools remained relatively static between 1990 and 1997, both in real terms and as a percentage of all sources of funding (US Census Bureau 2000a: 154). In that time, federal funding as a percentage of all schools' funding rose from 8.3 to 8.4 percent; for elementary and secondary schools from 5.6 to 6.1 percent; but for higher education declined from 12.3 to 12 percent.

Chart 4.13 shows that, over the two terms of the Clinton presidency, total federal expenditure on education and training as a percentage of GDP was actually 0.003 percent *less* than if the 1993 level of 0.0059 percent had been sustained.

As part of the Telecommunications Act of 1996, Clinton introduced Vice President Gore's E-Rate program for providing low-cost Internet connections for schools, libraries, rural health clinics, and hospitals (CEA 2001: 108). Between 1994 and 2001 the number of classrooms connected to the Internet rose from 3 to 65 percent and the number of schools rose from 35 to 95 percent (Clinton 2001a). Clinton believes access to technology as well as skills is crucial to succeeding in the "knowledge economy" and told Congress in 2000: "opportunity for all requires...having access to a computer and knowing how to use it" (Clinton 2000c).

Education, Burns and Sorenson (1999: 120, 338) observe, was "a good middle-class issue, a good bipartisan issue" which appealed to Clinton not least because it appealed to these two constituencies, yet they conclude that "no teacher or parent could enjoy the illusion in 1999 that public education as a whole had been dramatically improved.... Education was still in crisis." Brainard *et al*. (2000)

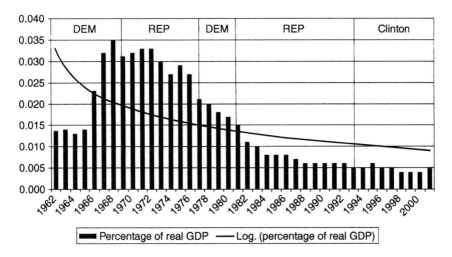

Chart 4.13 US federal government educational and training expenditure 1962–2001.
Source: OMB 2003: tables 9.9 and 10.1.

agree that "many of [Clinton's] education achievements came about because of...the Republican takeover of Congress in the 1994 elections. And educators remain divided over some of Mr. Clinton's promises." For example, after two years of working with a Democratic Congress, Clinton had raised the maximum Pell Grant by only $40 and had not increased funding for the campus-based student-aid programs.

In testimony to the National Summit on High Technology held in June 1999, the president of the Massachusetts Institute of Technology, Charles Vest, testified that between 1993 and 1997 federal government funding for basic and applied research had fallen by 12 percent as a share of GDP (Johnson, H. 2001: 45). He concluded his testimony by asking whether the US Government was investing sufficiently in research and ended with the unequivocal reply: "No. We are reducing our investments. We are going in the wrong direction" (Johnson, H. 2001: 46). In addition to funding, and as part of an effort to "re-invent" government, Clinton (2001a) also reduced government regulation in the Department of Education by two-thirds.

Public school choice

Clinton strongly supported public school choice and sought to improve the quality of state education by introducing competition within the state sector through the creation of charter schools (Coates and Lawler 2000: 38). A charter school is "an independent public school organized as a non-profit organization funded on a per-pupil basis from the state school aid fund and operated under a contract [or charter] issued by a state authorizing body" (MAPSA 2001). Despite falling short of his goal of increasing the number of charter schools to 3,000, their number still increased markedly from 1 to 1,700 by the year 2000 (Clinton 2000c). By 1998, 200,000 of 53 million students were enrolled in charter schools (Clinton 1998b). Clinton opposed the use of public funds for private school vouchers at a federal level but he was not opposed to them at a state or local level (*What Works in Teaching and Learning* January 24, 2001).

Employment policy

When Clinton assumed office in January 1993 the unemployment rate was a relatively high 7.5 percent. Employment had featured prominently during the campaign and in his policy agenda, summed up in his campaign slogan "putting America to work" (Clinton and Gore 1992: 3; OMB 2001: 13). Clinton's performance in employment policy is distinguished by increased deregulation (known as labor market flexibility in neoclassical theory), significant reductions in public employment, growth in private employment, and increased wage inequality.

Labor law reform

One of Clinton's first acts on taking office was to initiate a wide-ranging investigation of the state of worker–management relations in the United States. Appointed by Secretary of Labor Robert Reich and the Secretary of Commerce, and headed by John Dunlop (who had been Secretary of Labor under Republican President Gerald Ford), the Commission on the Future of Worker–Management Relations (the "Dunlop Commission") held hearings across the United States in 1993 and 1994. The assumptions behind its inquiries were that because the US economy had changed during the past six decades, the time had come to consider restructuring the mode of labor regulation to increase US workers' competitiveness in the global marketplace (Herod 1997: 167).

Herod (1997: 171) observes that the Dunlop Commission recommendations, the TEAM Act, and negotiated regulations ("reg-neg") represent a significant change of policy direction: devolution of workplace regulation from the federal government to the level of the individual workplace and the privatization of workplace relations through a diminishing government role. Moreover, whereas workplace regulations developed prior to Clinton stipulated minimum standards below which firms could not fall, under Clinton it was increasingly a ceiling on standards that was being imposed above which states and communities would not be able to go for fear of losing capital investment to other less-regulated states (Peck 1996). These shared policy directions point to an emerging consensus between Democrats and Republicans on increasing labor market flexibility so that the United States might become more competitive in the global economy, taking the form of greater use of market forces in industrial relations reform (Herod 1997: 168; Jaenicke in Coates and Lawler 2000: 35). Thus, just as in other economic policy areas, the influence of neoclassical theory in promoting labor flexibility is clear.

As discussed in Chapter 3, neoclassical theory promotes labor market flexibility in the belief that the sole cause of unemployment is wage rigidities that prevent the labor market from clearing and therefore, by definition, failing to attain full employment.

In his January 1999 *State of the Union Address*, Clinton announced that "we should eliminate the limits on what seniors on Social Security can earn." In April 2000, Clinton signed the Senior Citizen's Freedom to Work Act, which abolished means testing for people above the "normal retirement age" of 65 years. Under prior legislation, retirees aged 65 through 69 had their retirement benefits reduced by one dollar for every three dollars earned above $17,000 in 2000. Thus, any such retirees earning about $68,000 per annum would lose their retirement benefits. This acted as the major disincentive to paid employment amongst that age cohort (Clinton 2000b; Ford 2000).

Importantly, the legislation actually increases federal revenue in three ways (Ford 2000). First, by removing the disincentive to work, retirees who engage in employment transfer the cost of their health care from the national Medicare-Medicaid programs to the employer's private health insurer. Second, as older workers extend their careers, they continue paying 1.45 percent of their earnings into the Medicare-Medicaid programs for a longer period. In sum, the Medicare-Medicaid programs spend less and receive more income. Third, the US Treasury receives revenue benefits as older workers extend their liability to income taxes by working longer.

The "Middle-Class Bill of Rights"

On December 15, 1994, in an Oval Office Address to the Nation ("Clinton's 'Middle-Class Bill of Rights,' " *Historic Documents of 1994*: 610–6), Clinton proposed a "Middle-Class Bill of Rights" which embraced $60 billion in tax cuts over five years in four major proposals designed to reverse the decline in real incomes and living standards:

- full tax deductibility for education and retraining of up to $10,000 per year for families earning up to $120,000 a year;
- a tax cut of up to $500 for every child up to age 13 in families with incomes below $75,000;
- allowing families with incomes of less than $100,000 to place $2,000 a year in a tax-deferred Individual Retirement Account. People could withdraw the money without a tax penalty to pay for college, a first home, a major illness, or the care of an elderly parent;
- eliminating 60 different federal job retraining programs and instead giving people who qualify vouchers for $2,000 to $3,000 each to use at private facilities.

The package would be paid for by "continuing to reduce government spending" by $24 billion over five years in five government departments. Clinton said his "test will be: Does an idea expand middle-class incomes and opportunities? Does it promote values like family, work, responsibility, and community? Does it

contribute to strengthening the new economy? If it does, I'll be for it..."
("Clinton's 'Middle-Class Bill of Rights,'" *Historic Documents of 1994*: 614).

The Clinton Administration successfully enacted a tax credit worth up to $1,500 per annum for the cost of the first two years of post-secondary tuition. This was, according to Jaenicke (in Coates and Lawler 2000: 38), clearly targeted at the "middle class" since only those paying at least $1,500 of federal income tax receive the full benefit, while those paying little or no federal income tax receive little or nothing.

Public sector employment

Clinton's professed commitment to "putting America to work" did not, however, extend to public employment. In fact, Clinton pared federal public employment down to the lowest level since 1960 (OMB 2001: 38).

During the Clinton presidency, executive branch civilian employment fell by 302,000 to 2,645,000 and uniformed military personnel by 360,000 to 1,384,000, reducing total federal personnel by 666,000 to 4,092,000, and the ratio of federal executive branch civilian employees per 1,000 population fell from 11.4 to 9.6 (OMB 2002: table 17.5). The federal government lost more employees than any other industry, except for the apparel and other textiles products industry, and the Department of Defense suffered the greatest losses – 333,000 civilian workers (Hatch and Clinton 2000: 15).

Clinton proudly declared to the Congress on February 17, 1993, three days short of his first month in office, that he had fulfilled his promise to cut White House staff by 25 percent, saving $10 million, and had cut the federal bureaucracy by 100,000 positions, for combined savings of $9 billion (Clinton 1993d). According to the OMB, Clinton actually eliminated 138,000 positions in his first year in office (2002: table 17.5).

The Clinton Administration credits the National Performance Review and the National Partnership for Reinventing Government with abolishing an estimated 377,000 full-time equivalent federal civilian positions, as shown in Chart 4.14 (OMB 2001: 38).

Unemployment

Historically, Democratic presidents have tended to focus on lowering unemployment at the expense of higher inflation (Tufte 1978; Hibbs 1987; Burns and Taylor 2001). Chart 4.15 shows that unemployment has been lower under Democratic administrations than Republican: the mean unemployment rate for Democrats (excluding Clinton) is 5.1 percent, for Republicans 6.4 percent, and for the Clinton Administration 5.2 percent. The declining unemployment rate under Clinton is striking, from 6.9 percent in 1993 to 4 percent in 2000 – the lowest rate since 1969 (CEA 2001: 188, 324).

It is generally accepted that Clinton presided over the longest running expansion in US history and a large growth in employment, with estimates of 13.25 million new jobs between 1992 and 1999 (Wray and Pigeon 2000: 811) and

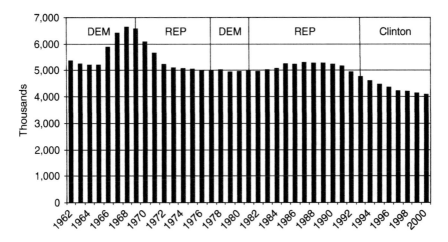

Chart 4.14 US total federal government personnel 1962–2000.
Source: OMB 2002: table 17.5.

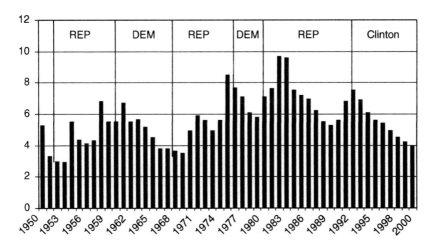

Chart 4.15 US civilian unemployment rate (%) 1950–2000.
Source: CEA 2001: table B-42.

21 million between 1989 and 1999 (Hatch and Clinton 2000: 3). Note that this is jobs growth that Clinton argues occurred due to – not despite of – fiscal discipline (CEA 2001: 3, 43, 249).

In employment policy too, deficit reduction was central to policy-making. According to Clinton's Secretary of Labor, Robert Reich, Clinton was unwilling to tax the "economic winners" of the past two decades to pay for the necessary education and training which would help welfare recipients and the unemployed obtain decent jobs (Reich 1997: 155–6, 213–14; Jaenicke in Coates and Lawler 2000: 40). The one innovation which Reich claims to have supported and which was enacted – the Workforce Investment Act 1998 – actually *saved* the government money (Reich 1997: 130–1; Jaenicke in Coates and Lawler 2000: 40).

Reich complained that all policy-making was framed within what he calls the "conceptual prison" of deficit reduction:

> [T]he Wall Street and Federal Reserve … bankers argue that a lower deficit leads to more private savings, that more savings result in more capital investment, that more capital investment means higher productivity, and that higher productivity translates, as night follows day, into higher wages.
>
> (1997: 29)

According to the administration, the other key ingredient to economic growth besides deficit reduction was labor market flexibility as the "flexibility of labor markets has been an important aspect of economic success in the United States … [by assisting] firms to adapt their workforce to changing economic prospects" (CEA 2001: 166).

Hatch and Clinton (2000) find that between 1989 and 1999 the largest job losses occurred in the federal government followed by the manufacturing and mining sectors. The largest job gains occurred in the services sector, specifically the personnel supply industry followed by the personal service and financial services sectors.

During the 1990s, employment in manufacturing declined due to technological innovations combined with the effects of the Asian financial crisis on manufacturing exports (Hatch and Clinton 2000: 7). The only exception to the industry as a whole was construction, which boomed as home purchases increased due to low rates of interest and unemployment.

The services sector was the driving force behind the jobs growth of the 1990s (Hatch and Clinton 2000: 13). Table 4.4 shows that between 1998 and 1999, the services sector generated 99 percent of the 21 million new jobs created and that the average weekly earnings from those jobs increased by 7.6 percent over the decade – four times faster than the private sector average (Bureau of Labor Statistics 2001).

Of the 10 specific industries adding the most jobs, 7 were in services. Business services in particular generated more jobs than any other industry group during the decade. Personnel supply services tops the list of most jobs added and is ranked third by growth rate during the decade, with an increase of 147.6 percent. Demand for contract or temporary personnel, especially for the highly skilled, soared as firms adopted more "flexible" labor practices such as contracting-out and "just-in-time labor" – rather than direct hiring of employees – to help them quickly adjust their labor forces to stay competitive (Clinton, A. 1997; Hatch and Clinton 2000: 13).

Employment in computer and data processing services increased by 148.6 percent due to the increasing role of technology in business practices. Demand for personal services, such as health care, beauty, and hospitality, also soared, by

Table 4.4 Change in US employment by industry 1989–99

Industry	1989	1999	Change in number	%
Total nonfarm employment	107,884,000	128,786,000	20,902,000	19.4
Total private employment	90,105,000	108,616,000	18,511,000	20.5
Total service-producing employment	82,630,000	103,304,000	20,674,000	25.0
Transportation and public utilities employment	5,614,000	6,826,000	1,212,000	21.6
Wholesale trade employment	6,187,000	6,924,000	737,000	11.9
Retail trade employment	19,475,000	22,788,000	3,313,000	17.0
Finance, insurance, and real estate	6,668,000	7,569,000	901,000	13.5
Services employment	26,907,000	39,027,000	12,120,000	45.0
All government employment	17,779,000	20,170,000	2,391,000	13.4
Federal	2,988,000	2,669,000	−319,000	−10.7
State	4,182,000	4,695,000	513,000	12.3
Local	10,609,000	12,806,000	2,197,000	20.7

Source: Bureau of Labor Statistics 2001.

Note
Average weekly earnings are expressed as constant 1999 dollars.

160.8 percent and 77.8 percent respectively, due to reforms expanding Medicare benefits for home health care coverage and increasing disposable incomes.

The financial services industry, which includes finance, insurance, real estate, and securities, enjoyed rapid job growth also. Historically low interest rates and higher incomes combined to increase the number of households owning stocks to 50 percent by the end of the decade, earning Wall Street record profits and increasing securities' employment by 120.4 percent.

The Clinton administration claims that income "gains were shared by Americans at all income levels" during its two terms and that, in addition, "the most disadvantaged groups tended to experience the greatest improvements in financial well-being" (CEA 2001: 188–9). Wolff's analysis of income and wealth distribution (Table 4.5) challenges these claims, finding that the years between 1983 and 1998 were a period of increasing income and wealth inequality (Wolff 2001). Throughout that time, only the top 1 percent of households increased their share of total net worth (assets minus debts), financial wealth (liquid assets), and income, while the rest either stagnated or declined. The bottom 40 percent's share of total net worth, financial wealth, and income declined significantly. Wolff also finds that, between 1982 and 1997, the average real income of non-Hispanic black households remained unchanged. He concludes that "the results point to stagnating living conditions for the average American household, with median net worth growing by only 4 percent and median income by 5 percent between 1989 and 1998" (Wolff 2001).

Table 4.5 The distribution of US wealth and income (percentage share of wealth or income held by)

Year	Gini coefficient	Top 1%	Bottom 40%
A. Net worth			
1983	0.799	33.8	0.9
1989	0.832	37.4	−0.7
1992	0.823	37.2	0.4
1995	0.828	38.5	0.2
1998	0.822	38.1	0.2
2001	0.826	33.4	0.3
B. Financial wealth			
1983	0.893	42.9	−0.9
1989	0.926	46.9	−2.5
1992	0.903	45.6	−1.1
1995	0.914	47.2	−1.3
1998	0.893	47.3	−1.1
2001	0.888	39.7	−0.7
C. Income			
1982	0.480	12.8	12.3
1988	0.521	16.6	10.7
1991	0.528	15.7	10.5
1994	0.518	14.4	10.7
1997	0.531	16.6	10.5

Source: Adapted from Wolff 2001.

Bernstein and Mishel (1997: 16) also note the accelerating rate of wage inequality during the 1990s, and find that its "pattern...does not comport well with the oft-repeated description of an economy in which all are doing well except 'less educated, less skilled workers' " but, on the contrary, suggests that only the wages of the high-wage workforce grew, while those of the rest either stagnated or declined. In other words, they find that the 1990s was a decade in which "the rich got richer" not necessarily the educated, thus continuing a trend begun in the 1980s. Even Reich concedes that the United States "has the widest inequality of income and wealth of any advanced country – wider than it has experienced in more than a century – but no strategy for how to reduce it, and none is being discussed" (Reich quoted in Hartcher 2001: 52).

Wray and Pigeon (2000) examine how widely the Clinton economic expansion distributed new employment opportunities. They find that opportunities were distributed very narrowly as 98.3 percent of the 13.25 million new jobs created between 1992 and 1999 went to 13.033 million of the 16.5 million persons with some college education and only 217,000 – or less than 2 percent – went to the half of the population without a college education. This, they argue, means those with a college education "crowded out" low-skilled job seekers. They conclude that "neither the Reagan rising tide nor the Clinton rising tide has been sufficient to lift the boats at the bottom in terms of job opportunity" (Wray and Pigeon 2000: 835).

Handel (2001) claims the evidence indicates that the labor market behaved according to Say's Law: the increased supply of the college-educated generated its own demand as employers selected employees from the top, casting doubt on the popular Clinton claim that there has been an accelerating demand for higher skills in the workforce (Reich 1991, 1997). According to Handel:

> [I]t is hard to find evidence that information technology has done much to alter either the skills content of work within occupations or the occupational composition of the workforce..... It appears that the skills requirements of postindustrial technology have had far less influence on wages than the state of the overall economy.
>
> (2001)

If, as Reich (1991) has argued in a reversal of Say's Law, the demand for more educated employees creates its own supply, we would expect all 16.5 million college-educated persons to have been employed. Other commentators (Mishel *et al.* 1999) also argue that the data contradict Clinton's argument that higher education necessarily leads to real income gains, much less to reductions in economic inequality.

Chart 4.16 shows historical data collected by the US Bureau of the Census (2000b: table A-3) in which there appears to be a correlation between education and income, but that fact by itself is by no means new or unique to the 1990s. It also shows evidence of accelerating real income growth for college graduates

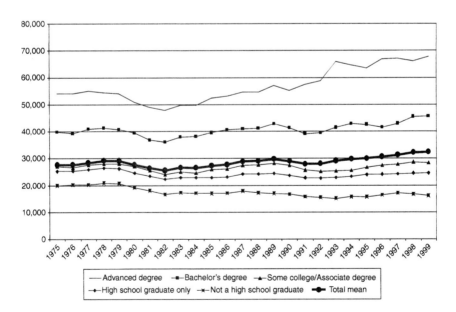

Chart 4.16 US mean earnings by education (constant 1999 dollars) 1975–99.

Source: US Census Bureau 2000b: table A-3.

over the decade as opposed to declining real incomes for non-college graduates, which would appear to support Clinton's claim that "today's income gap is largely a skills gap" (Clinton 1999c) as "the more you learn, the more you earn" (Clinton and Gore 1992: 16).

It should also be noted that whilst the official unemployment rate declined across all demographic categories, it may have been distorted by the increasing prison population. Like those in the armed forces, the prison population is excluded from the official unemployment statistics. Becket and Western (1997 in Wray and Pigeon 2000: 820) find that the unemployment rate between 1990 and 1994, for example, would have been 7.7 percent instead of the official 5.9 percent had it been adjusted to include the prisoner population. Moreover, the prisoner population consists disproportionately of young black men, a cohort which has a higher unemployment rate than the general population (11.3 percent). When adjusted to include this group, the official unemployment rate would have been an even higher 18.8 percent.

Bluestone and Rose (1998), meanwhile, call into question the Clinton Administration's claim that technological innovations have increased productivity without increasing wages, thereby generating the New Economy's inflation-free economic growth (CEA 2001: 19–25). They find that hours worked have increased consistently since the 1980s and throughout the 1990s, leading to a de facto labor supply increase equivalent to one-sixth of the additional supply that has kept a lid on wages, thereby increasing output without inducing inflation. The average annual hours worked by prime-age workers (age 25–54) increased by 2.5 percent to 2000 hours between 1991 and 1995 (Bluestone and Rose 1998: 32). Greenspan (1996 quoted in Bluestone and Rose 1998) and Reich (1997: 295) both attribute the longer (unpaid) hours to increasing job insecurity. Much of the evidence seems to suggest that labor intensity, rather than technology, has driven the majority of increased productivity (Greenspan 1996; Reich 1997; Bluestone and Rose 1998; Meeropol 2000).

The picture that emerges then is one of rising income and wealth inequality, along with displacement of the low-skilled by the high-skilled, longer working hours, and stagnating incomes. Quite a different picture to that painted by Clinton and one which could hardly be described as a case of "a rising tide lifting all boats."

Conclusion

This chapter has shown that the distinguishing features of Clinton's economic policy program are all drawn from neoclassical economic theory: fiscal discipline through spending cuts, deficit reduction, and tax cuts; competitiveness and deregulation; pro-market policies to attract private investment; privatization and labor market flexibility along with deregulation. Indeed, the defining feature of Clinton's agenda, as noted at the beginning of this chapter, is its fiscal discipline, at the expense of reduced public investment. The following chapter analyzes the economic policies of the United Kingdom's prime minister, Tony Blair, and finds that his New Labour Government has pursued a remarkably similar economic policy course to Clinton's.

5 The Third Way in the United Kingdom

This chapter will argue, first, that the overall macroeconomic framework of the Blair Government was contractionary – based on the twin-deficits proposition of standard neoclassical theory – and, second, that this constrained the key public investment elements of the Third Way program to such an extent that Blair, like Clinton, effectively abandoned them in favor of fiscal discipline. This will be shown through a detailed examination of public spending in the key areas of fiscal policy, investment policy, and education policy.

Fiscal policy

As with Clinton, Blair's fiscal policy performance is defined by its fiscal discipline along with lower rates of taxation and high revenue growth. The important point to note is that fiscal discipline or fiscal consolidation was achieved through reduced government spending rather than through higher tax rates, consistent with the standard neoclassical theory that lower taxes stimulate investment and that government spending crowds out private investment, the latter being, as discussed in Chapter 2, the standard neoclassical vehicle for economic growth.

Revenue

In an address to the financial community of the City of London, Blair said that the objective of any government should be to lower, rather than raise, taxes because "the presumption should be that economic activity is best left to the private sector" (quoted in Yergin and Stanislaw 1998: 373). The Blair Government has indeed abolished or reduced a wide range of taxes. Chancellor of the Exchequer Gordon Brown boasts of having reduced corporate tax from 33 to 30 percent, the lowest level of business taxation of the major industrial countries (Callinicos 2001: 53); abolished advance corporation tax; removed repayable dividend tax credits from pension funds; moved to a quarterly system of tax payments for large firms; and introduced a lower rate of corporate tax of 20 percent for companies with annual profits of less than £300,000 (Clark and Dilnot 2001: 3).

In April 1999, the starting rate of personal income tax on the first £1,520 per annum was reduced from 20 to 10 percent, and in the 2001–2 budget the upper limit of this tax rate was increased to £1,880. In 1997–8, the basic tax rate (on income between £1,521 and £28,400) was reduced from 24 to 23 percent and again in April 2000 from 23 to 22 percent. In April 2001, its upper limit was increased to £29,400 whilst the higher rate of 40 percent for income above £29,400 remained unchanged (New Labour 1997d; Inland Revenue 2001).

The Blair Government also increased the starting point for National Insurance Contributions (the pensions system) to £76 weekly in April 2000 and again to £87 in April 2001. In order "to reduce the burden on employers," the point at which they begin to pay National Insurance Contributions was raised by £17 weekly in April 2000, which, with some other measures, reduced the total contributions burden on employers by £1.35 billion (New Labour 1997d). In 1997, the Government reduced the Value Added Tax on fuel from 8 to 5 percent, the lowest level allowed under European Union law (New Labour 1997d).

The Government also introduced a range of tax credits to "help make work pay." The biggest change has been the Working Families Tax Credit (WFTC), which, much like Clinton's EITC, aims at guaranteeing any family with a full-time worker £214 per week from spring 2001 (Glyn and Wood 2001: 53). It was set at a considerably more generous level than the Family Credit program which it replaced, and was boosted by an additional subsidy to cover child-care expenses for the low-paid. Those on low earnings also benefit from adjustments to the bottom end of the tax and national insurance schedules. The 1999 Budget claimed that the number of those employed who face effective marginal tax (and withdrawal of benefit rates) of more than 70 percent had fallen from 715,000 to 230,000. Single-earner families would be £30–40 per week better off over a large range of weekly earnings (£120–280 per week).

Despite the Government's reduction of income and corporate tax rates, the buoyant economy saw government revenue rise from 37.4 percent of GDP in 1996–7 to 40.1 percent in 2000–1 (HM Treasury 2002b: table C23). Furthermore, and despite the reductions in corporate taxation, overall tax revenue from private firms also increased from 3.5 percent of GDP in 1998–9 to 3.9 percent in 2001–2 (Taylor 2001a: 53).

Expenditure

In 1998 Blair told the French Parliament: "First, we must maintain strong, prudent discipline over financial and monetary policy.... There is no right or left politics in economic management today. There is good and bad" (1998a: 3). The role of government, Blair explained in a 1998 interview, is "not to pile up big budget deficits and hope for the best" but "to run a prudent financial policy and combine that with government intervention to equip people and business to survive and compete in this new global market" (Blair quoted in Wilkinson, R. 2000: 141).

As Blair had promised in his 1997 election manifesto, his Government has adhered to the previous Major Conservative Government's spending limits for its first term in office (Foley 2000: 98). In its 2001 budget, the Blair Government restated its ongoing commitment to its two "fiscal rules" (HM Treasury 2001). The first is the "golden rule": that over the economic cycle it will borrow only to invest and not to fund current spending. The second is its "sustainable investment rule," which requires that public sector net debt as a proportion of GDP be limited to a "stable and prudent" level, which the Chancellor Gordon Brown has defined as a maximum of 40 percent over the economic cycle (HM Treasury 1998b). The "golden rule" restricts the government to running a surplus on the current budget.

In terms of aggregate spending, Blair's Government has adhered to the "golden rule" by pursing disciplined fiscal policy (Chart 5.1). Total managed expenditure declined every year from 41 percent of GDP in 1996–7 to 38.1 percent in 2000–1 – the lowest level since at least 1970–1 (the Treasury's earliest historical figure) (HM Treasury 2002b: table C24).[1] Public sector current expenditure also declined, from 38.7 percent in 1996–7 to 36.5 percent in 2000–1. As a consequence of the buoyant economy and the Government's spending restraint, the current budget surplus thus increased, from a deficit of 3 percent of GDP in 1996–7 to a surplus of 2.3 percent in 2000–1, the largest since 1970–1.

Public sector net borrowing – one key measure of the budget deficit – was reversed from 3.7 percent of GDP in 1996–7 to net savings of 1.7 percent in 2000–1 (HM Treasury 2002b: table C23). As a result, public sector net debt has declined massively: from 43.7 percent of GDP in 1996–7 to 31.3 percent in 2000–1 (HM Treasury 2001: table C23). As with the "golden rule," the Government has also adhered to the "sustainable investment rule" (Chart 5.2).

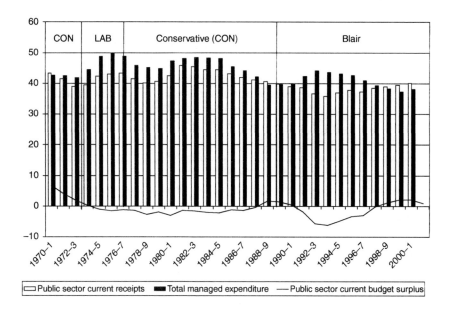

Chart 5.1 UK public expenditures, receipts, and budget surplus (% of GDP) 1970–1 to 2000–1.

Source: HM Treasury 2002b: tables C23 and C24.

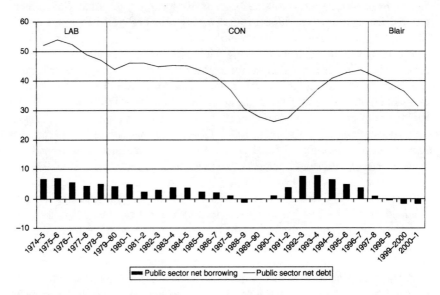

Chart 5.2 UK public sector net borrowing and net debt (% of GDP) 1974–5 to 2000–1.
Source: HM Treasury 2002b: table C23.

The Blair Government announced the results of its Comprehensive Spending Review at the end of July 2000. The Review set departmental spending plans for the next three years – from fiscal 2000–1 to 2003–4 (New Labour 1997d). Alongside the plans are quantified performance targets setting out what taxpayers can expect for this investment. Fifteen cross-departmental reviews addressed issues which cut across traditional departmental boundaries. Within limits for spending in line with the Government's fiscal rules, the Review provided new funding and set new performance outcomes as well as investment strategies for each department which set out detailed plans for how capital programs will contribute to their overall goals.

The move to three-year planning cycles from 1999 and the establishment of a link between planned expenditures and the performance of spending departments reflects what Moran and Alexander (2000: 114) describe as the "unusual authority" of the Chancellor of the Exchequer and the Treasury over other agencies. It also offers the Government greater control over spending, enabling it to better meet its fiscal "rules" (Emmerson *et al.* 2003b: 9).

According to the United Kingdom's Institute for Fiscal Studies, the Blair Government has spent significantly more on health and education than either the Major Conservative or the Thatcher Conservative governments but, due to its resistance to higher taxes, could only do so by internally reallocating from the defense and social security budgets (Table 5.1). In terms of total spending, however, the Blair Government is located exactly halfway between the Conservative

Table 5.1 UK government spending (average annual real percentage increase)

Portfolio	1979–92 (Thatcher)	1992–7 (Major)	1997–2002 (Blair)
Health	3.1	2.6	4.7
Education	1.5	1.6	3.8
Defense	−0.2	−3.1	−1.3
Social security	3.5	3.8	1.5
Total spending	1.6	2.0	1.8

Source: Adapted from Institute for Fiscal Studies in Glyn and Wood 2001: 58.

Note
Social security spending includes tax credits (revenue forgone) for comparability.

Thatcher and Major governments. Discussion and evidence of the Blair Government's spending on public investments and education is presented below that challenges the Institute for Fiscal Studies' view of education spending.

The Fabian Society's Commission on Taxation and Citizenship (2000: 3) and the commentator Samuel Brittan (Callinicos 2001: 54) both point out that New Labour's public spending plans for the period 2001–4 will leave public spending as a proportion of GDP lower than when the Major Conservative Government left office in fiscal 1996–7.

Redistribution

This section examines the redistributive impact of the Blair Government's policies as income redistribution is a standard test of a government's commitment to social democracy. It is, therefore, also a good test of Blair (1998d: 1) and Giddens' (2001: 2) claims that the Third Way is a form of "modernised social democracy."

There is some disagreement over the precise impact of New Labour's policies on income inequality. According to the Commission on Taxation and Citizenship (2000: 3), the first four Labour budgets (1997–2000) have been modestly redistributive in impact, both to low-income households and to families with children. By one estimate, the Blair Government's budgets have increased the incomes of the poorest 20 percent of households with children by 15 percent whilst the incomes of the richest 20 percent rose by only 1 percent (Moran and Alexander 2000: 115–16).

Clark and Dilnot (2001) agree that the incomes of the poorest households have risen under the Blair Government but argue that the richest households have benefited more. Whilst the incomes of households in the poorest quintile have grown by 1.4 percent, they calculate that the richest households' income have grown by 2.8 percent and the next richest quintile's by 2.4 percent (Clark and Dilnot 2001: 31). Glyn and Wood (2001: 57) argue that the Blair Government's refusal to reverse Conservative prime minister Margaret Thatcher's decision to index welfare benefits to prices rather than earnings has been a major contribution to the rise in inequality because, since the poorest households receive most of their incomes from benefits, this inevitably drags down the share of the poorest groups whenever real incomes rise.

Callinicos (2001: 52) accuses the Blair Government of raising inequality. He cites Gini coefficients (one key measure of inequality) which show income inequality rising from 33 in 1996–7 to 35 in 1998–9, the highest level since the Thatcher era. He also cites Department of Social Security figures which show the number of people living in households with less than half the average income (the United Kingdom's official definition of poverty) rising from 16.9 to 17.7 percent of the population during Blair's first two years in office. Moreover, the wealthiest 10 percent of the population saw their incomes rise by 7.1 percent compared with only 1.9 percent for the poorest 10 percent. Callinicos (2001: 53) agrees with Glyn and Wood (2001: 57) that the key cause is the Government's continuation of Thatcher's decision to index welfare payments to inflation rather than to the growth in real incomes.

Monetary policy

The only explicit monetary policy commitment New Labour offered was to transfer operational control over interest rates to the Bank of England's Monetary Policy Committee, which it did in June 1997, to "ensure that decision making on monetary policy is more effective, open, accountable and free from short-term political manipulation" (New Labour 1997e: 13).

The Government monetary policy framework requires that the Government sets the inflation target, which is 2.5 percent per year, while the Monetary Policy Committee sets interest rates to meet that target. By removing monetary policy from the control of political parties, the idea is that interest rates would be changed in a timely manner to offset inflationary or deflationary pressures as well as "enhance its credibility in the eyes of the financial markets" (Glyn and Wood 2001: 51).

This is one example among many of Blair's New Labour openly drawing upon the American experience by emulating both the machinery and stability of monetary policy established by the Federal Reserve Bank System in the United States. Foley explains that

> [T]he American linkage is unmistakable given that the choice undertaken by the Blair administration in May 1997 owed much to advice Mr Brown [then Shadow Chancellor of the Exchequer] had received from Mr Alan Greenspan, the chairman of the US Federal Reserve, two months prior to New Labour's victory in the [1997] general election.
>
> (2000: 7)

According to the Bank of England's (2001a) survey of selected retail bank interest rates, the last time the average retail rate was lower than the 5.25 percent of

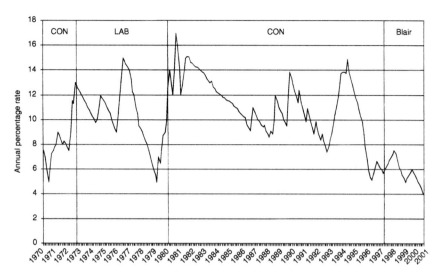

Chart 5.3 Bank of England base interest rates 1970–2001.

Source: Bank of England 2003.

May 10, 2001 was on June 12, 1972. Chart 5.3 shows the Bank of England's base (or discount) rates between 1970 and 2001 and similarly finds that the 5 percent base rate on June 10, 2001, was the lowest since October 17, 1977 (Bank of England 2003).

Like the United States, reduced government spending appears to have had the intended effect of reducing demand on the money supply, thus contributing to lower interest rates. Also like the United States, the United Kingdom has adopted the monetary practice of inflation targeting, whereby monetary policy is adjusted to maintain an inflationary target, 2.5 percent in the case of the United Kingdom.

Inflation

On November 27, 2001, New Labour's Chancellor of the Exchequer Gordon Brown told the House of Commons: "inflation has been at or near our target of $2\frac{1}{2}$ percent for four years... [which is] the lowest inflation rate since 1963" (Brown 2001) in fulfillment of New Labour's 1997 election commitment. Whilst this is probably overstating the case, price inflation has remained low, and F. Wilkinson (2000: 661–3) agrees that inflation, which was 3.1 percent in 1997, had by 1999 fallen to below 2 percent for the first time since the 1960s. However, he argues that this was more due to the "extraordinary decline" in the price of imports – which fell by 6.7 percent in 1997, 6.4 percent in 1998, and another 2.5 percent in 1999 – than to the effects of monetary policy.

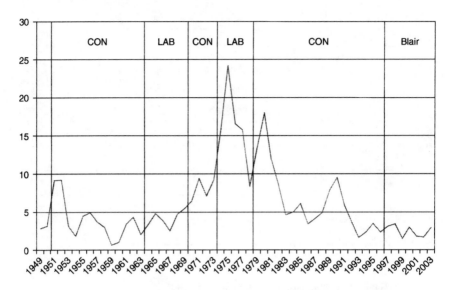

Chart 5.4 Annual percentage change in UK retail prices 1949–2003.

Source: ONS 2004.

Notes
Chart 5.4 uses the United Kingdom's Office for National Statistics' (ONS) longest time-series data for inflation, which excludes mortgage interest payments. Data which include this expense are only available from 1987.

Money supply

Chart 5.5 shows that between 1997 and 2000, growth in M4 (the broadest UK measure of money supply) was at its lowest rate since 1970 and most closely resembled the rates under Conservative governments between 1991 and 1996.

This analysis of monetary policy reveals the standard neoclassical logic to be at work: that by reducing government spending and government debt, interest rates decline, thereby stimulating private investment.

Investment policy

We have seen that the overall macroeconomic settings of the Blair Government were contractionary. As a result of its overriding commitment to a budget surplus, this prevented the Government from pursuing its Third Way program in the key policy areas of public investments in infrastructure, education, and R&D.

Public investment

In keeping with the evolutionary and endogenous growth theories, the Blair Government devoted a large portion of its *Spending Review 2000* (HM Treasury

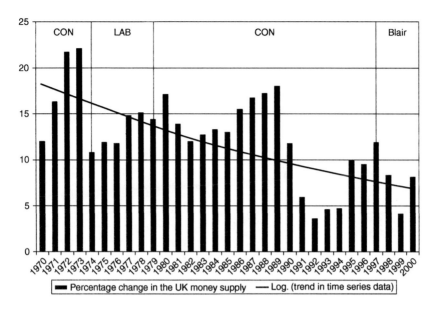

Chart 5.5 Annual percentage change in the UK money supply (M4) 1970–2000.

Source: Bank of England 2001b.

2000a) to stressing the importance of public investment, as it provides the infrastructure essential to improvements in output, productivity, and growth. Indeed, the Blair Government has accused its Conservative predecessors of cutting capital programs "as a way of meeting short-term current pressures, with long-term detrimental effects" (HM Treasury 2000b: 2). In its *Spending Review 2002*, it referred to estimated backlogs in 1997 of "in excess" of £7 billion in schools, over £3 billion for National Health Service (NHS) buildings, and up to £6.7 billion on roads (HM Treasury 2002a: 5). Despite its declared enthusiasm, however, increased public investment has not only failed to materialize under the Blair Government but has actually declined, as a share of GDP, to postwar lows (Clark and Dilnot 2001: 25–6; Clark *et al.* 2002: 305).

Chart 5.6 illustrates the long-term trend of declining public investment in the United Kingdom. Total gross public investment as a percentage of GDP has fallen almost continuously since its peak in 1967–8 and has continued to decline under the Blair Government.[2] In 1996–7, the financial year in which Blair won office, gross public investment represented 2.4 percent of GDP but, by 2000–1, it had reached a postwar low of 1.8 percent of GDP. Net public investment shows a similar continuous collapse from its peak of 7.1 percent in 1967–8 to 0.5 percent in 1999–2000 and again in 2000–1.

According to Clark and Dilnot (2001: 25–7), over the course of Blair's first term his government spent an average of less than 0.5 percent of GDP per year on public net investment, which is, they argue, "easily the lowest figure for any

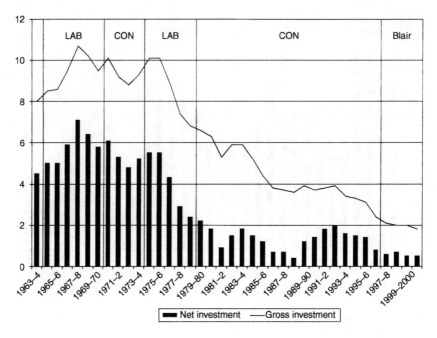

Chart 5.6 UK gross and net public investment (% of GDP) 1963–4 to 2000–1.
Source: HM Treasury 2003a.

four-year period since the Second World War." They calculate that, in that period, real investment spending declined by an average of 4.4 percent per annum, a total reduction of 16.4 percent over those four years.

Some commentators have considered the argument that the decline in public investment may simply reflect the attempts of successive governments to reduce the overall size of public spending (e.g. Clark *et al.* 2002: 312). If this argument were true, we would expect to see the public investment share of total public spending as relatively constant despite reductions in the total size of spending. Chart 5.7, which shows the UK public gross investment as a percentage of all government expenditure, reveals this not to be the case. Rather, it shows a significant and continuous decline in the public investment share of public spending from very high levels in the 1960s and 1970s to unprecedented lows of less than 5 percent under the Blair Government. It thus appears to contradict the Blair Government's claims of priority for public investment (e.g. HM Treasury 2000a,b) and exposes them to their own criticism that previous governments have diverted capital expenditure to recurrent spending programs.

Chart 5.8 shows gross public capital formation for education – a key Third Way policy area – and another important test of Blair's commitment to the Third Way program.

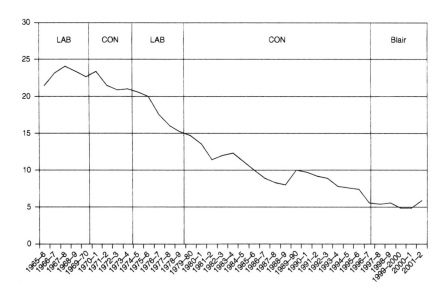

Chart 5.7 UK public gross investment as a percentage of total managed expenditure 1965–6 to 2001–2.

Source: HM Treasury 2003a,d.

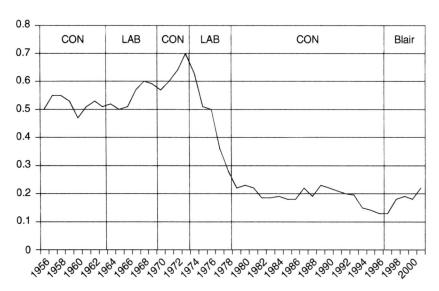

Chart 5.8 UK general government gross capital formation for education (% of GDP) 1956–2001.

Source: ONS 2003: table 11.2.

Chart 5.8 reveals that public investment in education peaked at just over 0.7 percent in 1973 and, after that, declined extremely rapidly, so that by 1982 it represented just under 0.2 percent of GDP. It has remained at a similar level ever since, fluctuating between 0.15 and 0.25 percent. Despite a slight recovery in the early 1990s, it declined again in the mid-1990s. Another recovery is evident during Blair's first term: gross capital formation rising to 0.22 percent in 2001, almost but still less than the level of investment at the end of the 1980s. Of particular concern, argue Clark *et al.* (2002: 336), is that in 1990 the rate of growth in pupil numbers turned positive yet education investment continued to decline as a share of GDP. The absolute number of pupils in 1999 had reached its 1970 level of 10.2 million; however, the level of gross capital formation in 1970 represented 0.57 percent of GDP, yet by 1999, in contrast, it had declined to only 0.19 percent.

Given the stated importance of R&D in economic theory as well as in Blair's New Economy rhetoric, it is particularly pertinent to examine his government's expenditure on R&D in comparison with that of earlier governments. As Chart 5.9 shows, the UK government expenditure on R&D peaked at 1.27 percent of GDP in 1981 and in the 21 years between 1967 and 1988 generally remained in a range of between 1 and 1.2 percent. Since 1988, however, a clear decline is evident and it has not been reversed by the Blair Government. In its first four years, average R&D represented half its average between 1967 and 1987.

Chart 5.10 shows public investment in health care continued rising until 1973, when it reached almost 0.4 percent of GDP. Thereafter, it fluctuated between 0.25 and 0.3 percent until 1991. It then appears to have collapsed to 0.02 percent in 2001. However, the creation of the NHS Trusts in 1990 may have a bearing on

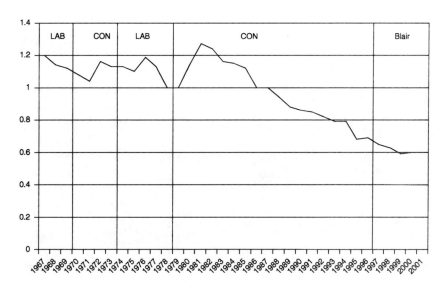

Chart 5.9 UK total net government expenditure on R&D (% of GDP) 1967–2001.

Source: ONS 2002: table 4.

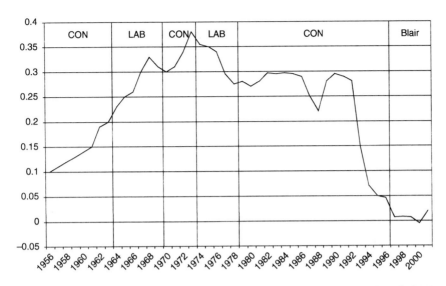

Chart 5.10 UK general government gross capital formation for health (% of GDP) 1956–2001.

Source: ONS 2003: table 11.2.

Notes
General government includes central and local governments but excludes public corporations. *Gross capital formation* is another measure of public investment, which includes the acquisition of fixed assets plus changes in the level of inventories less sales of assets and the improvement of land. Gross capital formation may be negative as the sale of assets may be larger than acquisitions.

these figures. NHS Trusts are classified as public corporations whose expenditure lies outside of the "general government" statistical category and is not included in the series. With their inclusion, Clark *et al.* (2002: 331) calculate that gross capital formation for health may be as much a full percentage point higher from 1992, yet the rapidly declining trend thereafter is identical to that in Chart 5.10 (Clark *et al.* 2002).

Chart 5.11 shows total public investment in the roads network as a percentage of GDP. It reveals that public investment in roads declined from 1.5 percent in 1970–1 to stabilize at about 0.7 percent in the 1980s. It then increased again in the early 1990s, only to decline to record lows of less than 0.5 percent under the Blair Government. This almost continuous decline is of particular concern considering the almost continuous growth in the number and use of motor vehicles (Department for Transport 2003) and the demands made upon the roads network for the transportation of goods and services.

Privatization

Many commentators have turned to the increased role of privatization and private financing of public services as one possible explanation for the decline in public

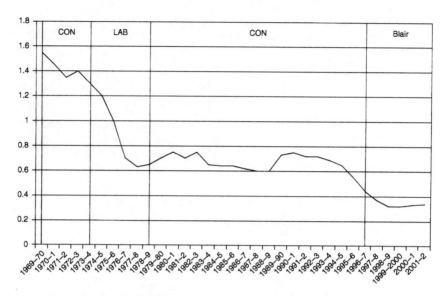

Chart 5.11 UK public investment in roads (% of GDP) 1969–70 to 2001–2.

Source: Department for Transport 2003.

investment shown in Chart 5.6 (e.g. Bloom and Bond 2001: 6; Clark *et al.* 2002: 310; Emmerson *et al.* 2003b: 36).

On coming to office, New Labour privatized public assets in air traffic control, student loans, and defense research as well as relaunching the Conservatives' Private Finance Initiative (PFI) (Coates and Lawler 2000: 129). The PFI is a method of privatization introduced by the Major Conservative Government in 1992 whereby private sector finance is used in the construction, maintenance, and delivery of public services in return for government payment of an income stream over a number of years. These payments are not classed as capital spending, so public investment appears lower than it otherwise would under traditional public procurement. The PFI is in many respects similar to Clinton's PPP initiative discussed in Chapter 4.

Several arguments have traditionally been put in favor of PFI (Institute for Public Policy Research 2000; Robinson, P. 2000). The principal argument is that the private sector can deliver public goods of a higher quality and more efficiently than the government. The other main argument is that by helping government overcome a perceived fiscal dilemma by securing new financing for public investment, the PFI appears to allow government to reconcile the desire for higher capital spending with the commitment to maintaining a policy of fiscal discipline and low taxation.

The Blair Government rebranded and relaunched the PFI as PPP and extended its use into the delivery of public services previously thought of as exclusively public. According to Toynbee and Walker (quoted in Taylor 2002), between 1997 and 2001, PFI contracts had been signed for 150 projects worth more than £12 billion, including 35 hospitals, 520 schools, and four prisons. According to HM Treasury (1998a: table B15, 2001: table C16), the total value of capital spending on public projects by the private sector increased 258 percent from £1,500 million in 1997–8 to £3,878 million in 2000–1.

Chart 5.12 shows gross public investment with the addition of private sector capital spending under the PFI. It reveals that even with the inclusion of PFI investment, and despite its rapid growth, total gross public investment in the fiscal year 2000–1 was only raised from 1.8 to 2 percent of GDP – still an historically low level and the overall trend remains unchanged. These data appear not to lend substance to the argument that public investment has made way for private investment – a key element of the neoclassical approach to 'sound' public finance known as the crowding-out hypothesis (discussed in Chapter 3).

Very controversially, New Labour has even begun a trial of privatized police officers it calls the "rent-a-bobby" scheme, whereby consumers, usually busi-nesses, can rent a police officer to guard client stores only (*Police News* 2001: 7). South Yorkshire police, for example, charge £3,000 a month to shopkeepers in a Sheffield shopping centre and that entitles them to one police officer to guard their stores during daylight hours. The shopkeepers may also purchase protection for night-time hours for an additional fee.

Blair's support for PFI and PPPs and his "plans to push privatization" further than Prime Minister Thatcher have proven extremely controversial and, because

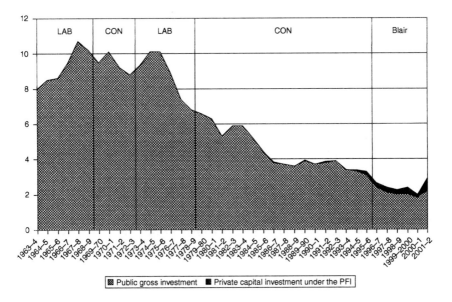

Chart 5.12 UK gross public investment including capital spending by the private sector under the PFI (% of GDP) 1963–4 to 2001–2.

Source: HM Treasury 2003a,b.

they transfer public sector services and jobs to the private sector, have incurred the opposition of the trade unions – the traditional constituency of the Labour Party – and accusations of betrayal (Taylor 2001b). Toynbee and Walker (quoted in *The Bulletin*, May 15, 2001) accuse Blair of using private sector finance to actually disguise the declining levels of public spending on infrastructure and services.

A final, and perhaps the most plausible, explanation for the decline in public investment considered by a number of commentators is the desire demonstrated by successive governments to contain public spending overall, and the budget deficit in particular, by diverting capital spending to current spending (Clark and Dilnot 2002; Clark *et al.* 2002). Politically, reductions in public investment, as opposed to current spending, are less likely to be immediately apparent and therefore provoke political reaction. During the past 25 years, public investment in fact appears to have been sacrificed to containing overall public spending and, indeed, this strategy has been practiced even more actively by the Blair Government. The risk this strategy runs, of course, is that such short-term political pressures may result in public investment that is below the optimal long-term level required for economic growth. Ironically, this is, as noted above, precisely the accusation the Blair Government had leveled at its Conservative predecessors. Yet, just as Clinton had done, Blair too sacrificed public investment for debt reduction.

According to the Commission on Taxation and Citizenship (2000: 33), as "Labour's commitment was not just to hold income tax rates, but to reduce the large budget deficit inherited from the Conservatives...the new [Labour] Government argued that high borrowing levels increase interest rates" and that this would crowd-out private investment. Just as with Clinton (e.g. CEA 2001: 43), this is the standard neoclassical argument with which by now we have become well acquainted.

Private investment

In late 1999, Blair became the first Labour prime minister to address the Confederation of British Industry. In his speech, he described the role of government intervention in industry as a policy that had "passed its sell-by date" (Blair 1999). He confirmed that under New Labour, the role of contemporary government was "to encourage innovation and entrepreneurship" and "to equip people and business for the New Economy, concluding that as a New Labour Prime Minister, he was proud to be pro-business and proud to have transformed [New Labour's] relations with business" (1999).

As with Clinton, Blair's policy for encouraging private investment contained the two components of lower interest rates and tax incentives. We have already seen how the Blair Government sought to induce lower interest rates by adhering to the standard neoclassical prescription of reducing the budget deficit and public net debt.

The other instrument Blair adopted to encourage private investment was tax incentives. As already noted, the Blair Government reduced the corporate tax rate from 33 to 30 percent, the lowest level of business taxation of the major industrial countries (Callinicos 2001: 53). It also introduced a new lower rate of corporate tax of 20 percent for companies with profits of less than £300,000 per annum.

Chart 5.13 shows private and public investment in the United Kingdom as a percentage of GDP. It shows that, at 14.2 percent, 1989 represents the highwater mark for business investment in the past 37 years. Overall in that period, business investment has fluctuated between 10 and 15 percent. However, the early 1990s is shown as a period of declining private investment until a slight resurgence emerges during the last two years of the Major Conservative Government (1995 and 1996) and the first two years of the Blair Government (1997 and 1998). Bloom and Bond (2001: 10) critically note that, despite the Blair Government's pro-investment rhetoric, suggestions that there has been an investment boom are not supported by the range of available evidence.

Interestingly, we would expect that if the neoclassical theory of crowding-out were to apply (discussed in Chapter 3), then an inverse relationship between private and public investment should emerge: the higher the level of public investment, the lower the level of private investment should be from crowding-out, and vice versa. Yet no discernible pattern is apparent.

It is also of interest to examine the portion of total business investment dedicated to R&D, which, as we can recall from earlier chapters, is, according to the Third Way, an important "driver" of the New Economy. As Chart 5.14 shows, after its reaching its highest point of 1.5 percent of GDP in 1981 and 1986, business investment in R&D has consistently declined until a very modest reversal in 1999, still at a considerably lower level than during the late 1980s.

Chart 5.15 shows that, as with Clinton, whilst the United Kingdom's private saving has fluctuated within a small range over the past 20 years, public saving has changed markedly and undergone a major reversal to budget surplus with the election of the Blair Government.

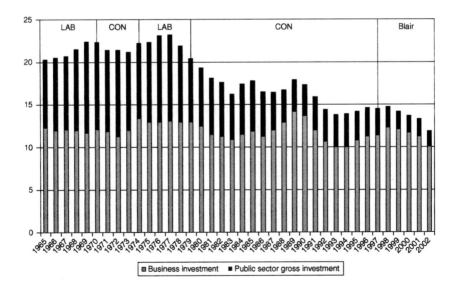

Chart 5.13 UK business and public sector investment (% of GDP) 1965–2002.
Source: ONS 2003.

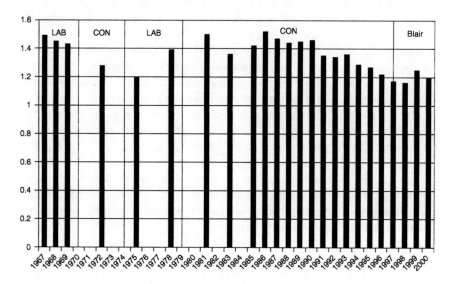

Chart 5.14 UK total business investment in R&D (% of GDP) 1967–2000.

Source: ONS 2002: table 7.

Note
As Chart 5.14 shows, the UK ONS' time-series data for business expenditure in research & development (BERD) are not complete.

Finally, in the endless quest for discernible patterns and valid theories, it is also worth comparing time series for national savings and private investment. If, as neoclassical growth theory would have it, increased savings are vital for increased investment, we would expect to see a positive relationship between them. Yet this is not the case. To the extent that any relationship is able to be discerned at all, a pattern emerges whereby private investment is greater during periods of public dissaving, that is, budget deficits. Whilst it is not suggested that this represents conclusive empirical evidence, it does seem to point, however, to the important economic role of the government and to the value of evolutionary growth theory (discussed in Chapter 2) and Keynesian public finance theory (discussed in Chapter 3).

Education policy

If, as Glennerster (2001: 3) has noted, sheer policy activity were the measure of success, the Blair Government would do very well indeed. However, on the question of funding – despite Blair's famous declaration that his "three priorities for government would be education, education and education" (Blair 1996a) – his Government scores considerably less well (Chart 5.16).

There have been no fewer than 36 major education policy initiatives between 1997 and 2001. In Opposition, the Labour Party identified educational standards

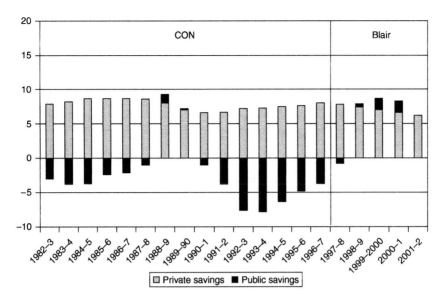

Chart 5.15 UK national savings (% of GDP) 1982–3 to 2001–2.

Source: HM Treasury 2003c; Bank of England 2004.

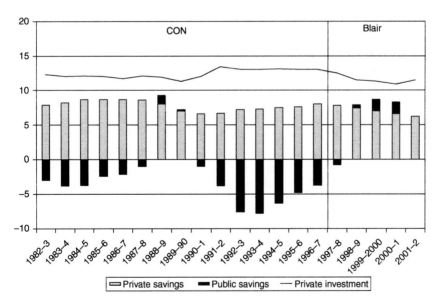

Chart 5.16 UK national savings and private investment (% of GDP) 1982–3 to 2001–2.

Source: HM Treasury 2003c; ONS 2003; Bank of England 2004.

as its central concern (New Labour 1997e) and its reforms in office are characterized by an intense focus on educational standards through performance testing, competition and the devolution of resources, responsibility, and accountability to the local level.

The importance of standards was illustrated by the subject of the Government's first White Paper *Excellence in Schools* in July 1997 and by the School Standards and Framework Act of July 1998. Under the Act, standards are centrally set in the *National Literacy Strategy* (1998) and the *National Numeracy Strategy* (1999) and centrally overseen by the Standards and Effectiveness Unit in the Department for Education and Skills and the Chief Inspector of Schools in the Office for Standards in Education (Ofsted), established by the Conservative Government in 1992.

In November 1998, the Government introduced national homework guidelines for primary and secondary schools after its 1997 *Excellence in Schools* White Paper proposed that these be published. The Government also introduced regular testing and assessment of both students and teachers and the publication of performance in controversial "league tables" of schools.

In addition to standards, the central Government exercises tremendous power over education through two programs known as "Fresh Start" and "Educational Action Zones." Introduced in July 1997, the Fresh Start program involves the closure of a school judged to be "failing" and the opening of a new school on the same site. A "failing school" is one subject to a formal Local Education Authority warning that it repeatedly failed to meet designated educational standards. The Government supplemented Fresh Start the following July with its "New Deal for Schools" program, a program aimed at raising educational standards by improving the condition of school buildings and technological facilities.

In September 1998, the Government established Educational Action Zones which are clusters of two to three secondary schools and their associated primary schools working with the Local Education Authority, parents, businesses, and other stakeholders to overcome obstacles to learning in areas of social and economic disadvantage. That same month, the Government identified "beacon schools," which are the best performing in the country and represent examples of best practice that less effective schools can learn from. Each beacon school is partnered with at least one school in a disadvantaged area. The scheme was piloted with 75 beacon schools in 1998 and, by 2001, their number had risen to 1,000.

The Government has also sought to increase the responsibility and accountability of both teachers and parents. It set out a series of reforms to the teaching profession in its 1998 Green Paper *Teachers: Meeting the Challenge of Change* to empower individual school leaders to more easily recruit, promote, and better reward teachers. It also enabled school leaders to more easily dismiss teachers identified as failing to achieve educational standards. Parents too are not exempt from their obligations. With the establishment of learning contracts, parents are obliged to assume responsibility for their child's attendance and preparedness to learn.

In addition to the devolution of staffing decisions, individual Local Education Authorities and schools have been given greater responsibility over budgetary resources such as funding and maintenance decisions. More funding has been devolved to the individual school level and each Local Education Authority receives a grant from the central government but has discretion over how it is spent on different functions.

The Government also brought competitive pressures to bear on schools as a means of improving educational outcomes (Glennerster 2001). In particular, competition between schools was introduced in the form of quasi-market measures such as the allocation of funding to individual students which schools then must compete to attract. The higher the quality of the school, the more students it attracts, and the more funding it receives. Conversely, schools that, for whatever reason, fail to attract students in sufficient numbers will find their funding reduced. The quality of a school is largely determined by its performance in the "league tables" of national examinations.

A further New Labour initiative was the publication of its discussion paper on lifelong learning, *The Learning Age*, in July 1998. The paper committed the Government to investing £150 million in 1 million individual learning accounts and reconfirmed New Labour's commitment to a University for Industry (Department for Education and Employment 1998). The University for Industry aims to stimulate demand for lifelong learning by providing information and advice on learning opportunities through its 70 "hubs" – local PPPs of colleges, universities, local governments and authorities, trade unions, private companies, and community organizations (Glennerster 2001: 36). As an example of New Labour's attraction to PPPs, Stedward (2000: 174) notes that the University for Industry "may provide one way of meeting the Government's aim of increasing participation in... education without increasing the resources" spent on the task.

The Government's reforms in funding for higher education – particularly the introduction of tuition fees and the abolition of grants – marked a distinct departure from the ideology of previous Labor governments, for whom free education had been a matter of faith (Stedward 2000: 177). After a major inquiry into higher education funding, the Dearing Committee recommended in 1997 that graduates should make a contribution equivalent to 25 percent of the average cost of their tuition on some income-related basis. Since 1998, new undergraduate students in full-time higher education courses and their parents are means-tested and charged up to £1,000 for each year of their course. As Glennerster (2001: 20) notes, this reform was much in line with what neoclassical economists had been recommending since Milton Friedman's (1955) proposals and similar to the scheme the Australian Hawke Labor Government had introduced in 1989. The introduction of fees was considered radical not just in the context of a departure from the policies of previous Labor governments but also in its willingness to implement a reform successive Conservative governments had canvassed but feared adopting (Stedward 2000: 178).

As noted, whilst the Blair Government performs well with respect to policy activity, it has performed less well, however, when it comes to funding education

(Chart 5.17). Overall, real public expenditure on education as a share of GDP actually declined from 4.9 percent of GDP in fiscal 1996–7 to 4.5 percent in 1999–2000 – less than even the lowest figure of the previous Thatcher and Major Conservative governments and the lowest figure since the early 1960s (Glennerster 2001: table 2: 7). By 2000–1, government spending had only risen slightly to 4.8 percent. Glennerster (2001: 6) attributes the relative decline in government spending on education to "the Labour Government's determination to keep to the Conservative [overall spending] plans." Thus, in its first term, the Blair Government failed to meet its 1997 manifesto commitment to "increase the share of national income spent on education" (New Labour 1997e: 8).

Chart 5.18 examines public expenditure on education by individual sector on a recurrent (not capital) basis for England only. It reveals that as a percentage of GDP, the higher and further education sectors have fared worst under the Blair Government. The further education sector – which includes adult education and lifelong learning – declined from 0.52 percent of GDP in 1996–7 to 0.43 percent in 2001–2. The higher education sector, which includes universities, similarly declined from 0.57 to 0.48 percent over the same period.

The three other sectors – under-fives, primary, and secondary education – have remained static over the period 1993–4 to 2001–2 at 0.2, 0.8 and 1 percent respectively. Very small recoveries in 2001–2 fall very short indeed of offsetting reductions in the first term.

We should note that the spending reductions shown in Chart 5.18 are similar in trend and additional to the declining public investment in education and R&D illustrated by Charts 5.8 and 5.9 respectively.

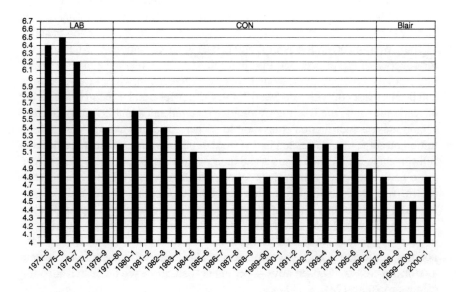

Chart 5.17 UK real public expenditure on education (% of GDP) 1974–5 to 2000–1.
Source: Glennerster 2001: 7.

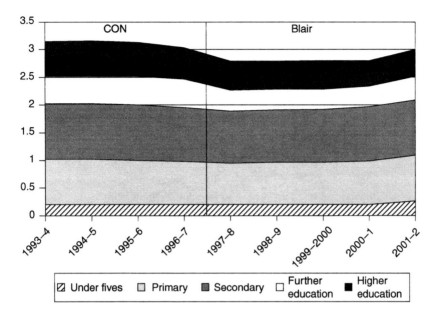

Chart 5.18 Real education expenditure by sector (% of GDP) for England only 1993–4
to 2001–2.

Source: Department for Education and Skills 2003a,b.

Conclusion

The similarities between the economic policies pursued by both the Clinton Administration and the Blair Government are striking: reduced government spending and public investment; debt reduction; reduced rates of taxation; deregulation and increased competitiveness; pro-market policies to attract private investment; privatization and increased private sector participation in public services.

From these analyses of both Clinton and Blair's economic policy practice, it is clear that the defining feature of the Third Way in practice is the similarity with which both governments sacrificed their stated commitment to public investment in favor of fiscal discipline. This feature confirms that the potential conflict that was acknowledged in Chapter 3, that is, the conflict between the two components of the Third Way economic program – public investment and 'sound' public finance – did in fact emerge and was resolved in favor of the latter.

In Chapter 2 it was established that the public investment component of the Third Way *program* is based on evolutionary and endogenous growth theories of economic growth due to its advocacy of active government intervention in the provision of NSI and infrastructure. Chapters 4 and 5 find, however, that the Third Way's policy *practice* is clearly based on neoclassical theory, demonstrated by its overriding commitment to fiscal discipline as a means of increasing savings for investment, which is the standard neoclassical vehicle for economic growth.

6   A Third Way or no way at all?

In a letter to John Maynard Keynes, Sir Dennis Robertson warned:

> [E]ducational disadvantages [can have] the tendency...to exaggerate
> differences and represent all knowledge as brand new: It doesn't breed a scien-
> tific spirit but the reverse, viz., a blind scramble to acquire the new orthodoxies
> for fear of being out of fashion.
>
> (quoted in Keynes 1973: 95–6)

His warning might well apply to proponents of the Third Way, and indeed the
purpose of this study has been, in the spirit of Sir Dennis' words, to attempt to
draw some meaningful conclusions by subjecting historical practice to theoretical
analysis.

This study has found that the Third Way's program for economic growth is
based on both evolutionary and endogenous growth theory, which advocate
increased government investment in the provision of certain types of public
goods, namely, national systems of innovation such as education and public infrastructure. The Third Way's program for 'sound' public finance, however, is based
on standard neoclassical theory's requirement for fiscal discipline and chose to
express itself in the form of neoliberal economic policies.

It was warned that there exists potential conflict between these two programs:
specifically, the economic growth program's advocacy for increased public
spending and 'sound' public finance's requirement for fiscal discipline.

The study then proceeded to test the Third Way's historical *practice* against economic theory and found that the conflict it warned of did in fact emerge and public
investment was sacrificed in favor of 'sound' public finance, so that the macroeconomic policies of the Third Way can best be described as neoliberal, more closely
associated with governments of the Right not the Left, and certainly not a "third" way.

It should be noted that while the adoption of 'sound' public finance and the
abandonment of alternative policies is a defining characteristic of the Third
Way, it is by no means unique to it; on the contrary, it has been an experience
common to many social democratic governments such as the Mitterand Socialist
Government in France (1981–95) and the Australian Hawke and Keating Labor
Governments (1983–96) (Pierson and Castles 2002), which are discussed in more

detail later. In fact, the process of the Third Way described has been characteristic of most governments that have initially pursued a non-standard neoclassical policy paradigm. This suggests that the 'failure' to really pursue a Third Way is symptomatic of a more general tendency inherent in capitalist liberal democratic systems to converge on the standard neoclassical approach. Schumpeter's warning, in *Capitalism, Socialism and Democracy* (1942), that a capitalist economy can only be governed according to capitalist logic resonates loudly. This suggests that a more complete explanation of the process described in this study must be sought in political theory and practice, not just in economic analysis.

As discussed in Chapter 1, a convincing interpretation of the Third Way which enjoys widespread support is that of a political strategy designed to reposition the Left within the political mainstream as a viable alternative to the Right, capable of successfully governing capitalist economies in the age of global capitalism (Reich 1997; Burns and Sorenson 1999; Dionne 1999; Harris 1999; Hay 1999; King and Wickham Jones 1999; Morris 1999; Scanlon 1999; Baer 2000; Campbell and Rockman 2000). Political strategy in this context should simply be understood to mean an electoral tactic designed to win sufficient electoral support from voters for political parties to govern.

As Dionne (1999, quoted in Temple, M. 2000: 303–4) argues, in order to win elections "parties on the left . . . have to prove they're comfortable with the market and accept its disciplines"; however, voters want capitalism tempered by other values, such as community and compassion.

Harris (1999: 52–61) too argues that the Third Way represents the Left's response to the New Right and the 'victory' of capitalism over socialism. According to Harris, if the Left were to persist in the redundant argument of socialism or social democracy versus capitalism, it would face certain political irrelevance. The Third Way therefore represents the Left's reinvention to enter the mainstream political debate by, first, accepting capitalism as the given economic system and, second, inventing the language of a "New Left" paradigm for "administering" capitalism. In fact, Blair explicitly acknowledges that a political ambition for the Third Way project is as "an attempt to marginalise the free-market Right" (Blair 1996b: 13–15). It should be noted that the principle of equality of opportunity for its citizens, as opposed to equality of outcome, is not distinctively Third Way but is, of course, a well-established liberal principle (Adams 1998: 85).

Hay (1999) also interprets the Third Way as a political strategy by applying Anthony Downs' framework in *An Economic Theory of Democracy* (1957). Downs (1957: 300) posited that "political parties tend to maintain the ideological positions that are consistent over time unless they suffer drastic defeats, in which case they change their ideologies to resemble those of the party that defeated them." Applying Downs' theory, Hay argues that Blair's New Labour, having been kept out of office by the Conservative Party for the 18 years to 1997, recrafted its agenda to more closely resemble that of its Conservative opposition, thereby reducing the difference and increasing its electoral appeal (1957: 94). Hay's argument can easily be extended to apply to the US Democratic Party, which had similarly been kept out of office for the 12 years to 1992 by its Republican opposition.

Duncan (1999) builds on Schumpeter's (1942) argument that if the Left were to govern a capitalist economy they would have to do so according to capitalist not socialist logic:

> Socialists had to govern in an essentially capitalist world...a social and economic system that would not function except on capitalist lines.... If they were to run it, they would have to run it according to its own logic. They would have to "administer" capitalism.

(1999: 32)

Baer's (2000) findings concur with those of Hay (1999) and Downs (1957). Baer's thesis is that the Third Way project was originally developed by the "New Democrat" faction of the Democratic Party and their most important organizational form, the DLC, to reposition the Democratic Party to appeal to the electoral mainstream and thus win elections. With the election of their former chairman Bill Clinton to the presidency, the New Democrats saw many of their ideas become national policy and some of their most prominent members enter the presidential cabinet and staff.

Adams (1998: 43) explains that in reshaping and repositioning New Labour, Blair was strongly influenced by Clinton's performance with the Democratic Party. Secretary of the British Fabian Society, Michael Jacobs, has also noted that Blair and his Chancellor of the Exchequer, Gordon Brown, have explicitly styled themselves on the United States' Democrats rather than in the tradition of European social democrats (Jacobs 2001a). Foley (2000) goes so far as to speak of Blair's as a "British presidency." Thus, a consensus has emerged that Blair imported the Third Way – amongst other ideas – from Clinton as a means to reposition the Labour Party to win elections, as it had been for Clinton and the Democratic Party in 1992 and again in 1996 (Adams 1998; Hay 1999; Claven 2000; Fairclough 2000; Foley 2000). Blair is also known to have been interested in the political success of the Australian Hawke and Keating Labor Government (Scott 2000), a point which is discussed in some detail later.

This literature offers a convincing account of the reasons for Clinton and Blair's adoption of neoliberal policy agendas, namely, that their political predecessors had installed the neoliberal economic paradigm to such an extent that it compelled them to believe that either they too adopt it as their own or they would face certain electoral irrelevance. Fukuyama (1992) goes so far as to describe the ideological dominance of the neoliberal paradigm over alternatives in contemporary macroeconomic management as "the end of history."

However, history has by no means ended as far as Blair is concerned. In July 2003, 14 heads of government including Tony Blair met in London to hold a conference for the purpose of developing "Third Way" policies for the new millennium under the banner "Progressive Governance." The joint communiqué of the conference identified as the first priority, under the heading "progressive strategies for growth," the need for governments to "invest in future prosperity through education, modern infrastructure and research and development; to support the shift into more resource efficient products and processes; and to maintain fiscal rigor and sound monetary policy" (Progressive Governance Summit 2003). Given the zeal of the Clinton and Blair governments to sacrifice the former to achieve the latter policy objectives, the persistence with the myth of practicing a "Third Way" is astonishing.

The Third Way has also been the subject of some debate in Australia. Politicians of different and even opposing political parties have sought to associate themselves with it. Their error, however, has been to interpret the Third Way as narrowly as Clinton and Blair, that is, as a standard neoclassical program.

The former Minister for Employment Tony Abbott, for instance, has invoked the Third Way to describe the outsourcing of employment services as part of the Jobs Network initiative:

> the Howard [Liberal/National] Government was already pursuing the Third Way.... While the political Left has been trying to create an ideology of the Third Way, the Howard Government has been making it happen in practice.... As the purchaser, but not the provider, of employment services, the Government has created what might best be described as a social market, a competitive market which exists because government has summoned it into being... [and therefore] the Third Way might even have come further in Australia than in Britain.
>
> (quoted in Tingle 2000: 6)

Following its 1996 federal election defeat, some members of the Australian Labor Party (ALP) – especially Latham (1998a) – began advocating the Third Way as a program for Labor's political renewal. The then Labor Leader of the Opposition, Kim Beazley, writes in the foreword to Claven (2000) – which examines New Labour's importation of the Clinton Third Way into Britain – that the Third Way is to his mind a term which describes well the neoliberal policies of the Hawke and Keating Labor Governments (Claven 2000: 9–10). As Beazley claims: "We invented the third way, and that was essentially the philosophical underpinning of the Hawke and Keating governments" (quoted in Seccombe 1999).

Former Prime Minister Keating strongly disagrees with Beazley's assessment. Keating insists that the Hawke and Keating Labor Governments' pursuit of policies for economic growth was in order to make the economic pie bigger for everyone, and as such is not at all novel but completely within the social democratic and Australian Labor traditions:

> [I]n continuing to pursue this growth objective, the Hawke Labor Government is operating completely in concert with the tradition of the Labor movement. In essence, in adopting practical, pragmatic measures to create growth and jobs, the Labor Party is doing nothing out of the ordinary from what the Labor Party in government has sought to do throughout its long history.
>
> (1987: 173)

Indeed, Keating, unlike Clinton and Blair, goes to some lengths to dissociate the Hawke and Keating Governments' policies from any suggestion of novelty, observing that "We didn't call what we were doing the Third Way. For Australia, we saw it as the only way" (Keating 1999, quoted in Pierson and Castles 2002: 683).

Nevertheless, a number of commentators find the neoliberal economic policies of the Hawke and Keating governments in breach (for some even a betrayal) of the Australian Labor tradition (Stilwell 1986; Maddox 1989; Frankel 1997). Others even find in those policies what Pierson and Castles (2002) call "Australian antecedents of the Third Way."

Stilwell (1986) critically examines the economic agreement between the Hawke and Keating Labor Governments and the Australian Council of Trade Unions known as "the Accord," which was presented as the centerpiece of national economic policy. It is interesting to note Stilwell's observation that the Accord emerged in response to "the perceived need [of the times] for a 'third way', a new economic strategy to replace, or at least supplement, the Keynesian and monetarist-oriented policies which had proved to be of such limited effectiveness" (Stilwell 1986: 8). He adds that this " 'third way' came increasingly to be seen in terms of a combination of a prices and incomes policy (to control inflation) and a stimulatory Keynesian fiscal policy (to restore the social wage and generate employment)" (1986: 8).

However, in the final analysis, argues Stilwell, the government expenditure component of the Accord was sacrificed in favor of the so-called "Trilogy" of fiscal discipline: (1) no increase in total taxation as a percentage of GDP; (2) no increase in total government expenditure as a percentage of GDP; and (3) no increase in the size of the budget deficit as a percentage of GDP (Stilwell 1986: 15, 117). These neoliberal policies are all based on neoclassical theories of crowding-out, increased efficiency, and private sector profitability, reflecting a central concern with reassuring investors and the financial markets of the government's commitment to capital accumulation in the private sector (1986: 67, 83, 111). In this respect, the Australian Labor experience could easily be said to anticipate that of Clinton and Blair.

Maddox (1989) accuses the Hawke Governments of betraying the Australian Labor tradition by pursuing neoliberal policies, such as the "Trilogy," which sacrificed social justice for private profitability. Maddox attributes these policies to the ALP's perceived political need to break from the image of the previous Whitlam Labor Government as profligate and economically irresponsible (1989: 149). It is interesting that Keating seems to agree with this observation, arguing that the Whitlam Government was insufficiently concerned with private profitability and fiscal discipline (Keating 1987: 178–9, 182). Maddox adds that this strategy "has helped Labor politicians to hold the *middle ground* of politics, pushing their conservative opponents into the narrow confines of reaction" (Maddox 1989: 12, italics added). In both of these respects too the Australian Labor experience uncannily resembles that of Clinton and Blair.

Other commentators believe that, more than Clinton's "New Democrats," the Hawke and Keating governments' economic policies explicitly represent the inspiration for Blair's Third Way. Frankel (1997) and Pierson and Castles (2002) argue that Tony Blair's celebrated visits to Australia in 1990 and again in 1995 convinced him to base his model of New Labour on the Hawke and Keating governments. Blair himself practically said as much. When asked what lessons he drew from Australian Labor, he replied that they were, first, the ALP's capacity to win and retain office and, second, the possibility (and popularity) of combining economic growth with communal well-being (Blair 1995).

Despite its possibly Australian origins, the Australian Third Way debate has not been without its opponents. Within Labor circles, the parliamentarian Lindsay Tanner and the union leader Doug Cameron have argued strongly against Labor adoption of the Third Way as a concession to vacuous pragmatism (Tanner 1999: 52) and "a panacea for its electoral woes" (Cameron 2002: 11). Tanner's critique of the Third Way is particularly trenchant:

> Hordes of earnest academics and spin doctors are debating the meaning of terms like the Third Way and the radical centre. The British intelligentsia in particular is absorbed by the search for a label which can provide intellectual respectability to New Labour. Unfortunately, much of this dialogue is very superficial. It has produced many good sound bites, but few insights.... It is mere cocktail politics: pour two nips of markets forces, throw in a few platitudes, add a dash of socialism, and stir vigorously. This approach is extremely simplistic. It threatens to reduce the search for a new political framework to an empty quest for the swinging voter and the middle ground. The process should not be weighed down with labels which were out of date before they were conceived. We don't need a new label for vacuous pragmatism.
>
> (1999: 51–2)

Cameron (2002: 11) warns that the ALP should not engage in "parroting the so-called Third Way agendas of British Labour or of the US Democrats." McGregor also warns that the Third Way represents no more than the Left's capitulation to the "fashionable new clothes" of neoliberalism:

> [T]he greatest triumph of neo-liberalism was to have its ideological wish list categorised as both [new and inevitable] during the '80s. Most parties of the Centre-Left clambered to don the fashionable imperial new clothes. The trouble was they were not especially new.
>
> (2001: 11)

Hutton too warns not to look to the British Labour Party for political inspiration as it

> [L]acks any governing ideology underpinned by a distinctive and coherent model of the way economy and society work. The Third Way is supposedly neither free market capitalism nor old socialism, but the advantage of both those models is that they rested on clear sets of guiding principles. Without such principles New Labour risks being no more than a group of well-intentioned men and women making it up as they go along.
>
> (1998: 23)

Some economists have correctly pointed to the contradictions within the Third Way generated by its lack of both a critical economic analysis and an alternative economic vision. Hamilton (2001: 13, 2003: 125) accurately observes that the Third Way's error is that it "is not based on any critical analysis of modern capitalism... [and that this] absence of social analysis... means that, in the end, it can do nothing other than endorse the prevailing system.... The Third Way therefore lacks a rationale." Stilwell (2000: 121) adds that the Third Way suffers from "the contradictions arising from grafting social democracy onto a capitalist economic base... [and that] this draws attention to the awkward tension in 'third way' politics between the concern for social justice and the fundamentally anti-egalitarian character of capitalist markets."

Some critics argue that the community is losing patience with facile slogans such as the "third way" and want better public services and increased public investment funded through tax revenues. McGregor (2001: 11), for example, in discussing the 2001 British election, warns: "voters want the social infrastructure repaired. They have had enough of dangerously neglected rail infrastructure and ramshackle health system. Nor are they interested in a Third Way. They issued an Old Labour mandate to Tony Blair. Fix [public services]." Similarly, the Australian clergyman and social commentator Tim Costello is critical of the Third Way's policy of "social entrepreneurship" whereby the private sector is involved in the delivery of social goods because, he argues, it has delivered more profits for the private sector than it has outcomes for the public and therefore "economic policy options like tax and fiscal policy will still be needed to battle economic inequality for some time yet" (quoted in Wade 2002: 46).

Even Latham, Australia's most vocal political proponent of the Third Way, has criticized the Howard Liberal-National Government for basing "its entire [neoclassical] budget strategy on a single, essentially flawed, economic theory – the twin deficits theory" (Latham 1998a: 344). Given that, as has been shown, the practice of the Clinton–Blair Third Way, which Latham has so strongly supported, is almost entirely based on the neoclassical theory of the twin deficits, this is a matter of intense irony if not outright contradiction.

A neoclassical counter-critique

A neoclassical economist might well challenge the critical tone of this study with the observation that, after all, given that economic growth was the primary objective, then Clinton and Blair's Third Way has been extremely successful (in the strictest economic sense) and the tone is not justified.

Such a challenge would, however, be missing the central argument of the study. This study has not sought to argue that the Third Way has been unsuccessful in delivering economic growth; on the contrary, it has in fact offered proof of that growth. The critical tone adopted is based on its central argument that the Third Way is a misnomer because it is not a third way at all but is in fact the first (neoclassical) way.

Furthermore, as, at the time of writing, the Third Way has occurred entirely within a period of economic growth, it is thus not possible to gauge its effectiveness in dealing with the entire business cycle, which clearly represents a litmus test of economic policy.

Interpreting the Third Way: economics, philosophy, or politics?

In Chapter 1, it was noted that existing evaluations of the Third Way have focused on its philosophical and political dimensions, that economic assessments are lacking, and that it is precisely the purpose of this study to analyze it as an economic program.

It was also noted that the Third Way's so-called chief philosopher, Anthony Giddens (1994, 1998, 2000a,b,c, 2001) has written extensively about the Third Way as an alternative public philosophy to the two other "ways" of "classical social democracy" and "neoliberalism." Pierson (2003), quoting Hobsbawm, uses the label "social democracy" to refer to any economic strategy which aims "to regulate and socialise the wealth-creating and directionless economic dynamism of capitalism, not replace it." Neoliberalism, on the other hand, is prepared to sacrifice economic equality in the pursuit of growth through policies that foster wealth creation based on the free market, minimal government, and maximum individual freedom and responsibility (Adams 1998: 28). Giddens thus portrays the Third Way project as "modernising social democracy" by uniting its traditional concern with equality through redistribution with the neoliberal values of economic growth, through competitiveness and public investment (Giddens 1998: 99, 2001: 2).

This study has sought to demonstrate that despite the social democratic rhetoric of public investment and equality, the Third Way abandoned these values and adhered most closely to standard neoclassical economic theory, which manifested itself in neoliberal policies concerned with economic growth and competitiveness.

The political dimension of the Third Way was also discussed at length in Chapter 1 and again more briefly in the preceding sections to offer an account of the Third Way as a political strategy designed to reinvent the image of parties of the Left as business friendly, low taxing, and low spending so as to achieve popular appeal and win elections.

By uniting social democratic rhetoric with neoliberal policies into a powerful political strategy, the Third Way has shown that policies lacking economic consistency nevertheless can have broad economic appeal and impact as they can be offered as "all things to all people." An important question generated by the Third Way experience is whether economics drives politics or politics drives economics. A useful way in which to consider this question is to ask whether governments consist primarily of political parties or policy-makers. If governments consist primarily of political parties then we would expect their principal concern to be winning and keeping office and therefore developing and *changing* policies to serve that end. This is clearly the position taken by the many commentators who argue that the Third Way should be understood above all as a political strategy. On the other hand, if governments consist primarily of policy-makers then we would expect the emergence of policies that do not change or at least change much less between campaigning for office and governing in office.

In applying this distinction to the Third Way, it is found to conform more closely to the former category, where governments consist primarily of political parties. Political parties, of course, serve one paramount purpose and that is as vehicles to win and keep office. The reason for this conclusion is that, in the case of the Third Way, it has been shown that despite campaigning on policies which placed emphasis on the social democratic values of public investment and equality, the economic policies implemented in office pursued the neoliberal values of economic growth and competitiveness. Thus, the evidence suggests that, in the case of the Third Way at least, politics drives economics.

Whilst Giddens' interpretation of the Third Way as "modernising social democracy" does not hold true in the cases of Clinton and Blair, the interpretation of the Third Way as a political strategy not only stands up to scrutiny but is reinforced by the evidence presented in this study that it is a neoliberal economic policy program.

The preceding discussion has emphasized the failure of most social democratic governments to pursue an economic policy program different from that of standard neoclassical theory, regardless of whether they consider themselves as pursuing a second, third, or another way. This begs the question: is an alternative economic policy paradigm possible? If such an alternative is to be possible, be it called a Third Way or something else, the following section will lay down some economic principles which I believe must be a necessary element.

Marrying Schumpeter and Keynes: a more genuine Third Way?

A central implication of this analysis of the Third Way is that it highlights the necessity for economic programs to possess, perhaps above all, theoretical coherence. Due to its theoretical incoherence – namely the incompatibility between its program of public investment and that of 'sound' public finance – the Third Way was not practiced in reality.

The fundamental problem – in fact error – in Third Way thinking was to attempt to reconcile two mutually exclusive programs: an evolutionary program of economic growth based on dynamic efficiency and the active role for government that it implies with a neoclassical program of 'sound' public finance based on static efficiency and the passive role for government that it requires.

The requirement for 'sound' public finance could be said to have doomed the Third Way program from the start. In particular, the requirements of 'sound' public finance for balanced budgets *and reduced taxation* meant that reductions in public expenditure were essential as a matter of arithmetic, negating the possibility for increased public investment.

An important outcome of the Third Way's theoretical incoherence is the renewed need for governments to reassess macroeconomic policy on sounder intellectual foundations. There is also an imperative for governments to restore the objective of full employment to the center of the macroeconomic policy program. Unlike the neoclassical program pursued by Clinton and Blair, it will be argued that a more genuine Third Way macroeconomic program that is theoretically coherent and places the objective of full employment at its center is not only possible, but in fact desirable.

The Third Way program suggested here proposes uniting an evolutionary program of economic growth with a Keynesian program of public finance in order to achieve what Phillimore (1998) calls the "high road to economic development": high growth with high real wages and high rates of innovation. These two programs have complementary but distinct roles: the program of economic growth is concerned with determining the average growth path of the economy, whilst the program of public finance is concerned with the business cycle around that path.

As discussed in Chapter 2, evolutionary growth theory points to the central role of government in the (supply-side) provision of national systems of innovation and infrastructure, such as education and training, R&D, transport and communications. However, just as it was noted earlier that the Clinton–Blair Third Way program is only concerned with the supply side or the productive capacity of the economy, so too evolutionary growth theory is mainly concerned with the supply side of the economy. Indeed, it was the absence of a demand side that allowed neoclassical theory – through its assumption of full employment – to fill the void in the Third Way.

Palley (2003: 84) has critically noted that economic growth models have tended to assume away the problem of reconciling demand and supply growth: neoclassical growth models have tended to assume away the demand side, while Keynesian models have tended to neglect the supply side. What is needed, therefore, is an economic program that focuses on full employment and economic growth by paying attention to both the supply and demand sides of the economy. In this sense, a program that transcends earlier programs singularly concerned with either the supply or the demand side but addresses both sides may come closer to constituting a genuine Third Way.

According to demand-led economic growth theory there is no supply-determined equilibrium towards which the level of output converges; instead, at any point in time, the utilization of existing productive resources is determined by demand conditions that are relatively autonomous from conditions of supply. Therefore the actual output path of the economy is demand-determined (Setterfield 2003). Any expansion of demand and output today will influence firms' investment expectations, their ability to execute these expectations, and hence the availability and productivity of capacity tomorrow.

In a simple insight with remarkable implications, Nell (1988, 1996) argues that the economic growth of the industrial capitalist economy is, through virtue of capitalist logic, always constrained by demand not supply. The reason is that firms in the industrial capitalist economy are always required to maintain some level of excess reserve capacity in their production so as to be capable of exploiting any sudden increases in demand. If they do not, their competitors will exploit any increased demand at their expense. Thus, excess reserve capacity is not only strategically desirable for the firm but is, in fact, essential to its ability to seize growth opportunities. Therefore, since firms maintain such an excess reserve capacity, the industrial capitalist economy cannot, by definition, be supply constrained.

Quite the contrary, the industrial capitalist economy is constrained by demand because economic growth requires that demand grow at a higher rate than the excess reserve capacity. Otherwise, firms will simply not invest as they are already carrying excess capacity for which there is insufficient demand.

Nell (1988: 163) adds that a "capitalist industrial system, being inherently dynamic, has two and only two long-run options – transformational growth or stagnation." "Transformational growth" is growth that transforms the economy by changing the relative size of its sectors through innovations which create new markets, increase productivity, and maintain high employment (1988: 162–3). For these reasons, transformational growth is dependent on demand.

Therefore, a demand-side is needed to complement the evolutionary (supply-side) program of economic growth. Hence, the government should look to developing a strategic public investment program capable of stimulating effective demand and economic growth which can therefore grow the economy out of public debt rather than depending solely on reducing public expenditure. This is where the second component of the proposed program – the Keynesian program of public finance – enters the picture to play an important role.

The role for a Keynesian program of public finance is to stimulate effective demand so as to satisfy the needs of economic growth for a demand-side strategy. The evolutionary program for economic growth can cater to the supply needs of growth and, as noted, is concerned with determining the average growth path of the economy. The purpose of a Keynesian program of public finance is to strategically manage fiscal policy so as to stimulate demand and (1) help achieve full employment and rising real wages and (2) move the economy from recession to boom *around* the average growth path.

Keynes famously argued in his *General Theory of Employment, Interest and Money* (1936) that the benefit of a program of public investment is the stimulation of investment, consumption, and effective demand leading to increased output, incomes, and employment. Keynes showed that this can occur through two mechanisms: the income multiplier and the redistribution of income.

Public investment in cases of less-than-full employment can stimulate consumption and effective demand by increasing aggregate income. The additional income will increase aggregate demand and consumption by more than unity through the multiplier effect. The total effect of the multiplier will be determined by the marginal propensity to consume of the recipients of that additional income. The marginal propensity to consume is the portion of additional income that an income-earner spends in consumption. The higher their marginal propensity to consume, the higher the multiplier effect of the public investment will be.

Keynes also posited that lower-income earners display a higher marginal propensity to consume than higher income earners. Therefore, government policy that redistributes income from higher to lower income earners will have a larger total effect on aggregate consumption and effective demand. Nell (1988: 165–8) adds that by redistributing income to lower-income earners, larger new markets can be created for consumer goods which would otherwise have been limited to the much smaller market composed of high-income earners. In effect, redistributive policy as well as government spending can and should be used to subsidize consumption (Kalecki 1943). These arguments lead to recommendations for increased public investment and redistribution through countercyclical budget policy in situations of less-than-full employment. Economists such as Eisner (1986, 1989, 1991a) and Heilbroner and Bernstein (1989) have pointed to the pressing need for a complete reconceptualization of the public finance accounting system to distinguish between recurrent consumption spending which benefits current generations (and should be funded by them) and public capital and investment spending which will benefit future generations and should therefore be funded through borrowing over the life-cycle of the investment.

Countercyclical budget policy requires budget deficits in times of recession and budget surpluses in times of boom. The principal objective is to avoid the excessive peaks and troughs of business cycles and thus employment. In this way, economic growth and full employment are restored as the central objectives of economic policy, and budget policy is an instrument enlisted in their pursuit. This argument is, of course, precisely the converse of the Third Way, in which economic growth and employment policy are enlisted in the pursuit of surplus budgets. As Tanner quite rightly observes: "The need to beautify government balance sheets should not be allowed to dictate the pattern of infrastructure investment" (1999: 131).

The concept of a countercyclical budget policy could hardly be described as radical. In fact, it is the official policy position of the Australian Commonwealth Government:

> The primary objective of the strategy is to maintain budget balance, on average, over the course of the economic cycle. This medium-term focus provides scope for fiscal policy to assist with short-term demand management, while providing an anchor to ensure that spending during periods of weaker economic activity is made possible by savings during periods of stronger economic activity ... [that is] to moderating cyclical fluctuations in economic activity.
>
> (Commonwealth of Australia Treasury 2002: 1–7 and 1–8)

As discussed in Chapter 3, Aschauer (1988, 1989, 1990) goes much further than Keynes in arguing that *even at full employment* government capital spending complements private sector productivity and can increase aggregate output with consequent benefits for economic growth, without implying the need for deficit budgets. An important implication of this argument is that due to the returns of public capital investment, the 'sound' public finance requirement for balanced budgets can still be satisfied with the increased revenue collected from the higher economic growth generated through public capital spending.

Full employment, in turn, benefits both labor and capital (Kalecki 1943). It benefits labor through higher aggregate income and consumption, and benefits capital through higher effective demand for output, and thus higher profits. Full employment can also deliver rising real wages, the benefits of which are three-fold for economic growth (Phillimore 1998; Argyrous 2000). First, rising real wages prevent less efficient firms from competing through means of lower wages rather than innovation. Second, rising real wages stimulate investment in innovation and the capital stock as firms will seek innovations with which to replace expensive labor costs. Third, rising real wages increase effective demand for innovations as consumers receiving rising real incomes will demand increasingly innovative consumer products, such as home electronics.

The advantage of developing a demand-side program of redistribution and public investment in national systems of innovation would be to simultaneously capture the benefits of improvements to supply-side inputs as well as the benefits of full employment. Public investments in national systems of innovation of the kind discussed are of the supply side but, especially if financed through a deficit, would stimulate increased investment, innovations, employment, and real wages. Increasing employment and real wages (demand side) also augment demand for investment and innovations (supply side). More investment and innovations (supply side) lead to rising employment and real wages, and thus demand. All would lead to economic growth and therefore rising government revenue to reinvest in the national systems of innovation. In short, it would enable the stimulation of both the demand and supply growth rates and thus overall economic growth. The process of economic growth described here is, of course, a form of the process known as circular and cumulative causation made famous by, amongst others, the economists Gunnar Myrdal (1944, 1957) and Nicholas Kaldor (1966).

An economic program such as that described here would indeed represent a marriage between Schumpeter and Keynes and deliver the high road to economic development; a virtuous cycle in which public investment in economic growth would actually be funded through economic growth. No insignificant feat for any government of any political persuasion.

However, a macroeconomic program such as that described is not without its own potential political and economic limitations. The dominant ideology of free-market liberalism is so powerful that it could encounter fierce resistance from the electorate. The quest for full employment and rising real wages may well meet with opposition from employers concerned with the opportunities it creates for labor – especially organized labor – to extract higher wages. Nor are employers likely to welcome the effect of rising real wages on their firms' profitability. Employers are also likely to resist government demands for higher regulatory standards due to the often large costs of compliance. Higher-income earners may oppose the higher marginal taxes associated with a redistributive incomes policy. Moreover, there are likely to be citizens and organizations, powerful interests in particular, that oppose the large economic and regulatory role for government such a program calls for. Finally, and in addition to all these potential limitations, there is also disagreement over unresolved theoretical issues such as the functions of money, credit, and debt in the economy. Overall, the economic (and therefore political) costs are likely to be felt sooner than the benefits. Clearly, this is a program that demands strong political leadership as an essential but by no means sufficient criteria for success.

Notes

3 The Third Way and public finance

1 Blinder and Solow (1973: 320), however, do warn that if deficit-financed spending is not accompanied by new issues of money, and therefore requires issuing public debt instruments which compete with private debt instruments in financial markets, the resulting upward pressure on interest rates will reduce any private expenditures which are sensitive to interest rates, which may include private investment, thus resulting in crowding-out.

5 The Third Way in the United Kingdom

1 *Total managed expenditure* is the total amount of public expenditure by all levels of government in the United Kingdom comprising central government, local authorities, and public corporations.
2 There are two components to investment: *net investment* and *investment to offset depreciation*. The former is spending on new fixed assets and the latter is spending to replace and/or repair existing fixed assets. *Gross investment* is the sum of net investment and investment to offset depreciation.

Bibliography

Abramovitz, M. (1956) "Resource and Output Trends in the United States Since 1870," *American Economic Review*, 46: 5–23.

Adams, I. (1998) *Ideology and Politics in Britain Today*, Manchester: Manchester University Press.

Aghion, P. and Howitt, P. (1992) "A Model of Growth through Creative Destruction," *Econometrica*, 60(2): 322–52.

—— (1998) *Endogenous Growth Theory*, Cambridge, MA: MIT Press.

Akerlof, G. (1970) "The Market for 'Lemons': Quality, Uncertainty and the Market Mechanism," *Quarterly Journal of Economics*, 84: 207–19.

Akerlof, G. and Yellen, J. (1985) "A Near-Rational Model of the Business Cycle, With Wage and Price Inertia," *Quarterly Journal of Economics*, Supplement.

—— (eds) (1986) *Efficiency Wage Models of the Labor Market*, New York: Cambridge University Press.

Akerlof, G., Rose, A., and Yellen, J. (1988) "Job Switching and Job Satisfaction in the US Labor Market," *Brookings Papers on Economic Activity*, (2): 495–582.

Alesina, A. and Sachs, J. D. (1988) "Political Parties and the Business Cycle in the United States," *Journal of Money, Credit, and Banking*, 20: 63–81.

Allison, G. (1996) "Get Ready for the Clinton Doctrine," *New Statesman*, November 8.

Anderson, P. (2000) "Renewals," *New Left Review*, January/February, 2(1): 16.

Ando, A. K. and Modigliani, F. (1963) "The Life Cycle Hypothesis of Saving: Aggregate Implication and Tests," *American Economic Review*, 53: 55–84.

Archibugi, D. and Michie, J. (eds) (1997) *Technology, Globalisation and Economic Performance*, Cambridge: Cambridge University Press.

Arestis, P. (1985) "Is There Any Crowing-out of Private Expenditure by Fiscal Actions?," in P. Arestis and T. Skouras (eds) *Post Keynesian Economic Theory: a Challenge to Neoclassical Economics*, Sussex: Wheatsheaf Books.

—— (1992) *The Post-Keynesian Approach to Economics: An Alternative Analysis of Economic Theory and Policy*, Hants: Edward Elgar.

Arestis, P. and Sawyer, M. (eds) (2001) *The Economics of the Third Way*, Cheltenham: Edward Elgar.

Argy, F. (1998) *Australia at the Crossroads: Radical Free Market or a Progressive Liberalism*, St Leonards: Allen & Unwin.

Argyrous, G. (1999) "Can the Budget Surplus Last? A Review of the 1999–2000 Commonwealth Budget," *Journal of Economic and Social Policy*, 4: 27–44.

—— (2000) "The High Road and the Low Road to International Trade: Emerging Exporters Revisited," *Journal of Australian Political Economy*, 45: 46–67.

Argyrous, G. and Sethi, R. (1996) "The Theory of Evolution and the Evolution of Theory: Veblen's Methodology in Contemporary Perspective," *Cambridge Journal of Economics*, 20: 475–95.

Argyrous, G. and Stilwell, F. (eds) (2003) *Economics as a Social Science: Readings in Political Economy*, Annandale, VA: Pluto Press.

Arrow, K. J. (1962) "The Economics Implications of Learning by Doing," *Review of Economic Studies*, 29: 155–73.

Aschauer, D. A. (1988) "Rx for Productivity: Build Infrastructure," *Chicago Fed Letter*, Federal Reserve Bank of Chicago, September 13.

—— (1989) "Is Public Expenditure Productive?," *Journal of Monetary Economics*, 23: 177–200.

—— (1990) *Public Investment and Private Sector Growth: The Economic Benefits of Reducing America's Third Deficit*, Washington, DC: Economic Policy Institute.

Ascher, K. (1987) *The Politics of Privatisation*, Basingstoke: Macmillan Education.

Aucoin, P. (1995) *The New Public Management: Canada in Comparative Perspective*, Canada: IRRP.

Australian Broadcasting Corporation (2000) "PM Tony Blair," *Foreign Correspondent*, September 5.

Babbage, C. (1835) (1963 edition), *On the Economy of Machinery and Manufactures*, London: Frank Cass & Co.

Baer, K. S. (2000) *Reinventing Democrats*, Kansas: University Press of Kansas.

Bank of England (2001a) *Changes in Selected Retail Banks' Base Rates*, London: Bank of England. Online. Available http://www.bankofengland.co.uk/Links/setframe.html, May 14 (accessed May 15, 2001).

—— (2001b) *Statistical Abstract: Part 1, Table 1: Monetary Aggregates: Amounts Outstanding at Year-Ends, and Growth Rates*, London: Bank of England. Online. Available http://www.bankofengland.co.uk/Links/setframe.html, September 6 (accessed March 4, 2002).

—— (2003) *Changes in Bank Rate, Minimum Lending Rate, Minimum Band 1 Dealing Rate and Repo Rate*, London: Bank of England. Online. Available http://www.bankofengland.co.uk/mfsd/rates/baserate.pdf, February 6 (accessed April 1, 2003).

—— (2004) *National Savings*, London: Bank of England. Online. Available http://www.bankofengland.co.uk (accessed January 29, 2004).

Barro, R. J. (1974) "Are Government Bonds Net Wealth?," *Journal of Political Economy*, 82: 1095–117.

—— (1991) "The Ricardian Model of Budget Deficits," in J. Rock (ed.) *Debt and the Twin Deficits Debate*, Mountain View, CA: Mayview Publishing Company.

—— (1997) *Determinants of Economic Growth: a Cross-Country Empirical Study*, Cambridge, MA: MIT Press.

Barro, R. J. and Sala-I-Martin, X. (1995) *Economic Growth*, New York: MacGraw-Hill.

Becker, G. S. (1975) *Human Capital: A Theoretical and Empirical Analysis with Special Reference to Education*, New York: Colombia University Press.

Beckett, M. (1997) *Speech at the Launch of the Confederation of British Industry's Report of its National Manufacturing Council*, London: September 23.

—— (1998) *Speech to the European Union's Industry Council*, London: May 6.

Bell, S. (2000) "Do Taxes and Bonds Finance Government Spending?," *Journal of Economic Issues*, 34: 603–20.

Berman, W. C. (2001) *From the Center to the Edge: The Politics and Policies of the Clinton Presidency*, Lanham, MD: Rowman & Littlefield.

Bernheim, D. (1989) "A Neoclassical Perspective on Budget Deficits," *Journal of Economic Perspectives*, 3: 55–72.

Bernstein, J. and Baker, D. (2003) *The Benefits of Full Employment: When the Markets Work for People*, Washington, DC: Economic Policy Institute.

Bernstein, J. and Mishel, L. (1997) "Has Wage Inequality Stopped Growing?," *Monthly Labor Review*, 120: 3–16.

Bevir, M. and O'Brien, D. (2001) "New Labour and the Private Sector in Britain," *Public Administration Review*, 61: 535–47.

Blair, T. (1995) Press Conference, July 16, Canberra: Australian Labor Party.

—— (1996a) *Speech to the Labour Party Conference*, Blackpool: Labour Party.

—— (1996b) *New Britain: My Vision of a Young Country*, London: Fourth Estate.

—— (1997) *Speech to the Commonwealth Business Forum*, London: October 22.

—— (1998a) *Speech to the French National Assembly*, Paris: March 24.

—— (1998b) "Modernising Central Government," *Speech to the First Senior Civil Service Conference*, London: October 13.

—— (1998c) "Foreword," *Fairness at Work*, London: The Stationery Office.

—— (1998d) *The Third Way: New Politics for the New Century*, London: Fabian Society.

—— (1999) *Speech to the Confederation of British Industry*, Birmingham. Online. Available http: www.number-0.gov.uk/public/news/index.html, November 2 (accessed March 22, 2001).

—— (2001) "Third Way, Phase Two," *Prospect*, March, 61: 10–13.

—— (2002) *The Courage of Our Convictions: Why Reform of the Public Services is the Route to Social Justice*, London: Fabian Society.

Blair, T. and Schröeder, G. (1998) "Europe: The Third Way/Die Neue Mitte," in B. Hombach (2000) *The Politics of the New Centre*, Cambridge, MA: Polity Press.

Blanchard, O. and Kiyotake, N. (1987) "Monopolistic Competition and the Effects of Aggregate Demand," *American Economic Review*, September, 77(4): 647–66.

Blaug, M. (1980) *Economic Theory in Retrospect*, Cambridge: Cambridge University Press.

—— (1985) *Economic Theory in Retrospect*, Cambridge: Cambridge University Press.

—— (2001) "Is Competition Such a Good Thing?: Static Efficiency versus Dynamic Efficiency," *Review of Industrial Organization*, 19: 37–48.

Blinder, A. S. and Solow, R. M. (1973) "Does Fiscal Policy Matter?," *Journal of Public Economics*, 2: 319–37.

—— (1976) "Does Fiscal Policy Matter?: A Correction," *Journal of Public Economics*, 5: 183–4.

Blinder, A. S. and Yellen, J. L. (2001) *The Fabulous Decade: Macroeconomic Lessons from the 1990s*, New York: The Century Foundation Press.

Bloom, N. and Bond, S. (2001) *UK Investment: High, Low, Rising, Falling?*, London: Institute for Fiscal Studies.

Bluestone, B. and Rose, S. (1998) "The Unmeasured Labor Force: The Growth in Work Hours," *Public Policy Brief*, Annandale-on Hudson, NY: The Jerome Levy Economics Institute of Bard College, No. 40.

Board of Governors of the US Federal Reserve (USFR) (2001) *Selected Interest Rates: Historical Data*, Washington, DC: United States Federal Reserve. Online. Available http://www.federalreserve.gov.au/releases/H15/data/a/cm.text, May 14 (accessed May 15, 2001).

Botsman, P. and Latham, M. (2001) *The Enabling State: People Before Bureaucracy*, Annandale, VA: Pluto Press.

Brainard, J., Burd, S., and Gose, B. (2000) "The Clinton Legacy in Higher Education," *The Chronicle of Higher Education*, 47(16): A27.

Braverman, H. (1974) *Labor and Monopoly Capital: The Degradation of Work in the Twentieth Century*, New York: Monthly Review Press.

Breusch, J. (2000) "Increase in Jobless an Aberration: Libs," *The Australian Financial Review*, January 21: 12.

Brivati, B. and Bale, T. (eds) (1997) *New Labour in Power: Precedents and Prospects*, London: Routledge.

Brown, G. (1994) "The Politics of Potential: A New Agenda for Labour," in D. Milliband (ed.) *Reinventing the Left*, Cambridge, MA: Polity Press.

—— (2001) "Pre-budget Report," *Hansard*, United Kingdom House of Commons, November 27.

Brown, R. H. (1994) "Bill's Shibboleth: Competing to Win," *Insight on the News*, 10(43): 34.

Brown, W. (2000) "Putting Partnership Into Practice in Britain," *British Journal of Industrial Relations*, 38(2): 299–316.

Brunner, K. (1968) "The Role of Money and Monetary Policy," *Review*, 50: 8–24.

Buchanan, J. M. (1958) *Public Principles of Public Debt: A Defense and Restatement*, Homewood, IL: R. D. Irwin.

Buchanan, J. M. and Wagner R. E. (1977) *Democracy in Deficit: The Political Legacy of Lord Keynes*, New York: Academic Press.

Buchanan, J. M., Rowley, C. K., and Tollison, R. D. (eds) (1986) *Deficits*, New York: Basil Blackwell.

Burch, M. and Holliday, I. (2000) "New Labour and the Machinery of Government," in D. Coates and P. Lawler (eds) *New Labour in Power*, Manchester: Manchester University Press.

Burd, S. (2001) "Outgoing Administration Seeks Dismissal of Lenders' Suit Against Education Dept," *The Chronicle of Higher Education*, 47(21): A24.

Bureau of Justice (2001) *Bureau of Justice Statistics Bulletin*, Washington, DC: Bureau of Justice Statistics. Online. Available ftp://ftp.bls.gov./pub/suppl/empsit.ceseeb2.txt (accessed November 30, 2001).

Bureau of Labor Statistics (BLS) (2001) *Employees on Nonfarm Payrolls by Major Industry*, Washington, DC: Bureau of Labor Statistics. Online. Available ftp://ftp.bls.gov./pub/suppl/empsit.ceseeb1.txt (accessed November 30, 2001).

Burns, J. M. and Sorenson, G. J. (1999) *Dead Center: Clinton-Gore Leadership and the Perils of Moderation*, New York: Lisa Drew Book.

Burns, J. W. and Taylor, A. J. (2001) "A New Democrat?: The Economic Performance of the Clinton Presidency," *The Independent Review*, V(3): 387–408.

Buttrick, J. (1960) "Toward a Theory of Economic Growth: The Neoclassical Contribution," in B. Hoselitz (ed.) *Theories of Economic Growth*, Chicago, IL: The Free Press of Glencoe.

Byers, S. (1999) "Wealth Creation is the Priority," *The Guardian*, February 3: 9.

Callaghan, J. (2002) "Social Democracy and Globalisation: the Limits of Social Democracy in Historical Perspective," *British Journal of Politics and International Relations*, 4(3): 429–51.

Callaghan, J. and Tunney, S. (2001) "The End of Social Democracy," *Politics*, 21(1): 63–72.

Callinicos, A. (2001) *Against the Third Way*, Cambridge, MA: Polity Press.

Cameron, D. (2002) "The Workers' Party Needs to Relocate its Soul," *The Australian*, 10 April: 11.

Campbell, C. and Rockman, B. A. (eds) (2000) *The Clinton Legacy*, New York: Seven Bridges Press.

Carlsson, B. (ed.) (1995) *Technological Systems and Economic Performance: The Case of Factory Automation*, Dordrecht: Kluwer.

Carlsson, B. and Jacobsson, S. (1997) "Diversity Creation and Technological Systems: A Technology Policy Perspective," in C. Edquist (ed.) *Systems of Innovation: Technologies, Institutions and Organizations*, London: Pinter.

Carlsson, B. and Stankiewicz, R. (1995) "On the Nature, Function and Composition of Technological Systems," in B. Carlsson (ed.) *Technological Systems and Economic Performance*, Dordrecht: Kluwer.

Cass, D. (1965) "Optimum Growth in an Aggregative Model of Capital Accumulation," *Review of Economic Studies*, 32: 233–40.

Castles, F. G. and Pierson, C. (1997) "A New Convergence? Recent Policy Developments in the United Kingdom, Australia and New Zealand," *Policy and Politics*, 24(3): 233–45.

Cesaratto, S. (1999) "Savings and Economic Growth in Neoclassical Theory," *Cambridge Journal of Economics*, 23: 771–93.

Cesaratto, S., Serrano, F., and Stirati, A. (2003) "Technical Change, Effective Demand and Employment," *Review of Political Economy*, 15(1): 33–52.

Chappell, H. W. (1993) "Partisan Monetary Policies: Presidential Influence Through the Power of Appointment," *Quarterly Journal of Economics*, 108: 185–218.

Chesnais, F. (1994) *La Mondialisation du Capital*, Paris: Syros.

(The) Child Care Partnership Project (2001) "Innovative Approaches: What is a Public-Private Partnership?" Online. Available http://www.nccic.org/ccpartnerships/facts/fs1.htm (accessed November 11, 2001).

Clark, C. (1951) *The Conditions of Economic Progress*, London: Macmillan.

Clark, C. and Corbett, D. (eds) (1999) *Reforming the Public Sector: Problems and Solutions*, St Leonards: Allen & Unwin.

Clark, T. and Dilnot, A. (eds) (2001) *Election Briefing 2001*, London: Institute for Fiscal Studies.

—— (2002) *Long-Term Trends in British Taxation and Spending*, London: Institute for Fiscal Studies.

Clark, T., Elsby, M., and Love, S. (2001) *Twenty-Five Years of Falling Investment?: Trends in Capital Spending on Public Services*, London: Institute of Fiscal Studies.

—— (2002) "Trends in British Public Investment," *Fiscal Studies*, 23(3): 305–42.

Claven, J. (2000) *The Centre Is Mine: Tony Blair, New Labour and the Future of Electoral Politics*, Annandale, VA: Pluto Press.

Cleary, P. (2001) "Why Not Scrap Budget Speech Altogether?," *The Australian Financial Review*, May 18: 15.

Clinton, A. (1997) "Flexible Labor: Restructuring the American Workforce," *Monthly Labor Review*, 120(80): 3–15.

Clinton, W. J. (1991) "The New Covenant," *Remarks by Arkansas Gov. Bill Clinton to Students at Georgetown University*, October 23.

—— (1993a) *A Vision for Change in America*, Washington, DC: The White House.

—— (1993b) *Inaugural Address*, Washington, DC: The White House. Online. Available http://frwebgate6.access.gpo.gov, January 20 (accessed September 9, 2001).

—— (1993c) *Statement on Signing the Family and Medical Leave Act of 1993*, Washington, DC: The White House. Online. Available http://www.access.gpo.gov...pd08fe93_txt-29, February 5 (accessed November 3, 2001).

—— (1993d) *State of the Union Address*, Washington, DC: The White House. Online. Available http://www.washingtonpost.com/ws...tics/special/states/docs/sou93.htm, February 17 (accessed May 15, 2001).

—— (1993e) *Remarks and a Question-and-Answer Session on the Economic Plan at Chillicothe, Ohio*, Washington, DC: The White House. Online. Available http://frwebgate1.access.gpo.gov, February 26 (accessed November 3, 2001).

—— (1993f) *Remarks by President Clinton Announcing the Initiative to Streamline Government*, Washington, DC: The White House. Online. Available http://govinfo.library.unt.edu./npr/library/speeches/030393.html, March 3 (accessed September 11, 2001).

—— (1993g) *Remarks Announcing the Community Development Banking and Finance Initiative*, Washington, DC: The White House. Online. Available http:www.frwais.access.gpo.gov/pd19jy93_txt-31, July 15 (accessed December 15, 2001).

—— (1993h) *Interview with the Nevada Media*, Washington, DC: The White House. Online. Available http://frwebgate1.access.gpo.gov/cgibin/waisgate.cgi?WAISdocID=02527119066+11+0+0&WAISaion=retrieve, August 6 (accessed October 14, 2001).

—— (1993i) *Address to a Joint Session of the Congress on Health Care Reform*, Washington, DC: The White House. Online. Available http://www.frwebgate6.access.gpo.gov, September 22 (accessed September 7, 2001).

—— (1993j) *Remarks Announcing the Clean Car Initiative*, Washington, DC: The White House. Online. Available http:www.frwebgate2.access.gpo.gov, September 29 (accessed November 11, 2001).

—— (1993k) *Statement on Signing the Unemployment Compensation Amendments of 1993*, Washington, DC: The White House. Online. Available http://frwebgate4.access.gpo.gov/cg-in/waisgate.cgi?WAISdocID=76808132296+1+0+0&WAISaction=retrieve, November 24 (accessed November 3, 2001).

—— (1994a) *State of the Union Address*, Washington, DC: The White House. Online. Available http://www.washingtonpost.com/wp-s...tics/special/states/docs/sou94.htm, January 25 (accessed May 15, 2001).

—— (1994b) "Remarks on Signing the School-to-Work Opportunities Act of 1994," *Weekly Compilation of Presidential Documents*, 30(18): 985–8.

—— (1994c) "Remarks on Signing the Violent Crime Control and Law Enforcement Act of 1994," *Weekly Compilation of Presidential Documents*, 30(37): 1758–61.

—— (1994d) *Remarks on Signing the Riegle-Neal Interstate Banking and Branching Efficiency Act of 1994*, Washington, DC: The White House. Online. Available http://frwebgate4.access.gpo.gov/cgi-bin/waisgate.cgi?WAISdocID= 8319395420+3+0+0&WAISaction=retrieve, September 29 (accessed September 30, 2001).

—— (1994e) *Statement on Signing the Government Management Reform Act*, Washington, DC: The White House. Online. Available http://www.frwebgate5.access.gpo.gov/c...35723970+1+0+0&WAISacti on=retrieve, October 14 (accessed November 18, 2001).

—— (1995a) *State of the Union Address*, Washington, DC: The White House. Online. Available http://www.washingtonpost.com/wp-s...tics/special/states/docs/sou95.htm, January 24 (accessed May 15, 2001).

Clinton, W. J. (1995b) "Executive Order 12954 – Ensuring the Economical and Efficient Administration and Completion of Federal Government Contracts," *Weekly Compilation of Presidential Documents*, 31(10): 382–4.

—— (1996a) *Between Hope and History: Meeting America's Challenges for the 21st Century*, New York: Random House.

—— (1996b) "Statement on Signing the ICC Termination Act of 1995," *Weekly Compilation of Presidential Documents*, 32(1): 1–19.

—— (1996c) *State of the Union Address*, Washington, DC: The White House. Online. Available http://www.washingtonpost.com/wp-s...tics/special/states/docs/sou96.htm, January 23 (accessed May 15, 2001).

—— (1996d) "Statement on Signing the Telecommunications Act of 1996," *Weekly Compilation of Presidential Documents*, 32(6): 218–20.

—— (1997) *State of the Union Address*, Washington, DC: The White House. Online. Available http://www.washingtonpost.com/wp-s...tics/special/states/docs/sou97.htm, February 4 (accessed May 15, 2001).

—— (1998a) "Statement on Senate Action on the Internet Tax Freedom Act," *Weekly Compilation of Presidential Documents*, 34(41): 2011.

—— (1998b) "Statement on Congressional Action on the Charter School Expansion Act of 1998," *Weekly Compilation of Presidential Documents*, 34(42): 2030.

—— (1998c) *State of the Union Address*, Washington, DC: The White House. Online. Available http://www.washingtonpost.com/wp-s...tics/special/states/docs/sou98.htm, January 27 (accessed May 15, 2001).

—— (1999a) *Statement on Signing Legislation to Reform the Financial System*, Washington, DC: The White House. Online. Available http://frwebgate2.access.gpo.gov/cgi-bin/waisgate.cgi?WAISdocID=83366518613+0+0+0&WAISaction=retrieve (accessed September 30, 2001).

—— (1999b) "Remarks on the Welfare to Work Initiative," *Weekly Compilation of Presidential Documents*, 35(4): 119–22.

—— (1999c) *State of the Union Address*, Washington, DC: The White House. Online. Available http://www.washingtonpost.com/wp-s...tics/special/states/docs/sou99.htm, January 20, 1999 (accessed May 15, 2001).

—— (2000a) "Statement on the Workforce Investment Act," *Weekly Compilation of Presidential Documents*, 36(32): 1852.

—— (2000b) "Remarks on Signing the Senior Citizens' Freedom to Work Act of 2000," *Weekly Compilation of Presidential Documents*, 36(14): 761–4.

—— (2000c) *State of the Union Address*, Washington, DC: The White House. Online. Available http://www.washingtonpost.com/wp-s...tics/special/states/docs/sou00.htm, January 27 (accessed May 15, 2001).

—— (2001a) "Remarks at James Ward Elementary School in Chicago, Illinois," *Weekly Compilation of Presidential Documents*, 37(2): 57–63.

—— (2001b) "Statement on Efforts to Toughen Child Support Enforcement," *Weekly Compilation of Presidential Documents*, 37(3): 111–208.

—— (2001c) *Remarks on the 2001 Economic Report and an Exchange With Reporters*, Washington, DC: The White House. Online. Available http://frwebgate.access.gpo.gov...al_documents&docid=pd15ja01_txt-30, January 12 (accessed September 1, 2001).

(1993) "Clinton Letter to Congress on Renewal of Trade Agreement," *Historic Documents of 1993*, December 15: 997–1002 (author unknown).

(1993) "Clinton Remarks of House Passage of NAFTA," *Historic Documents of 1993*, November 17: 953–8 (author unknown).

(1993) "Clinton's Five-Year Economic Plan," *Historic Documents of 1993*, February 17: 181–96 (author unknown).

(1994) "Clinton's 'Middle-Class Bill of Rights'," *Historic Documents of 1994*, December 12: 610–16 (author unknown).

(1994) "Clinton's Remarks on GATT," *Historic Documents of 1994*, November 28: 555–9 (author unknown).

(1995) "Clinton on Unfunded Mandates Legislation," *Historic Documents of 1995*, March 22: 141–4 (author unknown).

(2001) "Clinton Set New Vision for Special Ed Students," *Special Education Report*, 27(2): 1 (author unknown).

Clinton, B. and Gore, A. (1992) *Putting People First: How We Can All Change America*, New York: Times Books.

Coates, D. and Lawler, P. (eds) (2000) *New Labour in Power*, Manchester: Manchester University Press.

Coates, K. (ed.) (1999) *The Third Way to the Servile State*, Nottingham: Spokesman Books.

Coleman, J. J. (1996). *Party Decline in America: Policy, Politics, and the Fiscal State*, Princeton, NJ: Princeton University Press.

Coleman, J. S. (1990) *Foundations of Social Theory*, Cambridge, MA: Harvard University Press.

(The) Commission on Taxation and Citizenship (2000) *Paying for Progress: A New Politics of Tax for Public Spending*, London: Fabian Society.

Commonwealth Heads of Government Meeting (1997) *Promoting Shared Prosperity: Edinburgh Commonwealth Economic Declaration*, Edinburgh: October 25.

Commonwealth of Australia Treasury (2002) *Budget Strategy and Outlook 2002–03*, Canberra: Commonwealth Government Printing Service.

Congressional Budget Office (CBO) (1999) *Trends in Public Infrastructure Spending*, Washington, DC: Congress of the United States. Online. Available http://www.cbo.gov/ showdoc.cfm?index=1256&sequence=0&from=5 (accessed September 2, 2001).

—— (2000) *An Economic Analysis of the Taxpayer Relief Act of 1997*, Washington, DC: Congress of the United States.

—— (2001) *Historical Effective Tax Rates 1979–1997*, Washington, DC: Congress of the United States.

Coombs, R., Saviotti, P., and Walsh, V. (1987) *Economics and Technological Change*, Totowa, NJ: Rowman & Littlefield.

Council of Economic Advisers (CEA) (1993) *Economic Report of the President*, Washington, DC: US Government Printing Office.

—— (1994) *Economic Report of the President*, Washington, DC: US Government Printing Office.

—— (1995) *Economic Report of the President*, Washington, DC: US Government Printing Office.

—— (1996) *Economic Report of the President*, Washington, DC: US Government Printing Office.

—— (1997) *Economic Report of the President*, Washington, DC: US Government Printing Office.

—— (1998) *Economic Report of the President*, Washington, DC: US Government Printing Office.

Council of Economic Advisers (CEA) (1999) *Economic Report of the President*, Washington, DC: US Government Printing Office.

—— (2000) *Economic Report of the President*, Washington, DC: US Government Printing Office.

—— (2001) *Economic Report of the President*, Washington, DC: US Government Printing Office.

Cowhey, P. (1994) "The Clinton Technology Policy: Boon or Boondoggle," *USA Today Magazine*, 122: 2584.

Crafts, N. (1996) "Post-Neoclassical Endogenous Growth theory: What are its Policy Implications?," *Oxford Review of Economic Policy*, 12(2): 30.

(2001) "Cruel Brittania," *The Bulletin*, May 15: 42–5 (author unknown).

Currie, D. A. (1981) "Macroeconomic Policy and Government Financing," in M. Artis and M. Miller (eds) *Essays in Fiscal and Monetary Policy*, Oxford: Oxford University Press.

Dahrendorf, R. (1999) "The Third Way and Liberty: an Authoritative Streak in Europe's New Center," *Foreign Affairs*, 78(5): 13–17.

David, P. A. and Scadding, J. L. (1974) "Private Savings: Ultrarationality, Aggregation and 'Denisons Law'," *Journal of Political Economy*, 82(2): 225–49.

Davidson, P. (1981) "Post Keynesian Economics," in D. Bell and I. Kristol (eds) *The Crisis in Economics Theory*, New York: Basic Books.

Davis, E., Parodi, C., and Rexford, E. (1996) "Structuring an [US] Asian Pacific Foreign Policy," *Journal of Contemporary Asia*, 26(3): 392–404.

Deavers, K. L. and Hattiangadi, A. U. (1998) "Welfare to Work: Building a Better Path to Private Employment Opportunities," *Journal of Labor Research*, 19(2): 205–28.

DeMartino, G. (1998) "Industrial Policies versus Competitiveness Strategies: In Pursuit of Prosperity in the Global Economy," in P. Arestis and M. Sawyer (eds) *The Political Economy of Economic Policies*, London: Macmillan.

Democratic Leadership Council (DLC) (1990) *The New Orleans Declaration: Statement Endorsed at the Fourth Annual DLC Conference*, New Orleans: Democratic Leadership Council. Online. Available www.ndol.org, March 1 (accessed January 17, 2001).

—— (1991) *The New American Choice Resolution: Resolutions adopted at the DLC Convention*, Cleveland: Democratic Leadership Council.

—— (1999) *The Third Way: Progressive Governance for 21st century*, Washington, DC: Democratic Leadership Council. Online. Available http://www.ndol.org/ndol_ci.cfm?kaid=128&subid=185&contentid=880, April 25 (accessed May 24, 2002).

—— (2001a) *President W. J. Clinton: Eight Years of Peace, Progress and Prosperity*, Washington, DC: Democratic Leadership Council. Online. Available www.lib.umich. edu/libhome/Documents.center/pdf/eightyears.pdf (accessed April 24, 2001).

—— (2001b) *National Service: A New Democrat Chronology*, Washington, DC: Democratic Leadership Council. Online. Available http:www.ndol.org/ndol (accessed November 24, 2001).

Democratic Party (1992) "Democratic Party Platform," *Historic Documents of 1992*, Washington, DC: Congressional Quarterly Inc.

De Muth, C. C. (2000) "Why the Era of Big Government Isn't Over," *Commentary*, 109(4): 23–9.

Denison, E. F. (1962) *The Sources of Economic Growth in the United States and the Alternatives Before Us*, New York: Committee for Economic Development.

—— (1985) *Trends in American Economic Growth, 1929–1982*, Washington, DC: The Brookings Institution.

Denton, R. E. (ed.) (1996) *The Clinton Presidency: Images, Issues, and Communication Strategies*, Westport, CT: Praeger Publishers.

De Parle, J. (1993) "Free Vaccine Program Creates Unusual Array of Skeptics," *New York Times*, April 22: A1.

Department for Education and Employment (1998) *The Learning Age: a Renaissance for a New Britain*, London: The Stationery Office.

Department for Education and Skills (2003a) *Departmental Annual Report*, London: The Stationery Office.

—— (2003b) *Statistics of Education: Education and Training Expenditure since 1989–90*, London: Department for Educations and Skills. Online. Available http:www.dfes.gov.uk/rsgateway, August 8 (accessed February 3, 2004).

Department of Trade and Industry (1998) *Our Competitive Future: Building the Knowledge Driven Economy*, London: The Stationery Office.

Department of Transport (2003) *Transport Statistics Great Britain 2003*, London: Department of Transport. Online. Available http://www.dft.gov.uk (accessed January 20, 2004).

Dervarics, C. (1998) "Clinton Signs Higher Education Act Reauthorization," *Black Issues in Higher Education*, 15(8): 8.

Dionne, E. J. (1999), "Mr Marx meet Mr Friedman," *Washington Post*, March 23.

Domar, E. D. (1946) "Capital Expansion, Rate of Growth and Employment," *Econometrica*, XIV: 137–47.

—— (1947) "Expansion and Employment," *American Economic Review*, 37: 34–55.

Dornbusch, R. and Fischer, S. (1990) *Macroeconomics*, Singapore: McGraw-Hill.

Downs, A. (1957) *An Economic Theory of Democracy*, New York: HarperCollins.

Dowrick, S. (1992) "A Review of New Theories and Evidence on Economic Growth: Their Implication for Australian Policy," *Discussion Paper No. 275*, Canberra: ANU Centre for Economic Policy Research.

—— (ed.) (1995) *Economic Approaches to Innovation*, Aldershot: Edward Elgar.

Drucker, P. (1969) *The Age of Discontinuity: Guidelines to Our Changing Society*, London: Heinemann.

—— (1993) *Post Capitalist Society*, New York: HarperBusiness.

Duncan, G. (1999) "Blurred, Bland and Blair," *Australian Quarterly*, May–June: 32–5.

Eatwell, J. and Milgate, M. (eds) (1983) *Keynes's Economics and the Theory of Value and Distribution*, London: Duckworth.

Eatwell, J., Milgate, M., and Newman, P. (eds) (1987) *The New Palgrave: A Dictionary of Economics*, London: Macmillan Press.

—— (1991) *The New Palgrave: The World of Economics*, London: Macmillan Press.

Edquist, C. (ed.) (1997) *Systems of Innovation: Technologies, Institutions and Organizations*, London: Pinter.

Edquist, C. and Johnson, B. (1997) "Institutions and Organizations in Systems of Innovation," in C. Edquist (ed.) *Systems of Innovation: Technologies, Institutions and Organizations*, London: Pinter.

Edwards, J. (2000) *Australia's Economic Revolution*, Sydney: UNSW Press.

Eichner, A. (1979) *A Guide to Post-Keynesian Economics*, White Plains, NY: M. E. Sharpe.

Eichner, A. S. and Kregel, J. A. (1975) "An Essay on Post Keynesian Theory: A New Paradigm in Economics," *Journal of Economic Literature*, 13: 1293–314.

Eisner, R. (1986) *How Real is the Federal Deficit?*, New York: The Free Press.

—— (1989) "Budget Deficits: Rhetoric and Reality," *Journal of Economic Perspectives*, 3(2): 73–93.

—— (1991a) "Deficits and Us and Our Grandchildren," in J. Rock (ed.) *Debt and the Twin Deficits Debate*, Mountain View, CA: Mayfield Publishing Company.

—— (1991b) "Infrastructure and Regional Economic Performance," *New England Economic Review*, September/October: 47–58.

—— (1998) *The Keynesian Revolution, Then and Now*, Cheltenham: Edward Elgar.

Emmerson, C. (2001) *Institute of Fiscal Studies Green Budget 2001*, London: Institute of Fiscal Studies. Online. Available http:www.ifs.org.uk/gb2001/carl.shtml (accessed January 31, 2002).

Emmerson, C., Frayne, C., and Love, S. (2003a) *The Government's Fiscal Rules*, London: Institute for Fiscal Studies.

—— (2003b) *A Survey of Public Spending in the UK*, London: Institute for Fiscal Studies.

Esping-Andersen, G. (1994) "Equality and Work in the Post-industrial Life-cycle," in D. Milliband (ed.) *Reinventing the Left*, Cambridge, MA: Polity Press.

Etzioni, A. (1993) *The Spirit of Community: Rights, Responsibilities and the Communitarian Agenda*, New York: Crown Publishers.

—— (ed.) (1995) *New Communitarian Thinking: Persons, Virtues, Institutions and Communities*. Charlottesville, VA: University Press of Virginia.

Fairclough, N. (2000) *New Labour, New Language*, London: Routledge.

Fallows, J. (1995) "A Triumph of Misinformation," *The Atlantic Monthly*, 275(1): 26–37.

Faux, J. (2002) "Bait and Switch: How Alan Greenspan Snookered the Democrats," *The American Prospect*, February 25.

Federal Reserve Board (2001) *Community Reinvestment Act*, Washington, DC: The Federal Reserve. Online. Available http:www.federalreserve.gov/DCCA/CRA (accessed December 15, 2001).

Federal Trade Commission (FTC) (2000) *Performance Report Fiscal Year 2000*, Washington, DC: Federal Trade Commission. Online. Available http://www.ftc.gov/opp/gpra/report2000.pdf (accessed September 30, 2001).

Fine, B. (2000) "Endogenous Growth Theory: A Critical Assessment," *Cambridge Journal of Economics*, 24: 245–65.

Finlayson, A. (1999) "Third Way Theory," *The Political Quarterly*, 271–9.

Fisher, A. G. B. (1933) "Capital and the Growth of Knowledge," *Economic Journal*, XLIII: 379–89.

—— (1935) (1966 edition) *The Clash of Progress and Security*, New York: A. M. Kelley.

—— (1939) "Production, Primary, Secondary and Tertiary," *Economic Record*, XV: 24–38.

Foley, M. (2000) *The British Presidency*, Manchester: Manchester University Press.

Ford, R. and Poret, P. (1991) *Infrastructure and Private-Sector Productivity*, Paris: OECD.

Ford, W. H. (2000) "Economic Implications of the Senior Citizens' Freedom to Work Act of 2000," *Business Economics*, 35(3): 59–62.

Foster, J. (1981) "The Reality of the Present and the Challenge of the Future," *Journal of Economic Issues*, 15: 963–8.

Frankel, B. (1997) "Beyond Labourism and Socialism: How the Australian Labour Party Developed the Model of 'New Labour'," *New Left Review*, 221: 3–33.

Frantzen, D. (2000) "Innovation, International Technological Diffusion and the Changing Influence of R&D on Productivity," *Cambridge Journal of Economics*, 24: 193–210.

Freeden, M. (1999) "The Ideology of New Labour," *The Political Quarterly*, 70(1): 42–51.

Freeman, C. (1987a) "Innovation," in J. Eatwell, M. Milgate, and P. Newman (eds) *The New Palgrave: A Dictionary of Economics*, London: Macmillan Press.

—— (1987b) *Technology and Economic Performance Lessons from Japan*, London: Pinter.

—— (1994) "The Economics of Technical Change," *Cambridge Journal of Economics*, 18: 463–514.

—— (1997) "The 'National System of Innovation' in Historical Perspective," in D. Archibugi and J. Michie (eds) *Technology, Globalisation and Economic Performance*, Cambridge: Cambridge University Press.

Freeman, C. and Soete, L. (1994) *Work for All or Mass Unemployment? Computerised Technical Change into the Twenty-first Century*, London: Pinter.

Free Trade Area of the Americas Secretariat (FTAAS) (2001) *Overview of the FTAA Process*, Free Trade Area of the Americas. Online. Available www.ftaa-alca.org (accessed September 22, 2001).

Friedman, B. M. (1991) "US Fiscal Policy in the 1980s: Consequences of Large Budget Deficits at Full Employment," in J. Rock (ed.) *Debt and the Twin Deficits Debate*, Mountain View, CA: Mayfield Publishing Company.

Friedman, M. (1955) "The Role of Government in Education," in R. Solo (ed.) (1982) *Economics and the Public Interest*, Westport, CT: Greenwood Press.

—— (1956) "The Quantity Theory of Money: a Restatement," in M. Friedman (ed.) *Studies in Quantity Theory*, Chicago, IL: University of Chicago Press.

—— (1957) *A Theory of the Consumption Function*, Princeton, NJ: Princeton University Press.

—— (1960) *A Program for Monetary Stability*, New York: Fordham University Press.

—— (1962) *Capitalism and Freedom*, Chicago, IL: University of Chicago Press.

—— (1968) "The Role of Monetary Policy," *The American Economic Review*, 18(1): 1–17.

—— (1970) *The Counter-Revolution in Monetary Theory*, London: IEA.

—— (1972) "Comments on the Critics," *Journal of Political Economy*, September/ October, 80(5): 906–50.

—— (1974) "A Theoretical Framework for Monetary Analysis," in R. Gordon (ed.) *Milton Friedman's Monetary Framework*, Chicago, IL: University of Chicago Press.

—— (1975) *There's No Such Thing as a Free Lunch*, La Salle, IL: Open Court Publishing.

—— (1983) "Monetarism in Rhetoric and Practice," *Monetary and Economic Studies*, 1: 1–14.

—— (1988) "Why the Twin Deficits are a Blessing," *Wall Street Journal*, December 14: 1.

Friedman, M. and Kuznets, S. (1945). *Income From Independent Professional Practice*, New York: National Bureau of Economic Research.

Friedman, T. L. (1999) *The Lexus and the Olive Tree*, London: HarperCollins.

Fukuyama, F. (1992) *The End of History and the Last Man*, London: Penguin.

Fukuyama, F. (1999) *The Great Disruption: Human Nature and the Reconstitution of Social Order*, London: Profile Books.

Fusfield, D. R. (1999) *The Age of the Economist*, Massachusetts, MA: Addison-Wesley.

Galbraith, J. K. (1975) *Money: Whence It Came, Where It Went*, London: Andre Deutsch Ltd.

—— (1994) *The World Economy Since The Wars*, London: Sinclair-Stevenson.

Giddens, A. (1994) *Beyond Left and Right: The Future of Radical Politics*, Cambridge, MA: Polity Press.

—— (1998) *The Third Way: the Renewal of Social Democracy*, Cambridge, MA: Polity Press.

—— (2000a) *On the Edge: Living With Global Capitalism*. London: Jonathan Cape.

—— (2000b) *The Third Way and its Critics*, Cambridge, MA: Polity Press.

—— (2000c) *Runaway World: How Globalization is Reshaping Our Lives*, New York: Routledge.

—— (ed.) (2001) *The Global Third Way Debate*, Cambridge, MA: Polity Press.

Glennerster, H. (2001) *United Kingdom Education 1997–2001*, London: Centre for Analysis of Social Exclusion, London School of Economics.

Glyn, A. and Wood, S. (2001) "Economic Policy under New Labour: How Social Democratic is the Blair Government?," *The Political Quarterly*, 72(1): 50–66.

Gordon, R. J. (1990) "What is New Keynesian Economics?," *Journal of Economic Literature*, XXVIII: 1115–71.

Gore, A. (1993) *Report of the National Performance Review: Creating a Government that Works Better and Costs Less*, Washington, DC: US Government Printing Office.

—— (1995) *Common Sense Government: Works Better and Costs Less*, New York: Random.

Gotsch, T. (2001) "The Clinton Years: Special Education Grows Up," *Education Daily*, 34(11): 5.

Gramlich, E. M. (1989) "Budget Deficits and National Savings: Are Politicians Exogenous?," *Journal of Economic Perspectives*, 3(2): 23–35.

—— (1994) "Infrastructure Investment: A Review Essay," *Journal of Economic Literature*, 32(3): 1176–96.

Greenberg, S. B. (ed.) (1997) *The New Majority: Toward a Popular Progressive Politics*. New Haven, CT: Yale University Press.

Greenwald, B. C. and Stiglitz, J. E. (1986) "Externalities in Economics with Imperfect Information and Incomplete Markets," *Quarterly Journal of Economics*, May: 229–64.

—— (1988) "Financial Markets Imperfections and Business Cycles," Cambridge, MA: National Bureau of Economic Research Working Paper No. 2494.

Grier, K. B. (1991) "Congressional Influence on U.S. Monetary Policy: An Empirical Test," *Journal of Monetary Economics*, 28: 201–20.

Grossman, G. M. and Helpman, E. (1991) *Innovation and Growth in the Global Economy*, Cambridge, MA: MIT Press.

—— (1994) "Endogenous Innovation in the Theory of Growth," *Journal of Economic Perspectives*, 8(1): 23–44.

Grunwald, M. (1997) "Welfare-to-Work Isn't Cheap: How She Got a Job," *The American Prospect*, 33: 25–9.

Haavelmo, T. (1945) "Multiplier Effects of a Balanced Budget," *Econometrica*, 13: 311–18.

Haberler, G. (1958) *Prosperity and Depression: A Theoretical Analysis of Cyclical Movements*, London: Ruskin House.

Hale, J. F. (1995) "The Making of the New Democrats," *Political Science Quarterly*, 110(2): 210.

Hall, P. (1994) *Innovation, Economics and Evolution: Theoretical Perspectives on Changing Technology in Economics Systems*, Hertfordshire: Harvester Wheatsheaf.

Hall, S. (1987) "Gramsci and Us," *Marxism Today*, June, 6: 16–21.

—— (1988) "Manifesto for New Times," *Marxism Today*, October.

—— (1998) "Nowhere Man," *Sunday Times*, October 18.

Hall, S. and Jacques, M. (eds) (1989) *New Times: The Changing Face of Politics in the 1990s*, London: Lawrence & Wishart.

Halpern, D. and Mikosz, D. (eds) (1998) *Third Way Debate*, London: Nexus. Online. Available www.netnexus.org/library/papers/3way.html#Background, February 12 (accessed February 25, 2000).

Hamilton, C. (2001) "Politics of Passion Abandoned Along the Third Way," *The Australian*, July 13: 13.

—— (2003) *Growth Fetish*, Crows Nest: Allen & Unwin.

Handel, M. (2001) "Is There A Skills Crisis?," *Public Policy Brief* (No. 62A), Annandale-on-Hudson, NY: Jerome Levy Economics Institute of Bard College.

Hansen, A. (1949) *Monetary Theory and Fiscal Policy*, New York: McGraw-Hill.

—— (1953) *A Guide to Keynes*, New York: McGraw-Hill.

Hardi, J. (2001) "Clinton Brought Direct Loans, Tax Breaks to Students," *Education Daily*, 34(12): 3.

Hargreaves, I. and Christie, I. (eds) (1998) *Tomorrow's Politics: the Third Way and Beyond*, London: Demos.

Harris, M. (1999) "New Labour: Government and Opposition," *The Political Quarterly*, 52–61.

Harrod, R. F. (1939) "An Essay in Dynamic Theory," *Economic Journal*, XLIX: 14–33.

Hartcher, P. (2001) "America: The Big Sleep," *The Australian Financial Review Magazine*, December: 46.

Hatch, J. and Clinton, A. (2000) "Job Growth in the 1990s: a Retrospect," *Monthly Labor Review*, December: 3–18.

Havrilesky, T. (1995) *The Pressures on American Monetary Policy*, Boston, MA: Kluwer Academic.

Hay, C. (1999) *The Political Economy of New Labour: Labouring Under False Pretences*, Manchester: Manchester University Press.

Hecht, J. (2001) "Classical Labour-displacing Technological Change: the Case of the US Insurance Industry," *Cambridge Journal of Economics*, 25: 517–37.

Heilbroner, R. (1990) "Analysis and Vision in the History of Economic Thought," *Journal of Economic Literature*, XXVIII: 1097–114.

Heilbroner, R. and Bernstein, P. (1989) *The Debt and the Deficit: False Alarms/Real Possibilities*, New York: W.W. Norton & Company.

Held, D. (1999) *Globalization*, London: The Foreign Policy Centre.

Herod, A. (1997) "Back to the Future in [US] Labor Relations: from the New Deal to Newt's Deal," *Urban Affairs Annual Reviews*, 48: 161–80.

Hibbs, D. A. (1987) *The American Political Economy: Macroeconomics and Electoral Politics*, New York: Cambridge University Press.

Hicks, J. (1937) "Mr. Keynes and the Classics: A Suggested Interpretation," *Econometrica*, 5: 147–59.

HM Treasury (1998a) *The Financial Statement and Budget Report: March 1998*, London: HMSO.

—— (1998b) *Economic and Fiscal Strategy Report*, London: The Stationery Office.

—— (1998c) *Modern Public Services for Britain: Investing in Reform*, London: HMSO.

—— (1999) *Public Expenditure Statistical Analyses 1999–2000*, London: HM Treasury. Online. Available http://www.hm-treasury.gov.uk/media//4D5F8/10.pdf (accessed January 14, 2004).

—— (2000a) S*pending Review 2000: New Spending Plans 2001–2004*, London: The Stationery Office.

—— (2000b) *Planning Sustainable Public Spending: Lessons from Previous Policy Experience*, London: HM Treasury.

—— (2001) *Budget 2001: Investing for the Long Term: Building Opportunity and Prosperity For All: Economic and Fiscal Strategy Report and Fiscal Statement and Budget Report*, London: HM Treasury. Online. Available http://www.archive.official-documents.co.uk/document/hmt/budget2001 (accessed February 17, 2002).

—— (2002a) *2002 Spending Review Departmental Investment Strategies: a Summary*, London: HM Treasury. Online. Available http://www.hm-treasury.gov.uk/media//343A6/dis_whitepaper02.pdf, December (accessed January 21, 2004).

—— (2002b) *Budget 2002*, London: HM Treasury. Online. Available http://www.hm-treasury.gov.uk/budget/bud_bud02/budget_report (accessed January 15, 2004).

—— (2003a) *Public Sector Capital Expenditure*, London: HM Treasury. Online. Available http://www.hm-treasury.gov.uk/economic_data_and_tools/national_statistics/main_public_spending_totals/natstat_spentotal_pubcap.cfm (accessed January 19, 2004).

—— (2003b) *PFI Signed Projects List*, London: HM Treasury. Online. Available http://www.hm-treasury.gov.uk/documents/public_private_partnerships_/ppp_pfi_stats.cfm July, (accessed January 13, 2004).

—— (2003c) *Public Finances Databank*, London: HM Treasury. Online. Available http://www.hm-treasury.gov.uk/Economic_Data_and_Tools/data_index.cfm, August (accessed January 29, 2004).

—— (2003d) *Public Expenditure Statistical Analyses 2003*, London: HM Treasury. Online. Available http://www.hm-treasury.gov.uk/media//C6E3A/pesa_03_indexed.pdf, May (accessed January 14, 2004).

Hobhouse, L. T. (1911) *Liberalism*, London: Williams & Norgate.

Hobsbawm, E. (1994) *Age of Extremes: The Short Twentieth Century, 1914–1991*, London: Michael Joseph.

Hodgson, G. M. (1993) *Economics and Evolution: Bringing Life Back Into Economics*, Cambridge, MA: Polity Press.

Holtham, G. (2001) *The Left's Long March*, London: Nexus. Online. Available http://www.netnexus.org/library/papers/holtham.html (accessed April 10).

Holtz-Eakin, D. (1994) "Public-Sector Capital and the Productivity Puzzle," *The Review of Economics and Statistics*, 76: 12–21.

Hombach, B. (2000) *The Politics of the New Centre*, Cambridge, MA: Polity Press.

Hoselitz, B. (ed.) (1960) *Theories of Economic Growth*, Chicago, IL: The Free Press of Glencoe.

(1994) "House Republican 'Contract With America'," *Historic Documents of 1994*, September 27: 374–8 (author unknown).

Hughes, O. (1994) *Public Management and Administration*, New York: St. Martin's Press.

Hutton, W. (1998) "Didn't He Do Well? Well . . . Did He?," *The Observer*, April 26: 23.

Inland Revenue (2001) *Chancellor of the Exchequer: Budget Proposals 2001*, London: HMSO.

Institute for Public Policy Research Commission on Public Private Partnerships (2000) *The New Partnership Agenda*, London: Institute for Public Policy Research.

Jacobs, M. (2001a) "The Blair Government," Personal Communication (June 26, 2001).

—— (2001b) *The Third Way*, London: Nexus. Online. Available http://www.netnexus.org/library/papers/jacobs.html (accessed April 10, 2001).

Jenkins, P. (1983) "The Vainglorious Vulnerable Style of Mrs Thatcher," *The Guardian*, October 3.

Johnson, H. (2001) *The Best of Times: America in the Clinton Years*, New York: Harcourt, Inc.

Johnson, R. A. (ed.) (2001) *Privatization 2001: The 15th Annual Report on Privatization*, Los Angeles, CA: Reason Public Policy Institute.

Jones, C. I. (1998) *Introduction to Economic Growth*, New York: W.W. Norton & Company.

Jones, H. G. (1975) *An Introduction to Modern Theories of Economic Growth*, Surrey: Thomas Nelson & Sons.

Jorgenson, D., Gollop, F., and Fraumeni, B. (1987) *Productivity and U.S. Economic Growth*, Cambridge, MA: Harvard University Press.

Jungwirth, G. (ed.) (1998) *Labor Essays: New Visions for Government*, Annandale, VA: Pluto Press.

Kahn, H. (1982) *The Coming Boom: Economic, Social and Political*, New York: Simon & Schuster.

Kaldor, N. (1934) "A Classificatory Note on the Determinateness of Equilibrium," *Review of Economics Studies*, 2: 122–36.

—— (1940) "A Model of the Trade Cycle," *Economic Journal*, 50(197): 78–92.

—— (1956) "Alternative Theories of Distribution," *Review of Economic Studies*, 23(2): 83–100.

—— (1957) "A Model of Economic Growth," *Economic Journal*, 67: 591–624.

—— (1966) *Causes of the Slow Rate of Economic Growth in the United Kingdom*, Cambridge: Cambridge University Press.

—— (1970) "The Case for Regional Policies," *Scottish Journal of Political Economy*, November, 17(3): 337–48.

—— (1972) "The Irrelevance of Equilibrium Economics," *Economic Journal*, 82: 1237–55.

—— (1973) "Equilibrium Theory and Growth Theory," in M. Boskin (ed.) (1979) *Economic and Human Welfare: Essays in Honor of Tibor Scitovsky*, New York: Academic Press.

Kaldor, N. and Mirrlees, J. (1962) "A New Model of Economic Growth," *Review of Economic Studies*, 29: 174–92.

Kalecki, M. (1943) "Political Aspects of Full Employment," in M. Kalecki (1990) *Collected Works of Michael Kalecki Volume 1: Capitalism, Business Cycles and Full Employment*, Oxford: Oxford University Press.

—— (1944) "Three Ways to Full Employment," in M. Kalecki (1990) *Collected Works of Michael Kalecki Volume 1: Capitalism, Business Cycles and Full Employment*, Oxford: Oxford University Press.

—— (1971) *Selected Essays on the Dynamics of the Capitalist Economy 1933–70*, Cambridge: Cambridge University Press.

Kalecki, M. (1990) *Collected Works of Michael Kalecki Volume 1: Capitalism, Business Cycles and Full Employment*, Oxford: Oxford University Press.

Kamien, M. and Schwartz, N. (1982) *Market Structure and Innovation*, Cambridge: Cambridge University Press.

Keating, P. (1987) "Traditions of Labor in Power: Whitlam and Hawke in the Continuum," in Australian Labor Party (ed.) *Traditions for Reform in New South Wales*, Sydney: Pluto Press.

Keynes, J. M. (1936) *The General Theory of Employment, Interest and Money*, Cambridge: Macmillan.

—— (1937) "The General Theory of Employment," *Quarterly Journal of Economics*, 51.

—— (1973) "The General Theory and After: Part 2 – Defence and Development," in E. Johnson and D. Moggridge (eds) *The Collected Writings of John Maynard Keynes*, London: Macmillan.

King, D. and Wickham Jones, M. (1999) "From Clinton to Blair: the Democratic (Party) Origins of Welfare to Work," *The Political Quarterly*, 62–74.

King, J. E. (2002) *A History of Post Keynesian Economics since 1936*, Cheltenham: Edward Elgar.

King, R. G. and Rebelo, S. (1990) "Public Policy and Economy Growth: Developing Neoclassical Implications," *Journal of Political Economy*, 98(5): 1008–38.

Kirchoff, S. (1998) "Head Start is Growing, But Is It Improving?," *Congressional Quarterly*, June 27: 2603–10.

Kittower, D. (1997) *Privatization Guide: A Guide to Serving the Public With Private Partners*, Washington, DC. Online. Available http://www.governing.com/archive/1997/may/priv.txt (accessed November 18, 2001).

Klamer, A. (1984) *The New Classical Macroeconomics: Conversations With New Classical Economists and Their Opponents*, Brighton: Wheatsheaf Books.

Klein, B. H. (1977) *Dynamic Economics*, Cambridge, MA: Harvard University Press.

Knight, F. (1944) "Diminishing Returns from Investment," *Journal of Political Economy*, 52: 26–47.

Koopmans, T. C. (1965) "On the Concept of Optimal Economic Growth," *Study Week on the Econometric Approach to Development Planning*, Amsterdam: North Holland Publishing Company.

Korliras, P. G. and Thorn, R. S. (1979) *Modern Macroeconomics: Major Contributions to Contemporary Thought*, New York: Harper & Row.

Kotlikoff, L. J. (1986) "Deficit Delusion," *The Public Interest*, 84: 53–65.

Krause, G. A. (1994) "Federal Reserve Policy Decision Making: Political and Bureaucratic Influences," *American Journal of Political Science*, 38: 124–44.

Krugman, P. (1994) "Competitiveness: a Dangerous Obsession," *Foreign Affairs*, 73: 28.

—— (1996) *What Economists Can Learn from Evolutionary Theorists: a Talk Given to the European Association for Evolutionary Political Economy*, November.

Kuhn, T. S. (1962) *The Structure of Scientific Revolutions*, Chicago, IL: University of Chicago Press.

Kurtz, H. (1998) *Spin Cycle: Inside the Clinton Propaganda Machine*, New York: The Free Press.

Kurz, H. D. and Salvadori, N. (1998) "The 'New Growth Theory': Old Wine in New Goatskins," in C. Fabrizio, M. di Matteo, and F. Hahn (eds) *New Theories in Growth and Development*, New York: St. Martin's Press.

Laidler, D. (1982) *Monetarist Perspectives*, Cambridge, MA: Harvard University Press.

Latham, M. (1998a) *New Thinking for Australian Labour: Civilising Global Capital*, St Leonards: Allen & Unwin.

—— (1998b) "Economic Policy and the Third Way," *Speech to Australian Economic Review Policy Forum*, University of Melbourne: November 17.

—— (1999) "Economic Governance and the Third Way," *Speech to the Committee for Economic Development of Australia*, Sydney: April 14.

—— (2000) *Welcome to Third Way Australia*, Sydney: Third Way Australia. Online. Available www.thirdway-aust.com (accessed March 2, 2000).

Leadbeater, C. (1999) *Living On Thin Air: the New Economy*, London: Penguin Books.

(2000) "Leaders: trust and antitrust," *The Economist*, October 7: 21 (author unknown).

Le Grand, J. (ed.) (1989) *Market Socialism*, Oxford: Clarendon Press.

Lehrer, J. (1996) *New Connections*, Washington, DC: Online Newshour. Online. Available http://www.pbs.org/newshour/bb/cyberspace/telecom_2-8a.html (accessed September 30, 2001).

Leighninger, R. (2000) "Public Investment Or Pork: the Meaning of New Deal Public Works," *Journal of Progressive Human Services*, 11(2): 29–50.

Lerner, A. P. (1936) "Mr. Keynes' 'General Theory of Employment, Interest and Money'," *International Labour Review*, October, 135(3–4): 435–54.

—— (1943) "Functional Finance and the Federal Debt," *Social Research*, 10: 38–51.

—— (1961) "The Burden of the Debt," *The Review of Economics and Statistics*, May: 139–41.

—— (1977) "From Pre-Keynes to Post-Keynes," *Social Research*, 44(3): 387–415.

Leslie, D. (1993) *Advanced Macroeconomics: Beyond IS/LM*, London: McGraw-Hill.

Letiche, J. M. (1960) "Adam Smith and David Ricardo on Economic Growth," in B. Hoselitz (ed.) *Theories of Economic Growth*, Chicago, IL: The Free Press of Glencoe.

Lichter, D. T. (2001) "Marriage as Public Policy," *Policy Report*, September.

Lindbeck, A. and Snower, D. J. (1989) *The Insider-Outsider Theory of Employment and Unemployment*, Cambridge, MA: MIT Press.

Linder, S. H. (1999) "Coming to Terms with the Public-Private Partnership: A Grammar of Multiple Meanings," *The American Behavioral Scientist*, 43(1): 35–51.

Lipsey, R. G. (1997) *Macroeconomic Theory and Policy*, Cheltenham: Edward Elgar.

List, F. (1841) (1966 edition) *The National System of Political Economy*, New York: A. M. Kelley.

Lohr, S. (2001) "States Press U.S. to Take Tough Stand on Microsoft," *The New York Times*, September 8: C1.

Long, S. (2000) "The Truth About Who Wins in Australia's New Economy Jobs," *The Australian Financial Review*, December 9–10.

Lovrich, N. P. (1999) "Policy Partnering Between the Public and Not-for-profit Private Sectors," *The American Behavioral Scientist*, 43(1): 177–91.

Lucas, R. E. (1973) "Some International Evidence on Output-Inflation Trade Offs," *American Economic Review*, June.

—— (1986) "Principles of Fiscal and Monetary Policy," *Journal of Monetary Economics*, January.

—— (1988) "On the Mechanics of Economic Development," *Journal of Monetary Economics*, July 22: 3–42.

Lucas, R. E. and Sargeant, T. J. (eds) (1981) *Rational Expectations and Econometric Practice*, Minneapolis, MN: The University of Minneapolis Press.

Lundvall, B. A. (ed.) (1992) *National Systems of Innovation: Towards a Theory of Innovation and Interactive Learning*, London: Pinter.

McCallum, B. T. (1996) *Neoclassical vs. Endogenous Growth Analysis: an Overview*, Cambridge, MA: National Bureau of Economic Research.

McDonnell, J. (1999) "Is the Third Way a Dead Armadillo?," *Quadrant*, 43: 21.

McGregor, M. (2001) "Greed Gives Way to the Public Good," *The Australian*, June 21: 11.

Machlup, M. (1962) *The Production and Distribution of Knowledge in the United States*, Princeton, NJ: Princeton University Press.

McKay, S. (2001) "Between Flexibility and Regulation: Rights, Equality and Protection at Work," *British Journal of Industrial Relations*, 39: 285–303.

McKinsey Global Institute (2001) *U.S. Productivity Growth, 1995–2000*, Washington, DC: McKinsey Global Institute. Online. Available www.mckinsey.com/knowledge/mgi/feature/index.asp October 17 (accessed November 16, 2001).

Macmillan, H. (1938) *The Middle Way: a Study of the Problem of Economic and Social Progress in a Free and Democratic Society*, London: Macmillan.

McPherson, M. S. and Schapiro, M. O. (1997) "Financing Undergraduate Education: Designing National Policies," *National Tax Journal*, 50: 557–71.

Maddox, G. (1989) *The Hawke Government and Labor Tradition*, Ringwood: Penguin.

Malthus, T. R. (1798) (1976 edition) *An Essay on the Principle of Population*, New York: Norton Critical Edition.

Mandelson, P. and Liddle, R. (1996) *The Blair Revolution: Can New Labour Deliver?*, London: Faber and Faber.

Mankiw, N. G. (1985) "Small Menu Costs and Large Business Cycles: a Macroeconomic Model of Monopoly," *Quarterly Journal of Economics*, May, 100(2): 529–38.

Mankiw, N. G. and Romer, D. (1991) *New Keynesian Economics*, Cambridge, MA: MIT Press.

Mankiw, N. G., Romer, D., and Weil, D. (1992) "A Contribution to the Empirics of Economic Growth," *Quarterly Journal of Economics*, 107: 407–38.

Marginson, S. (1993) *Education and Public Policy in Australia*, Melbourne: Cambridge University Press.

Martin, B. (2001) *The New Old Economy*, Annandale-on-Hudson: Jerome Levy Economics Institute. Online. Available http://www.levy.org/docs/pn/01–7.html (accessed November 16, 2001).

Marx, K. and Engels, F. (1848) (1967 edition) *The Communist Manifesto*, Harmondsworth: Penguin Books.

—— (1867) (1986 edition) *Capital*, Harmondsworth: Penguin Books.

Matalin, M. and Carville, J. (1994) *All's Fair: Love, War and Running for President*, New York: Random House.

Mayer, T. (1990) *Monetarism and Macroeconomic Policy*, Brookfield: Edward Elgar.

Meeropol, M. (2000) *Surrender: How the Clinton Administration Completed the Reagan Revolution*, Ann Arbor, MI: University of Michigan Press.

Metcalfe, S. (1987) "Technical Change," in J. Eatwell, M. Milgate, and P. Newman (eds) *The New Palgrave: a Dictionary of Economics*, London: Macmillan.

—— (1997) "Technology Systems and Technology Policy in an Evolutionary Framework," in D. Archibugi and J. Michie (eds) *Technology, Globalisation and Economic Performance*, Cambridge: Cambridge University Press.

Meyer, L. H. (1983) *The Economic Consequences of Government Deficits*, Boston, MA: Kluwer-Hijhoff.

Michigan Association of Public School Academies (MAPSA) (2001) *Overview of Michigan's Charter School Law*, Michigan: MAPSA. Online. Available http:www.charterschools.org/qanda/overview.html (accessed September 9, 2001).

Mill, J. S. (1848) (1930 edition) *Principles of Political Economy: with Some of Their Applications to Social Philosophy*, London: Longmans Green.

—— (1865) (1930 edition) *A System of Logic, Ratiocinative and Inductive: Being a Connected View of the Principles of Evidence and the Methods of Scientific Investigation*, London: Longmans Green.

Milliband, D. (ed.) (1994) *Reinventing the Left*, Cambridge, MA: Polity Press.

Mishel, L., Bernstein J., and Schmitt, J. (1999) *The State of Working America 1998–99*, Ithaca, NY: Cornell University Press.

Modigliani, F. (1944) "Liquidity Preference and the Theory of Interest and Money," *Econometrica*, 12: 45–88.

—— (1961) "Long-run Implications of Alternative Fiscal Policies and the Burden of the National Debt," *The Economic Journal*, December, 52: 730–55.

—— (1966) "The Life-Cycle Hypothesis of Saving, the Demand for Wealth and the Supply of Capital," *Social Research*, 33(2): 160–217.

—— (1977) "The Monetarist Controversy or, Should We Forsake Stabilization Policies?," *The American Economic Review*, 67: 1–19.

—— (1980) *Collected Papers: Essays in Macroeconomics*, Cambridge, MA: MIT Press.

Modigliani, F. and Brumberg, R. (1954) "Utility Analysis and the Consumption Function: an Interpretation of Cross-Section Data," in K. Kurihara (ed.) (1955) *Post-Keynesian Economics*, Brunswick: Rutgers University Press.

Moran, M. and Alexander, E. (2000) "The economic policy of New Labour," in D. Coates and P. Lawler (eds) *New Labour in Power*, Manchester: Manchester University Press.

Morris, D. (1999) *Behind the Oval Office: Getting Reelected Against All Odds*, Los Angeles, CA: Renaissance Books.

Mulgan, G. (ed.) (1997) *Life After Politics: New Thinking for the Twenty First Century*, London: Fontana Press.

Mundell, R. (1963) "Inflation and Real Interest," *Journal of Political Economy*, 71: 280–3.

Munnell, A. H. (1990) "Why Has Productivity Declined? Productivity and Public Investment," *New England Economic Review*, January/February: 3–22.

—— (1992) "Infrastructure Investment and Economic Growth," *Journal of Economic Perspectives*, 6: 189–98.

Musgrave, R. A. (1959) *A Theory of Public Finance: a Study in Public Economy*, New York: McGraw-Hill Book Company.

—— (1988) "Public Debt and Intergenerational Equity," in K. Arrow and M. Boskin (eds) *The Economics of Public Debt*, London: Macmillan.

Musgrave, R. A. and Peacock, A. T. (1958) *Classics in the Theory of Public Finance*, London: Macmillan & Co.

Muth, J. (1961) "Rational Expectations and the Theory of Price Movements," *Econometrica*, 29: 315–35.

Myrdal, G. (1944) *An American Dilemma: the Negro Problem and Modern Democracy*, New York: Harper & Brothers.

—— (1957) *Economic Theory and the Underdeveloped Regions*, London: Duckworth.

National Economic Council (NEC) (2001) *National Economic Council*, Washington, DC: The White House. Online. Available http://www.whitehouse.gov/nec/ (accessed October 12, 2001).

Nell, E. (1988) *Prosperity and Public Spending: Transformational Growth and the Role of Government*, Boston, MA: Unwin Hyman.

Nell, E. (1996) *Making Sense of a Changing Economy: Technology, Markets and Morals*, London: Routledge.

Nelson, R. (ed.) (1993). *National Systems of Innovation: a Comparative Study*, New York: Oxford University Press.

—— (1998) "The Agenda for Growth Theory: a Different Point View," *Cambridge Journal of Economics*, 22: 497–520.

Nelson, R. and Winter, S. (1974) "Neoclassical vs Evolutionary Theories of Economic Growth: Critique and Prospectus," *Economic Journal*, December, 84(336): 886–905.

—— (1977) "In Search of a Useful Theory of Innovation," *Research Policy*, 6: 36–76.

—— (1982) *An Evolutionary Theory of Economic Change*, Cambridge, MA: Belknap and Harvard University Press.

—— (2002) "Evolutionary Theorizing in Economics," *Journal of Economic Perspectives*, 16: 23–46.

New Labour (1997a) *Our Policies: Business and Productivity*, London: New Labour. Online. Available http://www.labour.org.uk (accessed April 26, 2001).

—— (1997b) *Our Policies: Economic Stability*, London: New Labour. Online. Available http://www.labour.org.uk (accessed April 26, 2001).

—— (1997c) *Our Policies: Tax and Public Finance*, London: New Labour. Online. Available http://www.labour.org.uk (accessed May 3, 2001).

—— (1997d) *Manifesto Commitments*, London: New Labour. Online. Available http://www.no.10.gov.uk (accessed May 2, 2001).

—— (1997e) *New Labour: Because Britain Deserves Better*, London: New Labour.

Newman, H. E. (1968) *An Introduction to Public Finance*, New York: John Wiley & Sons.

North, D. C. (1990) *Institutions, Institutional Change and Economic Performance*, Cambridge: Cambridge University Press.

—— (1991) "Institutions," *Journal of Economic Perspectives*, 5(1): 97–112.

Nursey-Bray, P. and Bacchi, C. (eds) (2001) *Left Directions: is There a Third Way?* Crawley, WA: University of Western Australia Press.

Nye, J. S. (2001) "In Government We Don't Trust," in A. Giddens (ed.) *The Global Third Way Debate*, Cambridge, MA: Polity Press.

O'Connor, J. (1973) *The Fiscal Crisis of the State*, New York: St. Martin's Press.

O'Driscoll, G. (1977) "The Ricardian Non-equivalence Theorem," *Journal of Political Economy*, 85: 207–10.

Office for National Statistics (2001) *Quarterly National Accounts: 4th Quarter and Year 2000*, London: Office for National Statistics. Online. Available http://www.statistics.gov.uk/pdfdir/qna0301.pdf, March 27 (accessed June 26, 2001).

—— (2002) *Research and Experimental Development (R&D) Statistics 2000*, London: Office for National Statistics. Online. Available http:www.statistics.gov.uk/articles/economic_trends/ET_Aug02.Morgan pdf (accessed January 22, 2004).

—— (2003) *The United Kingdom National Accounts: The Blue Book 2003*, London: Office for National Statistics. Online. Available http://www.statistics.gov.uk (accessed January 20, 2004).

—— (2004) *Retail Prices Index*, London: Office for National Statistics. Online. Available http://www.statistics.gov.uk/STATBASE (accessed January 30, 2004).

Office of Management and Budget (OMB) (1993) *Budget of the United States Government*, Washington, DC: Executive Office of the President.

—— (1994) *Budget of the United States Government*, Washington, DC: Executive Office of the President.

—— (1995) *Budget of the United States Government*, Washington, DC: Executive Office of the President.

—— (1996) *Budget of the United States Government*, Washington, DC: Executive Office of the President.

—— (1997) *Budget of the United States Government*, Washington, DC: Executive Office of the President.

—— (1998) *Budget of the United States Government*, Washington, DC: Executive Office of the President.

—— (1999) *Budget of the United States Government*, Washington, DC: Executive Office of the President.

—— (2000) *Budget of the United States Government*, Washington, DC: Executive Office of the President.

—— (2001) *Budget of the United States Government*, Washington, DC: Executive Office of the President.

—— (2002) *Budget of the United States Government*, Washington, DC: Executive Office of the President.

—— (2003) *Budget of the United States Government*, Washington, DC: Executive Office of the President.

Office of Trade and Economic Analysis (OTEA) (2001) *GDP and US International Trade in Goods and Services, 1970–2000*, Washington, DC: OTEA. Online. Available http://www.ita.doc.gov/td/industry/otea/usfth/aggregate/HL00T05.txt, August 8 (accessed September 22, 2001).

O'Hara, P. (1999) "Neoclassical Economics," in P. O'Hara (ed.) *Encyclopaedia of Political Economy*, London: Routledge.

Ohmae, K. (1990) *The Borderless World: Management Lessons in the New Logic Of the Global Market Place*, New York: Harper.

Online NewsHour (1997a) *Cabinet Work*, Washington, DC: Online Newshour. Online. Available www.pbs.org, January 29 (accessed September 29, 2001).

—— (1997b) *NAFTA: Good Deal?*, Washington, DC: Online Newshour. Online. Available http://www.pbs.org/newshour/bb/economy/july97/nafta_7–11.html, July 12 (accessed October 14, 2001).

Organisation for Economic Co-operation and Development (OECD) (2002a) *Dynamising National Innovation Systems*, Paris: OECD.

—— (2002b) *Main Economic Indicators*, Paris: OECD.

Osborne, D. and Gaebler, T. (1992) *Reinventing Government: How the Entrepreneurial Spirit is Transforming the Public Sector*, Reading, PA: Addison-Wesley.

Painter, C. (1999) "Public Service Reform from Thatcher to Blair: a Third Way," *Parliamentary Affairs*, 52(1): 94–112.

Palley, T. I. (1996) *Post Keynesian Economics: Debt, Distribution and the Macroeconomy*, London: Macmillan.

—— (2003) "Pitfalls in the Theory of Growth: An Application to the Balance of Payments Constrained Growth Model," *Review of Political Economy*, 15(1): 75–84.

Parliament of the United Kingdom (1998) *Modern Local Government: in Touch with the People*, London: HMSO.

—— (1999) *Modernising Government*, London: HMSO.

Patinkin, D. (1948) "Price Flexibility and Full Employment," *American Economic Review* 38: 543–64.

—— (1956) *Money, Interest and Prices: an Integration of Monetary and Value Theory*, Evanston, IL: Row Peterson.

Peck, J. (1996) *Workplace: The Social Regulation of Labor Markets*, New York: Guilford.

Peet, R. (1999) *Theories of Development*, New York: The Guilford Press.

Perryman, M. (1996) *The Blair Agenda*, London: Lawrence & Wishart.

Phelps, E. S. (1962) "The New View of Investment: a Neoclassical Analysis," *Quarterly Journal of Economics*, 76: 548–67.

—— (1967) "Phillips Curves, Expectations of Inflation, and Optimal Unemployment Over Time," *Economica*, 34.

Phillimore, J. (1998) "Neo-Schumpeterian Economics: Political Possibilities and Problems," *Journal of Australian Political Economy*, 42: 48–74.

Phillips, A. W. (1958) "The Relation Between Unemployment and the Rate of Change of Money Wage Rates in the United Kingdom, 1861–1957," *Economica*, 25: 283–99.

Phillips, L. T. (2001) "Forward Momentum," *Regulation*, 24(2): 47–9.

Philpot, R. (1999) "Why Bill Clinton is a Hero," *New Statesman*, July 19: 21–2.

Pierre, J. (ed.) (2000) *Debating Governance: Authority, Steering and Democracy*, Oxford: Oxford University Press.

Pierson, C. (2003) *Social Democracy on the Back Foot: the ALP and the "New" Australian Model*, Nottingham: Nottingham University. Online. Available http://www.nottingham.ac.uk/politics/staff/backfoot.pdf (accessed December 23, 2003).

Pierson, C. and Castles, F. G. (2002) "Australian Antecedents of the Third Way," *Political Studies*, 50: 683–702.

Pigou, A. C. (1928) *A Study in Public Finance*, London: Macmillan.

—— (1943) "The Classical Stationary State," *Economic Journal*, 53: 343–51.

—— (1947) "Economics Progress in a Stable Environment," *Economica*, 14: 180–8.

Plender, J. (1998) "A New Third Way," *Prospect Magazine*, February.

Pollitt, C. (1995) "Justification by Works or by Faith? Evaluating the New Public Management," paper for the European Group for Public Administration Conference, Rotterdam, September.

Poole, W. (1975) "The Making of Monetary Policy: Description and Analysis," *Economic Inquiry*, 13(2): 253–65.

Porat, M. U. (1977) *The Information Economy*, Washington, DC: Office of Telecommunications.

Porter, M. (1990) *Competitive Advantage of Nations*, London: Macmillan.

Powell, D. (1998) *What's Left: Labour Britain and the Socialist Tradition*, London: Peter Owen Publishers.

Progressive Governance Summit (2003) *Communiqué: Countries Commit to Progressive Governance*, London: Progressive Governance Summit. Online. Available http://www.number10.gov.uk/output/page4146.asp, July 13–14 (accessed August 8, 2003).

(2001) "Public services: King Tony and the Barons," *The Economist*, September 13: 31 (author unknown).

Putnam, R. D. (1995) "Bowling Alone: America's Declining Social Capital," *Journal of Democracy*, 6: 65–78.

Putnam, R. D., Leonardi, R., and Nanetti, R. Y. (1993) *Making Democracy Work: Civic Traditions in Modern Italy*, Princeton, NJ: Princeton University Press.

Quiggin, J. (1999) "The Future of Government: Mixed Economy or Minimal State?," *Australian Journal of Public Administration*, 58(4): 39–53.

Quinn, D. P. and Shapiro, R. Y. (1991) "Economic Growth Strategies: the Effects of Ideological Partisanship on Interest Rates and Business Taxation in the United States," *American Journal of Political Science*, 35: 656–85.

Ramsey, F. P. (1928) "A Mathematical Theory of Saving," *Economic Journal*, 38: 543–9.

Rawls, J. (1971) *A Theory of Justice*, Oxford: Clarendon Press.

Reason Public Policy Institute (RPPI) (1999) *Privatization 1999*, Washington, DC: RPPI. Online. Available http://www.rppi.org/apr99.html (accessed November 18, 2001).

—— (2001) *Privatization 2001: the 15th Annual Report on Privatization*, Los Angeles, CA: RPPI.

Reich, R. B. (1990) "Who is Us?," *Harvard Business Review*, 68: 53–64.

—— (1991) *The Work of Nations: Preparing Ourselves for 21st Century Capitalism*, New York: Alfred A. Knopf.

—— (1992) "Clintonomics 101: and why it beats Bush-Reagan," *The New Republic*, 207(10).

—— (1996) "Secession of the Successful," *National Policy*, Spring: 18.

—— (1997) *Locked In the Cabinet*, New York: Alfred A. Knopf.

—— (1999) "We Are All Third Wayers Now," *The American Prospect*, 10(43): 46.

(2001) "Rent-a-Bobby Scheme," *Police News*, July: 7 (author unknown).

Renshon, S. A. (1998) *High Hopes: The Clinton Presidency and the Politics of Ambition*, New York: Routledge.

Ricardo, D. (1817) O*n the Principles of Political Economy*, in P. Sraffa (ed.) (1951) *The Works and Correspondence of David Ricardo*, Cambridge: Cambridge University Press.

—— (1820) *Funding System*, in P. Sraffa (ed.) (1951) *Pamphlets and Papers*, 1815–23, *The Works and Correspondence of David Ricardo*, Cambridge: Cambridge University Press.

Roberts, P. C. (1984) *The Supply-Side Revolution*, Cambridge, MA: Harvard University Press.

—— (1989) *Supply Side Economics, Theory and Results: an Assessment of American Experience in the 1980s*, Washington, DC: Institute for Political Economy.

Robinson, J. (1956) *The Accumulation of Capital*, London: Macmillan.

—— (1962a) "Review of Money, Trade and Economic Growth by H. G. Johnson," *Economic Journal*, 72(257): 690–2.

—— (1962b) *Essays in the Theory of Economic Growth*, New York: St. Martins.

—— (1980) "Time in Economic Theory," *Kyklos*, 33: 219–29.

Robinson, P. (2000) "The Private Finance Initiative: the Real Story," *Consumer Policy Review*, 10(3): 82–5.

Rock, J. (ed.) (1991) *Debt and the Twin Deficits Debate*, Mountain View, CA: Mayview Publishing Company.

Roemer, J. (1999) "Egalitarian Strategies," *Dissent*, Summer: 64–74.

Rogers, J. and Streeck, W. (1994) "Productive Solidarities: Economic Strategy and Left Politics," in D. Milliband (ed.) *Reinventing the Left*, Cambridge, MA: Polity Press.

Rom, M. C. (1999) "From Welfare State to Opportunity, Inc: Public–Private Partnerships in Welfare Reform," *The American Behavioral Scientist*, 43(1): 155–76.

Romano, F. (1996) "Economic Development and Environmental Policy During the Hawke and Keating Governments," unpublished thesis, University of New South Wales.

Romano, F. (2003) "Clinton & Blair: the Economics of the Third Way," paper presented at University New South Wales Seminar on Economic Policy, Sydney, October 2003.

—— (2004) "Third Way a Dead End for Public Spending," *The Australian Financial Review*, December 20: 47.

Romer, P. M. (1986) "Increasing Returns and Long-Run Growth," *Journal of Political Economy*, 94: 1002–37.

—— (1989) *Increasing Returns and New Developments in the Theory of Growth*, Cambridge, MA: National Bureau of Economic Research Working Paper 3098.

—— (1990) "Endogenous Technological Change," in R. Solow (ed.) (2001) *Landmark Papers in Economic Growth*, Cheltenham: Edward Elgar.

—— (1994a) "The Origins of Endogenous Growth," *Journal of Economic Perspectives*, 8(1): 3–22.

—— (1994b) "Beyond Classical and Keynesian Macroeconomic Policy," *Policy Options*, July/August: 16.

Rosen, S. (1987) "Human Capital," in J. Eatwell, M. Milgate, and P. Newman (eds) *The New Palgrave: A Dictionary of Economics*, London: Macmillan Press.

Rosenau, P. (1999) "Introduction: the Strengths and Weaknesses of Public–Private Policy Partnerships," *The American Behavioral Scientist*, 43(1): 10.

Rosenberg, N. (1976) *Perspectives on Technology*, Cambridge: Cambridge University Press.

—— (1982) *Inside the Black Box*, Cambridge: Cambridge University Press.

—— (1994) *Exploring the Black Box: Technology, Economics and History*, Cambridge: Cambridge University Press.

Rousseau, J. (1968 edition) *The Social Contract*, London: Penguin.

Rowley, C. K. (1986) "Classical Political Economy and the Debt Issue," in J. Buchanan, C. Rowley, and R. Tollison (eds) *Deficits*, New York: Basil Blackwell.

Rowthorn, R. (1981) "Demand, Real Wages and Growth," *Thames Papers in Political Economy*, Autumn: 1–39.

Ryan, A. (1999) "Britain: Recycling the Third Way," *Dissent*, Spring: 77–80.

Ryner, J. M. (2002) *Capitalist Restructuring, Globalisation and the Third Way: Lessons From the Swedish Model*, London: Routledge.

Salant, W. A. (1966) "Taxes, Income Determination, and the Balanced Budget Theorem," in J. Scherer and J. Papke (eds) *Public Finance and Fiscal Policy*, Boston, MA: Houghton Mifflin.

Samuelson, P. (1951) "Principles and Rules in Modern Fiscal Policy: a Neoclassical Reformulation," in J. Waitzman (ed.) *Money, Trade and Economic Growth: Essays in Honor of John Henry Williams*, New York: Macmillan.

Sargeant, T. J. and Wallace, N. (1976) "Rational Expectations and the Theory of Economic Policy," *Journal of Monetary Economics*, 2: 169–83.

Sawyer, M. C. (ed.) (1988) *Post-Keynesian Economics*, Aldershot: Edward Elgar.

Scanlon, C. (1999) "Promises, Promises: The Third Way Rewrites Neo-liberalism," *Arena Magazine*, February–March: 25–8.

Schier, S. E. (ed.) (2000) *The Postmodern Presidency: Bill Clinton's Legacy in U.S. Politics*, Pittsburgh, PA: University of Pittsburgh Press.

Schmookler, J. (1966) *Innovation and Economic Growth*, Cambridge, MA: Harvard University Press.

Schultz, T. W. (1962) "Reflections on Investment in Man," *Journal of Political Economy*, 70: 1–8.

Schultze, C. L. (1989) "Of Wolves, Termites and Pussycats: Or, Why We Should Worry About the Budget Deficit," *The Brookings Review*, (Summer): 26–33.

Schumpeter, J. A. (1934) *The Theory of Economic Development: an Inquiry into Profits, Capital, Credit, Interest and the Business Cycle*, Cambridge, MA: Harvard University Press.

—— (1939) *Business Cycles*, New York: McGraw-Hill.

—— (1942) (1981 edition) *Capitalism, Socialism and Democracy*, London: George Allen & Unwin.

(1998) "Scientists urge Clinton to expand R&D investment," *Sea Technology*, 39(12): 78 (author unknown).

Scott, A. (2000) *Running on Empty: "Modernising" the British and Australian Labour Parties*, Annandale, VA: Pluto Press.

Seccareccia, M. (1999) *What Type of Full Employment?: a Critical Evaluation of ELR Policy Proposal*, Toronto: University of Toronto.

Seccombe, M. (1999) "Labor Pains," *The Sydney Morning Herald*, February 6: 33.

Setterfield, M. (2003) "Supply and Demand in the Theory of Long-run Growth," *Review of Political Economy*, 15(1): 23–32.

Shackle, G. L. S. (1955) *Uncertainty in Economics*, Cambridge: Cambridge University Press.

Shoop, T. (1995) *Government for Sale*, Washington, DC: GovExec.com. Online. Available http://www.govexec.com/reinvent/downsize/0695s.htm, June 1 (accessed November 18, 2001).

Sik, O. (1976) *The Third Way: Marxist-Leninist Theory and Modern Industrial Society*, London: Wildwood House.

Singer, H. W. (1998) *Growth, Development and Trade*, Cheltenham: Edward Elgar.

Sinha, D. (2000) "What's 'New' in the New Growth Theory?," *The Indian Economic Journal*, 47(4): 55–7.

Skidelsky, R. (2003) "The Mystery of Growth," *The Australian Financial Review*, March 21: 1–2, 8.

Smith, A. (1776) (1976 edition) *An Inquiry Into the Nature and Causes of the Wealth of Nations*, Indianapolis, IN: Liberty Press.

Smith, K. (1997) "Economic Infrastructures and Innovation Systems," in C. Edquist (ed.) *Systems of Innovation: Technologies, Institutions and Organizations*, London: Pinter.

Smith, P. and Morton, G. (2001) "New Labour's Reform of Britain's Employment Law: the Devil is Not Only in the Detail But in the Values and Policies Too," *British Journal of Industrial Relations*, 39(1): 119–38.

Snowdon, B., Vane, H., and Wynarczyk, P. (1994) *A Modern Guide to Macroeconomics: an Introduction to Competing Schools of Thought*, Aldershot: Edward Elgar.

Solow, R. M. (1956) "A Contribution to the Theory of Economic Growth," *Quarterly Journal of Economics*, 70(1): 65–94.

—— (1957) "Technical Change and the Aggregate Production Function," *Review of Economics and Statistics*, 39: 312–20.

—— (1960) "Investment and Technical Progress," in K. Arrow (ed.) *Mathematical Methods in the Social Sciences*, Stanford, CA: Stanford University Press.

—— (1970) *Growth Theory: an Exposition*, New York: Oxford University Press.

—— (1991) "Growth Theory," in D. Greenaway (ed.) *Companion to Contemporary Economic Thought*, London: Routledge.

—— (1994) "Perspectives of Growth Theory," *Journal of Economic Perspectives*, 8(1): 45–54.

Sparer, M. S. (1999) "Myths and Misunderstandings: Health policy, the Devolution Revolution, and the Push for Privatization," *The American Behavioral Scientist*, 43(1): 138–54.

Specter, A. (1993) "Just What the Doctor Ordered... Big Government?," *Washington Post*, December 22: A21.

Spengler, J. J. (1960a) "Mercantilist and Physiocratic Growth Theory," in B. Hoselitz (ed.) *Theories of Economic Growth*, Chicago, IL: The Free Press of Glencoe.

—— (1960b) "John Stuart Mill on Economic Development," in B. Hoselitz (ed.) *Theories of Economic Growth*, Chicago, IL: The Free Press of Glencoe.

Stedward, G. (2000) "New Labour's Education Policy," in D. Coates and P. Lawler (eds) *New Labour in Power*, Manchester: Manchester University Press.

Stein, J. L. (ed.) (1976) *Monetarism*, Amsterdam: North-Holland Publishing Company.

—— (1984) *Monetarist, Keynesian & New Classical Economics*, New York: New York University Press.

Stephanopolous, G. (1999) *All Too Human: A Political Education*, Boston, MA: Little, Brown & Company.

Stern, N. (1991) "The Determinants of Growth," *Economic Journal*, 101: 122–33.

Stiglitz, J. E. (1989) *The Economic Role of the State*, Oxford: Basil Blackwell.

—— (2000) "The Contributions of the Economics of Information to Twentieth Century Economics," *Quarterly Journal of Economics*, 115(4): 1441.

Stiglitz, J. E. and Wallsten, S. J. (1999) "Public-Private Technology Partnerships: Promises and Pitfalls," *The American Behavioral Scientist*, 43(1): 52–73.

Stilwell, F. (1986) *The Accord... And Beyond: the Political Economy of the Labor Government*, Sydney: Pluto Press.

—— (2000) *Changing Track: A New Political Economic Direction for Australia*, Annandale, VA: Pluto Press.

Summers, L. (2001) *Keep Growth Alive!*, Washington, DC: Progressive Policy Institute. Online. Available www.ppionline.org April 25 (accessed May 4, 2001).

Swan, T. (1956) "Economic Growth and Capital Accumulation," *Economic Record*, 32: 334–61.

Tanner, L. (1999) *Open Australia*, Annandale, VA: Pluto Press.

(1994) "Taxing Times for Small Business," *The Washington Times*, April 15 (author unknown).

Taylor, L. (2001a) "No Real Contest," *The Australian Financial Review*, May 9: 53.

—— (2001b) "Crean Finds Cracks in Blair Model," *The Australian Financial Review*, August 16.

—— (2001c) "Global Gain For Those Who Play The Game," *The Australian Financial Review*, February 24–25: 40.

—— (2002) "Blair: Losing the Third Way," *The Australian Financial Review Weekend*, March 2–3: 25, 28.

Temple, J. A. (1998) "Recent Clinton Urban Education Initiatives and the Role of School Quality in Metropolitan Finance," *National Tax Journal*, 51(3): 517–29.

Temple, M. (2000) "New Labour's Third Way: Pragmatism and Governance," *British Journal of Politics and International Relations*, 2: 302–25.

(2001) "The Clinton Years: A Look Back – Education Policy Moves Into the Spotlight," *What Works in Teaching and Learning*, 33: 6 (author unknown).

(1997) "The Investment Deficit," *The Nation*, 264: 3 (author unknown).

(2000) "The New Enforcers," *The Economist*, October 5: 79–82 (author unknown).

(2001) "The New Workforce," *The Economist*, September 15: 8 (author unknown).

Thirwall, A. P. (1979) "The Balance of Payments Constraint as an Explanation of International Growth Rate Differences," *Banca Nazionale Del Lavoro Quarterly Review*, 128: 45–53.

Tingle, L. (2000) "Coalition's On the Job in Third Way, Says Abbott," *The Sydney Morning Herald*, July 21: 6.

Tobin, J. (1965) "Money and Economic Growth," *Econometrica*, 33(4): 671–84.

—— (1999) "A Liberal Agenda," in R. Freeman (ed.) *The New Inequality*, Boston, MA: Beacon.

Tobin, J. and Buiter, W. (1976) "Long-run Effect of Fiscal and Monetary Policy on Aggregate Demand," in J. Stein (ed.) *Monetarism*, Amsterdam: North-Holland Publishing Company.

Touraine, A. (1971) *The Post-industrial Society: Tomorrow's Social History, Classes, Conflicts and Culture in the Programd Society*, trans. L. Mayhew, New York: Random House.

Tufte, E. R. (1978) *Political Control of the Economy*, Princeton, NJ: Princeton University.

Tullock, G. (1986) "The General Irrelevance of the General Theory," in G. Buchanan, C. Rowley, and R. Tollison (eds) *Deficits*, New York: Basil Blackwell.

Undy, R. (1999) "New Labour's Industrial Settlement: the Third Way?," *British Journal of Industrial Relations*, 37(2): 315–36.

United States Trade Representative, (USTR) (1997) *Identification of Trade Expansion Priorities Pursuant to Executive Order 12901*, Washington, DC: USTR. Online. Available http://www.ustr.gov/pdf/ 12901report97.pdf (accessed September 29, 2001).

—— (1998) *WTO Initiative on Global Electronic Commerce*, Washington, DC: USTR. Online. Available http://www.ustr.gov/pdf/gec_expl.pdf (accessed September 29, 2001).

—— (2000) *Special 301 Report*, Washington, DC: USTR. Online. Available http://www.ustr.gov/html/special.html (accessed September 29, 2001).

—— (2001) *U.S. Membership in the WTO*, Washington, DC: USTR. Online. Available http://ww.ustr.gov/wtofact1.html (accessed September 29, 2001).

US Census Bureau (2000a) *Statistical Abstract of the United States*, Washington, DC: US Bureau of the Census.

—— (2000b) *Mean Earnings of Workers 18 Year and Over, by Educational Attainment, Race Hispanic Origin and Sex: 1975 to 1999*, Washington, DC: US Census Bureau. Online. Available http://www.census.gov/population/socdemo/education/tableA-3.txt (accessed December 1, 2001).

US Congress (USC) (1998) *Workforce Investment Act of 1998 – Conference Report*, Washington, DC: US Congress. Online. Available http://thomas.loc.gov/cgi-bin/query/ D?r105:2:./temp/~r105FKLNyc:e0 (accessed November 17, 2001).

US Department of Health and Human Services (2001) *National Evaluation of Welfare-to-Work Strategies*, Washington, DC: Department of Health and Human Services.

US Department of Housing and Urban Development (USDHUD) (2001a) *A Public/Private Partnership to Rebuild America: Opportunities for Businesses in EZ/EC Urban Communities*, Washington, DC: USDHUD. Online. Available http://www.ezec. gov/Invest/pwguide.html (accessed November 11, 2001).

—— (2001b) *Housing and Urban Development: Community Planning and Development*. Washington, DC: USDHUD. Online. Available http:www.hud.gov/offices/cpd/ezec/ about/ezecinit.cfm (accessed November 15, 2001).

US Department of Labor (Bureau of Labor Statistics) (USDL) (2001) *Consumer Price Indexes*, Washington, DC: USDL. Online. Available ftp://ftp.bls.gov/pub/ special.requests/cpi/cpiai.txt (accessed October 4, 2001).

US Department of State (USDS) (2001) *History of the Department of State During the Clinton Presidency (1993–2001)*, Washington, DC: USDS. Online. Available http://www.state.gov/www/about_state/history/ch5.html   (accessed   September 29, 2001).

US Federal Reserve Bank (USFR) (2001) *Selected Interest Rates: Historical Data: Federal Funds Rate*, Washington, DC: USFR. Online. Available http://www. federalreserve.gov/releases/H15/data/m/fedfund.txt (accessed October 7, 2001).

US General Accounting Office (GAO) (1994) *Vaccines for Children: Critical Issues in Design and Implementation*, Washington, DC: US General Accounting Office.

(1999) "US-Japan Enhanced Initiative on Deregulation and Competition Policy," *M2 Presswire*, May 5 (author unknown).

Uzawa, H. (1965) "Optimal Technical Change in an Aggregative Model of Economic Growth," *International Economic Review*, 6: 18–31.

Valdes, B. (1999) *Economic Growth: Theory, Empirics and Policy*, Cheltenham: Edward Elgar.

Veblen, T. (1898) "Why is Economics not an Evolutionary Science?," *Quarterly Journal of Economics*, 12.

—— (1919) *The Place of Science in Modern Civilization ad Other Essays*. New York: Huebsch.

Vickrey, W. (1994) *Public Economics*, Cambridge: Cambridge University Press.

Von Hippel, E. (1982) "Appropriability of Innovation Benefit as a Source of Innovation," *Research Policy*, 11(2): 95–115.

Wade, M. (2002) "Idealistic Entrepreneurs Not About to Change the World," *The Sydney Morning Herald*, April 6: 46.

Waring, P. (2001) "The Third Way, Employment and the Workplace in Australia," *The Economic and Labour Relations Review*, 12: 174–92.

Weatherford, S. M. and McDonnell, L. M. (1996) "Clinton and the Economy: the Paradox of Policy Success and Political Mishap," *Political Science Quarterly*, 11: 403.

(1998) "We Have to Make Way for the Third Way," *Maclean's*, 111: 60 (author unknown).

Weiss, L. (1998) *The Myth of the Powerless State: Governing the Economy in a Global Era*, Cambridge, MA: Polity Press.

White, S. (1998) *Interpreting the "Third Way": Not One Route But Many*, London: Nexus. Online. Available www.netnexus.org/library/papers/white2.html (accessed March 15, 2000).

Wildavsky, B. (1998) "A Taxing Question," *National Journal*, 28: 440–4.

Wilkinson, F. (2000) "Inflation and Employment: Is There a Third Way?," *Cambridge Journal of Economics*, 24: 643–70.

Wilkinson, R. (2000) "New Labour and the Global Economy," in D. Coates and P. Lawler (eds) *New Labour in Power*, Manchester: Manchester University Press.

Wolff, E. N. (2001) *Recent Trends in Wealth Ownership, 1983–1998*, Annandale-on-Hudson: Jerome Levy Economics Institute. Online. Available http://www.levy.org/docs/ wrkpap/papers/300.html (accessed November 16, 2001).

Woodward, B. (1994) *The Agenda: Inside the Clinton White House*, New York: Simon & Schuster.

—— (1996) *The Choice*, New York: Simon & Schuster.

Woolley, J. T. (1984) *Monetary Politics: the Federal Reserve and the Politics of Monetary Policy*, New York: Cambridge University Press.

Wray, L. R. (2002) *Monetary Policy: an Institutionalist Approach*, Annandale-on-Hudson, NY: Jerome Levy Economics Institute.

Wray, L. R. and Pigeon, M. (2000) "Can a Rising Tide Raise All Boats? Evidence from the Clinton-Era Expansion," *Journal of Economic Issues*, XXXIV: 811–45.

Yellen, J. L. (1989) "Symposium on the Budget Deficit," *Journal of Economic Perspectives*, 3: 17–21.

Yergin, D. and Stanislaw, J. (1998) *The Commanding Heights: the Battle between Government and the Marketplace That is Remaking the Modern World*, New York: Touchstone.

Zakaria, F. (2001) "Time to Make Room for Daddy," *Newsweek*, July 3: 95.

Index